Decolonizing Equity

Decolonizing Equity

Edited by
Billie Allan
V.C. Rhonda Hackett

Fernwood Publishing
Halifax & Winnipeg

Development editing: Fazeela Jiwa
Copyediting: Amber Riaz
Cover design: Evan Marnoch
Type setting: Jessica Herdman
Printed and bound in Canada

Published by Fernwood Publishing
32 Oceanvista Lane, Black Point, Nova Scotia, B0J 1B0
and 748 Broadway Avenue, Winnipeg, Manitoba, R3G 0X3

fernwoodpublishing.ca

Fernwood Publishing Company Limited gratefully acknowledges the financial support of the Government of Canada, the Canada Council for the Arts, the Manitoba Department of Culture, Heritage and Tourism under the Manitoba Publishers Marketing Assistance Program and the Province of Manitoba, through the Book Publishing Tax Credit, for our publishing program. We are pleased to work in partnership with the Province of Nova Scotia to develop and promote our creative industries for the benefit of all Nova Scotians.

Library and Archives Canada Cataloguing in Publication

Title: Decolonizing equity / edited by V.C. Rhonda Hackett & Billie Allan.
Names: Hackett, V. C. Rhonda, editor. | Allan, Billie, editor.
Description: Includes bibliographical references and index.
Identifiers: Canadiana (print) 20210354496 | Canadiana (ebook)
20210363371 | ISBN 9781773635156
(softcover) | ISBN 9781773635309 (EPUB) | ISBN 9781773635316 (PDF)
Subjects: LCSH: Multiculturalism. | LCSH: Diversity in the workplace. |
LCSH: Anti-racism. | LCSH:
Decolonization.
Classification: LCC HM1271 .D43 2022 | DDC 305.8—dc23

CONTENTS

Pedagogies of Dissent: Meditations on Decolonial Disruptions
Foreword by OmiSoore Dryden...1
Pedagogies of Dissent...2
Mutual Aid..5
Decolonial Disruptions...7

Opening the Circle
Billie Allan and V.C. Rhonda Hackett 10

Round 1: Visioning for and Conceptualizing Decolonial Equity / 17

1 Theorizing Decolonial Equity: Coyote Takes a Chapter
Billie Allan...19
Decolonizing Equity..22
Wading into the Water: Reimagining Equity as Balance...........................25
A Job You Get Without Even Applying: In/Equity and "Diversity Work"...29
Wisdom at the Shoreline..30
Decolonial Equity in Action..32
Conclusion...35

2 Decolonizing Equity Praxis
Shauneen Pete..40
Personal Reflection..42
Seeking the Leader We Need:
Because Decolonization and Resurgence Matters......................................43
Equity Policy Frameworks...45
Indigenous Experience in Equity Landscapes 46
Settler Logic of Elimination...48
The Contractual Benevolence of the Academy...49
The Price of (Indigenous) Access: Paying the Cultural Tax 51
The Assumptions of Access: Presuming Assimilation 53
Dreaming: The Possibilities of Decolonizing Equity Praxis.......................54

3   A Theorizing of De-colonializing Equity and the Nation-State
    Kathy Hogarth 60
    Framing Decolonization Within the Nation................................64
    Challenges to Decolonizing Equity 67
    Recolonization Through Decolonization..72
    A Path Forward 75

Round 2: Being and Doing:
Decolonial Equity in Practice / 81

4   Tkaranto Ondaadizi-Gamig: Birth Is a Ceremony
    Roberta Pike with contributors Cheryllee Bourgeois and Sara Booth 83
    Self-location/Introduction of Author and Contributors 84
    Indigenous Ways of Seeing, Knowing, Relating, and Doing
    as Foundations of Decolonial Equity 85
    Visioning for a Birth Centre..88
    Indigenous Framework 89
    Weaving Decolonial Equity in Leadership:
    Roberta's Story and Reflections..101
    Allies in Decolonial Equity..104
    Decolonial Equity: Looking Ahead 105
    Closing Words..106

5   Introducing Indigenous and Black Youth
    to a New Vision of Social Work
    Terry Gardiner 108
    Locating Myself in the Context of Canadian Colonization.......109
    Black and Indigenous Presence...109
    The Summer Mentorship Program..111
    Visioning the Future..127
    Conclusion..129

6   Decolonizing Urban Education
    Roland Sintos Coloma 132
    Defining "Urban" 134
    Decolonizing Representation 139
    Decolonizing Structure 142
    Decolonizing Affect...146
    Conclusion..150

Round 3: On Healing, Well-being and Sustainability: Taking Care in the Work of Decolonizing Equity / 157

7   A Call for Integrating Radical Healing and Imagination
    into Critical Race Education
    Ozioma Aloziem 159
    Critical Race Theory and Education 162
    The Relevance of CRT and the Need for Radical Healing 164
    Teaching to Transform 167
    Incorporating Pedagogies of Healing..169
    Encouraging Radical Self-care 170
    Promoting Collective Healing..171
    Implications...173
    Conclusion...174

8   Centring Subjectivity: Witnessing and Wellness
    V.C. Rhonda Hackett..179
    Self-location...179
    Situating Social Work...180
    Storying Out..181
    Witnessing 183
    Witnessing Ourselves..186
    Wellness as Resistance...187
    Implications for Decolonial Equity 191
    Conclusion...192

Closing the Circle
    Billie Allan and V.C. Rhonda Hackett 196
    Decolonizing Equity Matters Right Now......................................197
    Decolonial Equity Requires Decolonial Solidarity.......................200
    How Will We Know? 203

Contributors..209

Index 212

To all of the beautiful relatives who supported us on this journey, we offer our deepest gratitude to you.

PEDAGOGIES OF DISSENT
Meditations on Decolonial Disruptions

Foreword by OmiSoore Dryden

The essays in this necessary and urgent book detail the importance of building trusting and deeply caring relationships as a cornerstone of decolonizing equity with a commitment to decolonial equity. With this shift in gaze, we engage new meaning, deeper meaning, not quite yet finished or completed meaning, as a way of engaging with the destabilizing practices of radical equity. In this text we are pushed to explore why we are happily committed to a "diverse workplace," when that diversity seems to only serve to maintain the status quo, thus maintaining white settler colonialism and logics.

By centring the tenets of colonialism, including the afterlife of slavery in this region currently normatively known as "Canada," this text explores how slavery and genocide continue to linger in spaces and places we cannot yet fully understand. Tiffany Lethabo King writes in her seminal text, *The Black Shoals: Offshore Formations of Black and Native Studies,* "Genocide and slavery do not have an edge. While the force of their haunt has distinct feelings at the stress points and instantiations of Black fungibility and Native genocide, the violence moves as one" (King, 2019, x). And this violence moves as one into normative white settler practices of equity, diversity, and inclusion.

Decolonizing Equity incites us to understand that equity, diversity, and inclusion (EDI) practices will remain much the same—tools to maintain the status quo — until we are ready to take action and to engage more fully with the disquieting, eccentric, bizarre, puzzling, extraordinary, mysterious, uncommon, and unconventional opportunities that will result in the substantive structural change demanded by social justice undertakings.

PEDAGOGIES OF DISSENT

As I write this, I am located in Kjipuktuk/Halifax, the traditional unceded territory of the Wəlastəkewiyik (Maliseet) whose ancestors along with the Mi'kmaq / Mi'kmaw and Passamaquoddy Nations signed Peace and Friendship Treaties with the British Crown in the 1700s. Yet we must not forget that these treaties were signed roughly 140 years before the end of slavery in this region now called Canada. Halifax was imposed upon Kjipuktuk in 1749 and enslaved African peoples were used to dig out roads and build the city — including much of the citadel. On the southern shore of the Bedford Basin, Mi'kmaq people shared land with Black people, and this allowed Africville to be founded in the mid-1800s. Africville was, as we know, later demolished by the city government in the 1960s — bulldozed to the ground in the middle of the night. In this acknowledgement, I honour Indigenous and Black Peoples who continue to be here; and who continue to fight against genocide and the afterlives of slavery. I respectfully acknowledge our collective ancestors — Indigenous, Black, queer, trans, genderqueer, and Two Spirit — who collectively were born here, forced here, and continue to make home here.

Between 1992 and 2004, I worked in the Centre for Race & Ethnic Relations at York University (the traditional territory of many Nations including the Mississaugas of the Credit, the Anishnabeg, the Chippewa, the Haudenosaunee and the Wendat peoples) in a shared office space with the Sexual Harassment Education & Complaint Centre. I was the Advisory on both Race & Ethnic Relations, and Sexual & Gender Diversity, and brought with me into this dual role the excitement and power of student activism. I was committed to disrupting how anti-Black racism manifested within the university. Our commitment to anti-racism meant finding creative and strategic tools that would urge the university to move beyond minimum requirements (as outlined by provincial human rights legislation, and internal protocols) and engage in maximum efforts to disrupt racism. But more so, our commitment to lessening harms caused by systemic racism on Black, Indigenous

Peoples, and people of colour was our primary concern. The work was to hold the university accountable to make the sites of working, learning, and living, safe/positive spaces. It is important to note that at the time, I did find my work in the Centre exciting and filled with possibilities.

However, university systems (similar to other colonial systems in Canada) claimed commitments to objectivity, "colour-blind" frameworks, neutral assessments — all of which are embedded in white supremacist logics of fairness and ultimately uphold the doctrines of colonialism. These deeply flawed and false logics often begin with the belief that everyone is treated equally and that by not directly naming colonialism and anti-Black racism, by not specifically identifying Indigenous and Black people, one is actually doing the work of equality. Yet, it is impossible to be unaffected by colonial systems of oppression, which, of course, include the afterlife of slavery.

Although, in this work, I have watched the framing change. More radical notions of justice and accountability morph into (are set aside for) multiculturalist notions of employment equity and increased diversity, "political correctness" (Wilson 1995), unconscious bias, and bullying — ultimately evacuating the difficult realities of decolonial/anti-colonial anti-racism. I resisted and bristled against the spoken and unspoken pressure and expectations to soften the work and to operate as a gatekeeper that protected the university from complaints of harassment and discrimination. If systems are only able to address discrete "symptoms," the underlying social structures remain untouched and the complexity of meaning and representation is occluded. I began to think seriously about the effectiveness of equity, diversity, and inclusion, especially as I was watching the more progressive elements of the work slowly being eroded, morphed, into a systems-management type of endeavour. I'm reminded of Mohanty (2003) who argues that "cultures of dissent must work to create pedagogies of dissent rather than pedagogies of accommodation" (216).

I venture that there is an overlap between the desire to claim, "I don't see colour" (colour-blind objectivity) and the colonial Canadian claims of "all are welcome here." To operate in this realm is to continue to entrench white supremacist/settler colonial logics which are established as the norm/standard. Canada's enduring national narrative of multiculturalism makes it difficult to address colonialism and difficult to understand that anti-Blackness is endemic to, and within the fabric of, the colonial nation. In the article, "Resisting Inclusion: Decolonial Relations between Peoples of Afrikan Descent and Original Peoples," Moyo Rainos Mutamba (2014) states,

> History shows how the white supremacist colonial state of Canada strategically desires our inclusion at times, to further its colonial agenda, only to exclude us to sustain its racist, anti-black agenda. To be included in the nation-state is to be in a colonial relationship with Original Peoples of this land, and inclusion necessarily comes at the expense of Indigenous sovereignty and self-determination. (n.p.)

In this way, there is recognition that inclusion (as it is normatively operationalized) is not freedom, and sameness is actually a social injustice. Inclusion continues to be promoted as the antidote to many of the oppressions that hinder our material well-being. It is believed to be a corrective philosophy that finds its support in the basic belief that oppression happens exclusively through means of exclusion. However, the questions are the following: Into what are we being included? Who defines the terms of this inclusion, and under what conditions? For example, fighting for inclusion within the framework of a Canadian colonial and anti-Black state, the presumption is that the Canadian state is legitimate, stable and will/should always exist.

The use of "diversity" is a strategy that serves to manage normativity, harmony, and civility but ultimately does not facilitate a disruption of systems of oppressions (Ahmed, 2012; Mohanty, 2003). The baseline in the work of diversity remains the maintaining of the status quo. Diversity work produces a culture of silence (Alexander, 2005; Mohanty, 2003) and, in effect, gestures to more diversity than actually exists.

How does one manage being positioned as unruly or uncivil when mentioning these realities when the practices of racism, sexism, homophobia are left unexamined and unexplored? Inclusion is not a promise extended to all who attend the academic institution (including faculty). Sara Ahmed (2012) details this failure when she states

> we can note how commitments to antiracism can become performances of racism: as if to say "you are wrong to describe us as uncaring and racist because we are caring and committed to

being antiracist." When antiracism provides a discourse of organizational pride, then racism is not recognized and is enacted in the mode of non-recognition. (145)

One response to systems of "non-recognition" of white settler colonial practices, the afterlife of slavery, and institutional equity practices is a turn to mutual aid and social justice.

MUTUAL AID

Mutual Aid is collective coordination to meet needs of the community, without relying upon current state systems to provide this care. COVID-19 has resulted in a number of community mutual aid interventions in Indigenous and Black communities across Turtle Island. While we may now call this mutual aid, we have always had systems of community care — be it sharing of food, expanded child minding, or supports for purchasing school uniforms, ride shares and/or supporting families who may be out of work, on strike, or precariously employed. Mariame Kaba, community organizer and abolitionist, says of mutual aid that it

is premised on solidarity and not charity, and that's really important. It rejects saviorism. It rejects hierarchy and authoritarianism…it marries community service with political education and political activism that's actually focused on challenging power and oppressive systems. (qtd. in Alkhafaji 2021, n.p)

The Black Panther Party exhibited the transformative outcomes of connecting community service with political education and activism. In 1972, they included health as part of their radical mission — the Ten Point Program — calling on the government to "provide, free of charge, for the people, health facilities which will not only treat our illnesses" — most of which have come about as a result of continued colonialism and anti-Black racism — but to develop preventive medical programs. In addition, the Black Panther Party *called on researchers* to provide Black people with access to "scientific and medical information, *so we may provide ourselves* with proper medical attention and care" (Fullilove 2016: n.p.; original emphasis). This demand for health and wellness for all becomes a foundation of a more just and equitable world (Basset

2016). Moya Bailey and Whitney People (2017) also make this assertion. They argue that "health and wellness [must be seen] as an integral part of social justice labour" (2). They provide us with a reminder of the full meaning of Fannie Lou Hamer's statement that she is "sick and tired of being sick and tired" (Bailey and People 2017, 2). Many of us — Black and Indigenous women (cis and trans), Black and Indigenous Two Spirit and queer folks — have repeated this phrase in response to the relentless white supremacy, anti-Indigenous and anti-Black racism, homophobia, lesbophobia, and transphobia. However, Fannie Lou Hamer was also speaking to her very literal sickness. Hamer's declaration that she was sick and tired was not simply a metaphor for activist fatigue; it was a declaration of literal pain, illness, and physical exhaustion. Physical and mental health remains a metric for understanding both the process and impact of oppression in our lives, which is why it is significant that in this text, we are reminded that *wellness as resistance* is a necessary response/intervention to inequity.

As COVID-19 has reminded us, anti-Indigenous and anti-Black racism continues to shape institutions and social interactions including those related to health care. Claims of cultural and racial neutrality, particularly in the fields of medicine and health, hamper and obstruct our ability to fully realize better health outcomes. I too believe that the management of our health would look different if we centred and then deployed decolonial/anti-colonial social justice as our guide. And as Audre Lorde (1984) reminds us: "Revolution is not a one-time event. It is becoming always vigilant for the smallest opportunity to make a genuine change in established, outgrown responses" (140).

Mutual aid as a cornerstone of decolonial equity would require that we participate in collective decision making. This is not always easy as the relationships between Black and Indigenous people are mediated through the interlocking violence of genocide and slavery. As Tiffany Lethabo King (2019) outlines: "The terms of survival — or, said another way, the circumstances under which you as a Black or Indigenous person lived — were often tethered to the death of the Other" (xi).

Decolonizing equity demands radical relation making which then underscores and supports our collective multi-voiced decision making. Instead of placing our trust in the system, we place it in the transformative process of decolonial equity. Believing and then simply stating that "all are welcome" does not do the work of actually making a space welcoming, nor does it address the concerns of our communities. There is a rupture between incorporating intersectionality within the institution and the continued presentation of people being simplistically constituted — where women are "just" women, Black people are "just" Black, queer people are "just queer," and Indigenous people are "just" Native. This is a very effective tactic that continues to perpetuate the precarity of our presence while occluding our complex identities, experiences, and modes of thought. I remain appreciative of the work of Leanne Betasamosake Simpson, Audre Lorde, Kimberlé Crenshaw, Audra Simpson, the book *This Bridge Called My Back: Writings by Radical Women of Color* (Moraga and Anzaldúa 1981), and the Black Feminist Statement as written by the Combahee River Collective (1983) which states,

> The most general statement of our politics at the present time would be that we are actively committed to struggling against racial, sexual, heterosexual, and class oppression, and see as our particular task the development of integrated analysis and practice based upon the fact that the major systems of oppression are interlocking. (272)

This book guides us on the ways to be daring when engaging the colonial and anti-Black foundations of systemic racism in which decolonizing equity requires us to engage. And we need to be daring. Our lives depend on it. Not for survival in the system — universities, and others — but something different, something based in wholistic mutual aid, transformative justice, care of the mind, body and spirit, the critical engagement with accountability in our communities, for our selves. This book's focus on Indigenous and decolonizing thought, critical race theory, Black feminist/queer thought is instrumental in creating a text that is both insightful and inciting.

DECOLONIAL DISRUPTIONS

The process of grappling with different ways of moving through our various complicated experiences incites different contemplations which in turn facilitates building anew. Perhaps through this process, something transformative will be created and animated. However, we must take note of the cautions offered in the book, especially one from Dr. Kathy Hogarth in Chapter 3, where she states "Not all colonized subjects are treated equitably in the decolonizing discourse" (76** Page number to be updated here after typesetting. This quote currently appears on pg 76 of this manuscript**). If all subjects are not treated equitably, and this is a clear distinction and departure from equality arguments, then have we decolonized or have we in fact re-inscribed another version of colonization?

To be incited to think anew, to engage what is unknown and currently unthought, is to simultaneously create an internal rupture and one that also causes rupture within sites where we are precariously situated. Turning toward each other in response to harmful white supremacist systems, colonial and anti-Black systems, will guide us to greater well-being.

The pedagogies offered within take us through a tapestry of multiple spaces where knowledge is produced. It asks us to enter in the difficult work of liberation. Decolonizing equity demands that we refuse hegemonic bargains that continue to support the very system in need of change and disruption — and assures us that, in doing so, we will collectively create spaces of health and wellness.

Adupe. Ase-O.

References

Ahmed, Sara. 2012. *On Being Included: Racism and Diversity in Institutional Life*. Durham: Duke University Press.

Alexander, M. Jacqui. 2005. *Pedagogies of Crossing: Meditations on Feminism, Sexual Politics, Memory, and the Sacred*. Durham: Duke University Press.

Alkhafaji, Sarah. 2021. "Activist Mariame Kaba Calls Mutual Aid Key to Ending Prison Industrial Complex at bars Event." *The Daily Pennsylvanian*, February 22, 2021. thedp.com/article/2021/02/penn-bars-conference-mariame-kaba.

Bailey, Moira, and Whitney People. 2017. "Articulating Black Feminist Health Science Studies." *Catalyst: Feminism, Theory, Technoscience* 3, 2: 1–27. doi.org/10.28968/cftt.v3i2.28844.

Bassett, Mary T. 2016. "Beyond Berets: The Black Panthers as Health Activists." *American Journal of Public Health* 106, 10: 1741–1743. doi.org/10.2105/AJPH.2016.303412.

Combahee River Collective. 1983. "The Combahee River Collective Statement."

In *Home Girls: A Black Feminist Anthology*, edited by Barbara Smith. New York: Kitchen Table — Women of Color Press.

Fulilove, Robert. 2016. "The Black Panther Party Stands for Health." *Columbia University Mailman School of Public Health*. Blog. February 23. publichealth. columbia.edu/public-health-now/news/black-panther-party-stands-health.

King, Tiffany L. 2019. *The Black Shoals: Offshore Formations of Black and Native Studies*. Durham: Duke University Press.

Lorde, Audre. 1984. *Sister Outsider: Essays & Speeches*. Berkeley: Crossing Press.

Moraga, Cherrie and Gloria Anzaldúa (eds.). 1981. *This Bridge Called My Back: Writings by Radical Women of Colour*. Watertown: Persephone.

Mohanty, Chandra T. 2003. *Feminism Without Borders: Decolonizing Theory, Practicing Solidarity*. Durham: Duke University Press.

Mutamba, Moyo Rainos. 2014. "Resisting Inclusion: Decolonial Relations between Peoples of Afrikan Descent and Original Peoples," *Decolonization: Indigeneity, Education, and Society*, June 18, 2014. decolonization.word-press.com/2014/06/18/resisting-inclusion-decolonial-relations-be-tween-peoples-of-afrikan-descent-and-original-peoples/.

Wilson, John K. 1995. *The Myth of Political Correctness: The Conservative Attack on Higher Education*. New York: Duke University Press.

OPENING THE CIRCLE

Billie Allan and V.C. Rhonda Hackett

This edited collection aims to centre the knowledge, experiences, and voices of Indigenous, Black, and racialized peoples in articulating a vision for decolonial equity work. Specifically, the focus on decolonizing equity is an invitation to re-articulate what equity work can look like when we refuse to separate ideas of equity from the historical and contemporary realities of settler colonialism in the territories presently known as Canada and the United States, and when we insist on linking an equity agenda to the work of decolonizing our shared realities. The text aims to address three core themes to support Indigenous, Black, and racialized scholars, practitioners and students seeking to begin or further their efforts toward decolonizing equity: 1) theorizing or conceptualizing decolonial equity; 2) strategies, skills and practices for enacting decolonial equity; and 3) practices for sustainability and well-being while doing decolonial equity work.

The chapters in this collection consider the practicality and emancipatory possibilities of decolonizing equity. However, articulating decolonial equity necessarily means struggling against the risk of diluting or diminishing decolonial theorization and action (Tuck and Yang 2012). For us, this risk is both necessary and generative because equity without a decolonial lens cannot yield liberation for Indigenous, Black, and other racialized scholars whose inequitable workloads and work lives have been constructed and sustained through colonial architecture and the racism that underpins it. Equity, without a decolonial lens, bears little relevance to current or hoped for governmental, societal, organizational, and institutional commitments and responsibilities to, for example, reconciliation, reparations, Indigenous land and water sovereignty, or movements to centre Black Lives. It offers nothing in the face of appalling devastation to the earth, air, waters, and plant and animal relations we all rely on to survive. As equity departments, policies, and leadership roles spring up or rapidly expand in organizations and institutions across Turtle Island, decolonial thought and action offers pathways for restoring relationality and articulating and challenging limitations associated with conflating equity with recruitment, diversity, and inclusion (see Chapter 2). Minogiizhigokwe (Dr. Kathy Absolon; 2019a, 17) asserts that "to decolonize is to reject being a host of colonization; to reject being a carrier of Eurocentric dominance." Decolonizing equity and the departments, policies, and practices meant to support it necessarily confronts and rejects epistemic racism and cultural imperialism embedded in the terminology, and the terms and conditions of contemporary equity. It invites a reordering and redistribution of epistemic power, and builds on the ongoing work of epistemological healing (healing of knowledge systems and the relationships between them) being carried out in academia and community contexts by and between Indigenous, Black, racialized, and allied scholars, Elders, knowledge keepers, youth, families, and communities. Epistemological healing is unfolding at kitchen tables, community gatherings, the frontlines of land and water protection, limes, powwows, Black, Indigenous, and people of colour (BIPOC) scholar networks, language nests, beading and artist collectives, and in classrooms and Zoom rooms, but it must become core to the work of institutional spaces that wish to transform statements and commitments to goals of decolonization, anti-racism, Indigenization, reconciliation, and equity into lived realities.

We recognize that we stand in the light of significant collective efforts already made to identify the pitfalls of current constructions and operationalizations of equity in academic institutions (Ahmed 2009, 2012; Henry et al. 2017; Thobani 2021). For example, Dr. Sunera Thobani (2021, 6) warns of the "equity/diversity regime" that rapidly sprung into action in the face of global protest against appalling racial injustice including the murder of Mr. George Floyd, as a kind of "containment zone" meant to block, redirect or subvert "radical praxis and insurgent scholarship," particularly that of Indigenous women/Indigiqueers, and queers and women of colour. Containment can be understood as enacted through the enlistment of Indigenous, Black, and racialized scholars into the busywork of the project and perpetually deferred promise of equity within institutions simultaneously meant to dull anti-racist and anti-colonial efforts and subsume them into less threatening and more manageable forms of equity, diversity, and inclusion work (Thobani 2021, 18). Yet, the imagined promise of what Henry et al. (2017) refer to as the "equity myth" is seductive, and the efforts to forward collectivist approaches to reaching it are profoundly exhausting. This exhaustion and the related early death and dis/ease witnessed and experienced among Black, Indigenous, and racialized scholars marks the untenable cost of "mythical" equity and the critical need to envision a kind of equity that we can live rather than die for. This book examines, explores, and troubles decolonial equity as a generative, life giving, potential pathway forward that aims to centre the well-being and sustainability of racialized, Black, and Indigenous Peoples.

Indeed, this book is meant to highlight and share what we, as Indigenous, Black, and racialized peoples, *already know* and *are already doing* in our respective areas of scholarship, leadership, activism, frontline and community practice, and to offer a vision of what equity does, and can, look like through a decolonial lens both now and in the future. What helps us to make this work possible? How do we take care with ourselves and each other in this work? What does solidarity, collaboration, or "allyship" look like in decolonial equity work? What are the implicit and explicit barriers we face in shifting equity discourse, policy, and practice, and what strategies, skills, or practices can help us in creating environments and lived realities of decolonial equity? The Calls to Action of the Truth and Reconciliation Commission of Canada (2015) and a growing institutional and societal awareness of the virulence of anti-Black, anti-Indigenous, and anti-Asian racism have increased the pressure on postsecondary institutions to develop dynamic frameworks for equity work that can simultaneously hold commitments to Indigenization, decolonization, and anti-racism in the context of a continued legacy of colonial harm in education. This is reflected in the expansion of leadership positions addressing equity, diversity, and inclusion (EDI) and Indigenization efforts in postsecondary institutions. We hope that this text will help contribute to meaningful practice in the uptake of decolonial approaches to equity work in postsecondary education and beyond (for example, in healthcare, social services, and community-based settings). Although this is reflected differently in each chapter, this text is grounded in the theoretical traditions of

Indigenous and decolonizing thought, critical race theory, and Black feminist/queer thought.

In developing this text, we also sought to respond to an urgent need for knowledge to support the well-being and sustainability of Black, Indigenous, and racialized peoples taking up equity work, whether in formal or informal roles, recognizing that equity work is often an inherent expectation of Indigenous, Black, and racialized peoples in many workplaces as presumed representatives and champions of "diversity." Beyond imposed expectations, engaging in equity work may also be an important practice of survival and well-being in working to imagine and create workplaces and broader community environments in which equity, anti-racism, and decolonization are lived principles. In this way, engaging in equity efforts can reflect an act of critical hope as well as a tangible and generative act of refusal (Simpson 2018) of normalized systemic and interpersonal racism and ongoing colonial violence and consumption. However, equity efforts often come at a significant cost to BIPOC relatives who may experience the cold front of those who would prefer our silence, compliance, or absence. There is also a cost attributable to the spiritual, physical, mental, and emotional exhaustion that comes from repeatedly having to assert one's humanity, dignity, capacity, and contributions in the face of colonial policies and practices that support the erasure or discounting of the presence and work of Indigenous, Black, and racialized peoples. While our equity efforts may be critical to our own retention and well-being in our workplaces and community spaces, it necessarily raises the question of what remediation and reparation is offered to address the weight of an increasingly disproportionate (and often undervalued) workload and the "cultural tax" (Henry et al. 2017; Padilla 1994) associated with simultaneously addressing inequity while living it. As such, this text is deeply concerned with centring well-being and sustainability in decolonial equity work such that BIPOC faculty, staff, students, community leaders, activists, and advocates can not only survive the work, but thrive in the transformative environments that they labour to envision and create.

Through the following chapters, we centre BIPOC authors' visions for decolonial equity, reflecting on what we already know and are already doing to realize decolonial equity, and what is needed to help us be well and sustained in this work. From the classroom to community practice, these chapters aim to invite dialogue and to uplift the theorizing, strategies, skills, and practices of those for whom decolonizing is neither optional nor conceptual, and for whom the reimagining of equity is required. To aid readers in engaging with the content, we begin each section or "round" (in the spirit of circle work) with an opening to help contextualize the chapters within the core themes of the text. We use the framing of a round here to reflect our desire to situate the chapters in relation to, and in conversation with, each other — just as though the authors were gathered together in a circle in which everyone is understood as having something to share and something to receive, with each person recognized as being no more or no less important than anyone else in the circle, and where we recognize ourselves as interconnected, interrelated, and actively contributing to the creation of a collective knowledge bundle or *dbaagmowin* (Minogiizhigokwe 2009) to support our collective well-being and change-making efforts. Circle work itself is a practice of equity that aims to enact and embody inclusion and collectivist ways of knowing, being, and doing (Minogiizhigokwe 2019b, 56).

It has been a long journey to gather and prepare the knowledge shared within these chapters. What we could not have anticipated in planning for this text was the compounding effect of the COVID-19 pandemic with the ongoing, multi-century pandemic of racial injustice and colonial violence; it meant that many of the anticipated and actual contributors to this text necessarily turned their attention to personal, family, and community safety, and to continued efforts to end racialized colonial violence. We are grateful to all these relatives for the important gifts and knowledge bundles they carry, for their deep and practised commitment to social justice and decolonial equity, and for the ways in which their wisdom and efforts have shaped our own. *Chi miigwetch.*

References

Ahmed, Sara. 2009. "Embodying Diversity: Problems and Paradoxes for Black Feminists." *Race Ethnicity and Education* 12, 1.

___. 2012. *On Being Included*. Durham: Duke University Press.

Henry, Frances, Enakshi Dua, Carl E. James, et al. 2017. *The Equity Myth: Racialization and Indigeneity at Canadian Universities*. Vancouver: UBC Press.

Minogiizhigokwe (Kathy Absolon). 2009. "Navigating the Landscape of Practice: Dbaagmowin of a Helper." In *Wichitowin. Indigenous Social Work in Canada: Perspectives, Practice Futures*, edited by Raven Sinclair, Michael Hart, and Gord Bruyere. Black Point/Winnipeg: Fernwood Publishing.

___. 2019a. "Decolonizing Education and Educators' Decolonizing." *Intersectionalities: A Global Journal of Social Work Analysis, Research, Polity and Practice* 7, 1.

___. 2019b. Reconnecting to Creation: A Spirit of Decolonizing." In *Spirituality and Social Justice*, edited by Norma Jean Profitt and Cyndy Baskin. Toronto: Canadian Scholars' Press.

Padilla, Amado. 1994. "Ethnic Minority Scholars, Research, and Mentoring: Current and Future Issues." *Educational Researcher* 23, 4.

Simpson, Leanne. 2018. *Leanne Betasamosake Simpson | Indigenous Resurgent Mobilization*. blogs.law.columbia.edu/uprising1313/leanne-betasa-mosake-simpson-indigenous-resurgent-mobilization/.

Thobani, Sunera (ed.). 2021. *Coloniality and Racial (In)Justice in the University: Counting for Nothing?* Toronto: University of Toronto Press.

TRC (Truth and Reconciliation Commission of Canada). 2015. *Truth and Reconciliation of Canada: Calls to Action*. Winnipeg. www2.gov.bc.ca/as-sets/gov/british-columbians-our-governments/indigenous-people/aborigi-nal-peoples-documents/calls_to_action_english2.pdf.

Tuck, Eve and K. Wayne Yang. 2012. "Decolonization is Not a Metaphor." *Decolonization: Indigeneity, Education & Society* 1, 1.

Round 1

VISIONING FOR AND CONCEPTUALIZING DECOLONIAL EQUITY

The chapters within this first round offer theoretical considerations in visioning and undertaking decolonial equity work. The contributors articulate the need for, practicalities of, and tensions involved in working to decolonize equity, including the imperatives of attending to Indigenous sovereignty and anti-Black racism. In Chapter 1, decolonial equity is explored through the brief but glorious academic career of Coyote and through Anishinaabe teachings of *nibi* (water) and balance. This chapter unpacks the framing of equity, diversity, and inclusion, and explores the challenges presented to Black, Indigenous, and people of colour (BIPOC) faculty, students, and staff in institutions of higher education where decolonial equity is a necessary act of survival and well-being.

In Chapter 2, Dr. Shauneen Pete reflects on examples from her experiences as a scholar and academic leader to illustrate the pitfalls of equity efforts that fail to acknowledge Indigenous sovereignty, the historical and continuing context of colonial violence, and the need to decolonize organizational policies, practices, and culture. Situating decolonizing equity as one small step in a broader journey toward decolonizing the entire higher education system, Dr. Pete presents a clear analysis of the settler logics of current equity, diversity, and inclusion policies and practices. She asks how equity policies are experienced by Indigenous Peoples and shares some examples of strategies and practices to advocate for decolonial equity.

In Chapter 3, Dr. Kathy Hogarth theorizes about what decolonizing equity and equitable decolonizing can look like and mean in the context of the nation-state. Questioning how current decolonial theorizing accounts for the histories and contemporary realities of Black peoples, Dr. Hogarth also challenges how settlers are conceptualized. Dr. Hogarth articulates her concerns about the conflation of Indigenization and decolonization, and questions the possibilities that lie in delinking the two.

1

THEORIZING DECOLONIAL EQUITY

Coyote Takes a Chapter

Billie Allan

It turns out that a straggly dog-like being with limited educational qualifications, a somewhat questionable sense of humour, and an okay suit can do okay for themselves in academia. Coyote had heard of a happening party occurring in academia with theme nights like "Decolonial Dreaming," "Indigenize this sh*t up in here," and "Equity, Diversity, and Inclusion." They were pretty sure that happening parties were the kinds of places that coyotes were meant to be so they packed their okay suit, their haphazard degrees, and their lie detector (never know when you might need it) and headed for the nearest campus they could find to take up a tenure-track job.

Coyote was moderately disappointed to find that some humans took the "Decolonial Dreaming" a little too far and were actually sleeping right through the good stuff. Coyote wasn't completely sure what sh*t the humans were trying to Indigenize, but then remembered the rip-roaring "De-Indigenize this sh*t up in here" parties they had seen over the years at the frat houses better known as parliament, legislatures, city halls, and township offices. Coyote shuddered at the thought of the lengths some of those humans had gone to try to erase something they couldn't, steal something that could not be owned, and demonize what they could not even begin to understand.

Not long into their campus days, Coyote started to realize these happening parties were a lot of work and, despite some of the joy and beauty in the efforts to create them, some party guests seemed bored and distracted, busy sizing up what they could pocket, or complaining about how these parties got in the way of the "real" and "important" work like grant writing, publishing, presenting at conferences, and cultivating the minds of the humans who had to pay to come to campus. After attending the most confusing party of all — Equity, Diversity, and Inclusion — Coyote decided to hatch a plan.

We are living in and through an incredible time — one in which the voices of our Ancestors — heard in our dreams, written on our hearts, held in wampum belts and treaties, and echoed across time in the reports of the Royal Commission on Aboriginal Peoples (1996), the Truth and Reconciliation Commission of Canada (2015) and the National Inquiry into Missing and Murdered Indigenous Women and Girls (2019) — grow ever louder. This is a time of great healing, or at least the possibility of great healing, and of reconciling our relationships with All Our Relations — human and more-than-human — to halt the harms of the destruction of Mother Earth and the violence we enact upon her and each other. Our Ancestors fought for their breath and for ours in the face of policies that sought to separate us from ourselves, each other, the land, our memory, and our teachings. Decolonizing was what they did by waking up each morning, by fighting to remember who they were, even when that was incredibly painful to do. Decolonizing is what we do by waking up each morning, resisting our erasure, and insisting on our connection to ourselves, each other, the land, our memory, and our teachings (Minogiizhigokwe 2019b). It is what we do when we refuse to repeat the colonial harms that have been visited upon us; as Minogiizhigokwe (2019b, 48) states: "to decolonize is to disrupt the 'power over' that colonization carries."

Through this chapter and with the company of (a pleasantly genderless) Coyote, I aim to take up and share my own efforts to understand and theorize decolonial equity; I offer this knowledge as no more or no less important than anyone else's and as reflective of the best of what I know now. Human nature, Coyote reminds me, means that the best of what I know now may change in ten minutes or ten years, and I ought to remain humble to the challenges of the written word and the limited room it leaves for reflecting how our knowledge shifts like the tides and grows like the trees. I will articulate my own working understanding of decolonial equity, what it has looked like in my own journey so far and what I hope it can look like in the beauty of Black, Indigenous, and people of colour (BIPOC) futurisms. I begin by situating myself and my intentions and motivations in writing on this topic, and close with some reflections on where I hope this knowledge might go.

Ahniin, waynayboozhoo. zaagaateikwe ndizhinikaaz, makinaak ndo-dem, Sharbot Lake ndoonjiba. Anishinaabe-kwe ndow, niizh manitowag ndow. My name is Billie and my traditional name means sun comes up or rising sun woman; my home community is Sharbot Lake, a small community situated in between Ottawa and Toronto in Ontario. I iden-tify as a Two Spirit non-status Anishinaabe and I carry Anishinaabe and mixed European ancestry through both my mom and dad. I was raised in the fiercely loving matriarchies of both of my grandmothers — Donna Ladouceur and Fay Hollywood — who worked together to advocate and create spaces for connection to culture, land, language, and ceremony for community members, especially youth, through the development of a Native community centre in Sharbot Lake in the 1990s. While the cen-tre no longer stands and my grandmothers have both made their jour-neys home to the spirit world, I lovingly carry the gifts they seeded in me. I walk in the light of my mother, Susan Jackson, and in the love of my partner and children, aunties, and chosen siblings. I begin with my humble offerings of Anishinaabemowin, my best efforts to make my-self audible to my Ancestors past and future, and the Ancestors of the unceded Lekwungen territories where I reside as an uninvited relative. I also begin with offerings of gratitude, to *gitchi manidoo* (great spir-it, great mystery, or Creator) for another day and to All My Relations. I begin with gratitude to help me be humble and respectful with my words. I begin in this way to make myself visible to you, the reader, so that you can also hold the knowledge I share here in the context of who I am and where I come from and weigh its value and meaning in the context of who you are and where you come from. I name my inten-tions and motivations to practice transparency and accountability for my thoughts, words, and actions. My first intention in taking up this chapter is to contribute toward ways of reimagining and transforming equity work through a decolonial lens; this work is inherently tied up in my own healing, well-being, and sustainability in academia. My second intention is to make visible what I — and those who I have the privilege to work and walk alongside — already know and are already doing to support decolonizing equity efforts. I am motivated to contribute toward academic workplaces and learning environments that refuse and denaturalize colonialism and that support ideas of (or beyond) equity that are grounded in decolonial ethics.

After some time of prodding local hens and geese to find a willing volunteer to help them hatch their plan, Coyote finally had one. Coyote was pretty sure, from all of their mischievous adventures across time and space, that the answer was always to throw an even bigger party. Coyote imagined how much better campus could be if all the relatives attending the "Decolonial Dreaming," "Indigenize this sh*t up in here," and "Equity, Diversity, and Inclusion" parties would all just get together in one place. Surely, they would be a happier bunch and see how much more fun they could have and how much more work they could get done together. Besides, Coyote definitely needed more participants if their new take on round dancing (less corners, more sides) was ever going to take off. Coyote was in for what my Grandmother would have called one hell of a shock.

DECOLONIZING EQUITY

What does it mean to decolonize equity and why does it matter? As noted in the introductory chapter, there are serious challenges in attempting to decolonize anything let alone equity. Decolonization is not an intellectual exercise, nor is it restricted to the realm of humans, despite what must seem like (to non-human relations) our fascination with ourselves. As such, decolonization centres the "restoration of respect with Mother Earth, water, and all sources of human life" (Minogiizhigokwe, 2019a, 17) and cannot be invoked apart from Indigenous lands, lives, and lifeways (Kennedy-Kish [Bell] and Carniol 2019; Minogiizhigokwe 2019b). Minogiizhigokwe (2019a,17) describes decolonizing as an act of detoxifying, of "cleans[ing] one's spirit, heart, mind and body from the toxins of colonial knowledge." The cleansing of colonial toxins from our conceptualizations of, social agreements about, and practices toward equity is both individual and collective work; it means working to undo the insidious mechanisms of colonialism that have penetrated our ways of knowing, being, and doing, and shaped the stories we tell about ourselves, each other, and what equity might look like between us.

Equity is presented in workplaces and public discourse as an important framework for trying to achieve or contribute toward social justice in our social institutions and broader society. In contrast to this seemingly pleasant notion of equity, Dr. Sunera Thobani (2021, 18) describes equity as "a technology of power" and an "institutionalized derailment of struggles against racial injustice and coloniality within the 'woke' institutions of late modernity" that feeds itself and functions by co-opting and containing the labour of Indigenous, Black, and racialized faculty. In the landscape of postsecondary education, equity is almost always grouped with diversity and inclusion, seemingly implying that equity itself will result from diversity and inclusion. It is necessary to un-nest these terms, hold them up to the light for decolonial examination, and consider what value they offer to fostering a pathway forward that simultaneously refuses the colonial enterprise and contributes toward a shared vision of what equity can look like, and mean, within and beyond postsecondary education.

Unpacking Diversity and Inclusion

The concept of diversity invisibilizes or neutralizes the standard norm of settler colonialism and its requisite systems of domination (for example, white supremacy, racism, sexism, ableism, homophobia, transphobia, classism, and faith-based discrimination) that serve as the foundation of so-called Canada. Much like federal policies and discourses of multiculturalism aimed at neutralizing anti-racism and anti-colonialism, and at naturalizing racial hierarchies as cultural difference through a seemingly altruistic policy stance (Thobani 2007, 162), diversity and inclusion policies in educational institutions offer entry points to addressing the "Other" that are likely to be less threatening and more palatable to the dominant norm than anti-racism, Indigenization, and decolonization. Equity, when paired with diversity and inclusion, is readily co-opted into the matters and metrics of representation, more often concerned with recruitment than retention. In Chapter 2, Dr. Shauneen Pete further addresses this challenge of equity as inclusion through the "recruitment and retention of diverse peoples," when both equity and inclusion are predicated on settler logics. I share Dr. Pete's concern about the serious gap between admissions or hiring strategies that aim to increase representation and the need for efforts to ensure that the environment that "diverse" employees or students are being invited into is actually equitable, welcoming, and safe. In the context of efforts to Indigenize higher education, Gaudry and Lorenz (2018, 220) further describe this challenge as one in which universities undertake the "need to do better as a need to assist Indigenous faculty, staff, students, and communities in overcoming obstacles, rather than a more direct process of removing the obstacles."

The ways in which diversity efforts are measured and lauded are perhaps telling of the limits of diversity and inclusion as proxies to equity. For example, the winners of Canada's Best Diversity Employers are determined by reviewing the diversity and inclusiveness initiatives of employers (Mediacorp Canada 2021) rather than (or without the balance of information from) the experiences of employees coded as "diverse" who work within their respective institutions and organizations. Such approaches lend credence to what Dr. Sara Ahmed (2009, 44) describes as the use of diversity as a form of "image management" for universities, in which the focus is on "changing the perceptions of whiteness rather than changing the whiteness of organisations." Indeed, university strategic plans are far more likely to highlight diversity as an aim rather than, for example, anti-racism, which might feel more threatening to, or uncomfortable for, those who benefit from white supremacy and risk the contributions of donors or the recruitment of high-profile members for bodies like Boards of Governors. Ahmed (2009, 47) notes "To speak of racism is to introduce bad feeling[s]"; it is to hurt not only the image, but the feelings of the organization.

Under the microscope of a decolonial analysis, the admirable goal of "inclusion" raises the question: Inclusion in what? Inclusion in a colonial apparatus? Inclusion in structures of white supremacy? Inclusion in the writing-over and building-atop Indigenous territories, peoples, and ways of knowing, being, and doing? The aim of inclusion, without a relationship to local Indigenous Peoples, territories, and knowledge systems, necessarily becomes fraught with the peril of replicating colonial erasure. It also offers a critical possibility of reconsidering the notion of "inclusion" and redistributing (restoring) the power embedded in the idea of what we imagine ourselves being included in. Do we seek inclusion within the territories, lifeways, and protocols of local Indigenous

Peoples, or do we seek inclusion in the institutions built upon them? If inclusion is not spatially but, rather, relationally oriented, what does inclusion look like and feel like, and how is it recognizable through a decolonial lens?

WADING INTO THE WATER: REIMAGINING EQUITY AS BALANCE

Coyote realized that their plan for one large party was not as straightforward as they thought it might be. It turns out that the partygoers had some very different ideas about how things should go down and weren't all that interested in Coyote's not-so-round (read: appropriated square) dance. In fact, some partygoers were fiercely protective of their respective party plans, fearful that any collaboration or compromise might result in a loss of all they had worked to build in their prime partygoing years. Others were beginning to get the sense that this was no party at all and way more work than it was worth. Their spirits were tired and there was no amount of square dancing that could repair their exhaustion. Thinking the problem was music, Coyote found themselves regretting their cancelled Spotify account and longing for the 8-track collection they once pawned to some deer to buy their first pair of Air Jordans (a long and convoluted story really; let's just say it involved a Coyote-style misunderstanding involving the need for court shoes [Judge Judy] versus court shoes [Kyle Lowry] and a rather dapper appearance at a downtown Toronto courthouse). Coyote seemed to be missing the point; but hey, they still looked good in their okay suit, right?

The "Equity, Diversity, and Inclusion" party was increasingly suspect to Coyote. What did equity mean in eighth-fire times? Coyote was confused about what exactly all these humans wanted an equitable crack at or piece of. Was it an equitable chance to pull scotch broom from the homelands of the kwetlal (Corntassel and Bryce 2012)? An equitable chance to protect the waters of Mother Earth? An equitable chance to walk in balance and to live out of the teachings *mino-bimaadiziwin* (the good life)? As a respectable university employee, Coyote needed to rub their brains and heart together (an old-fashioned Anishinaabe style of thinking) and come up with a new way of imagining equity; one that could hold both where Coyote had come from and all they had seen, and what Coyote thought the humans were longing for and moving toward in their own (albeit very rhythmically challenged) healing dance way. Coyote decided to imagine equity as a being. Initially, a duck. Then a cat (Coyote was hungry). And finally, as a body of water. Unlike pies, ducks, or cats (pies being the unwitting food mascot of equity discussions), "water" as a being exceeded, informed, and constituted human life. Water was life.

Esteemed Gitxsan scholar, trailblazing Indigenous social worker and indomitable advocate for the rights of Indigenous children and family, Dr. Cindy Blackstock (2019), reflects on equity in the context of her Breath of Life (BOL) theory and emphasizes the relationship between equity and balance. She further elaborates that balance is neither static nor always possible; instead,

> it is a state achieved through deliberate and thoughtful actions made by people who position their own survival as co-dependent with the health of other people across generations and with the universe. It requires a dedication to nurture and pass on knowledge that has proven effective in achieving balance without binding it to the unrealistic expectation of non-adaptation. (2019: 858)

Dr. Blackstock, citing Atleo's 2005 work, notes the very practical example of potlatching practised by First Nations along the coast of what is presently known as British Columbia, which continues to provide a means to practice equity through redistribution today despite the outlawing of this practice through the Indian Act from 1885 to 1951. Minogiizhigokwe (2019b, 48) and Grandmother Banakonda Kennedy-Kish (Bell) (Kennedy-Kish [Bell] and Carniol 2019) also frame equity as balance and the pursuit of harmony, which includes the "rejection of forces that disrupt harmony" (Minogiizhigokwe 2019b, 48).

An Indigenous approach to understanding equity as balance offers a more nuanced entry point into reimagining our relations than fair-share equity that recentres (slice of the) pie politics (see, for example, Farrow 2019). Equity as balance extends beyond human-to-human interaction, centres our relationship and responsibilities to the land, and requires consideration of what equity means in the context of All Our Relations, of our more-than-human relatives (Kennedy-Kish (Bell) and

Carniol 2019; Minogiizhigokwe 2019b; ross 2021). In this way, equity must extend beyond conversations of fair and just access to resources, opportunities or seats at a table to consider what it means to imagine or approach redistribution and balance in ways that are accountable to Mother Earth, to the waters, plants, and animal relations that sustain us, to the air that we breathe, to our Ancestors' dreams and actions, and to those little faces yet to come (Minogiizhigokwe 2019b). For example, equitable access to clean and safe drinking water would not be an issue if humans were maintaining their relational accountability to the waters of Mother Earth and ensuring balance rather than valourizing greed through ongoing worship of the capitalist model. Likewise, monocropping, fracking, and on and offshore oil drilling demonstrates little if any concern for relational accountability, balance, or equitable relations with the land, waters, plant, and animal relations, nor with past or future generations.

Dr. Blackstock's (2019) invitation to revisit equity through or within Indigenous ontologies centres interconnectedness and interrelatedness, inviting those seeking equity to recall the ways in which our survival and well-being is bound together with the survival and well-being of others across time and space, calling in Indigenous notions of time, relationality, place, and space. Equity as relational rather than relative, requires mutual understanding, negotiation, consent, and relational accountability. In turn, mutual understanding requires an understanding of histories — our own, each other's, and those of the territories on which we reside and of the traditional caretakers of these territories. Historicizing our presence, relationships, intentions, and motivations is an anti-racist and decolonial ethic, emphasized in the writings of Queer Black Feminist scholars (Alexander 2005; Hackett 2016; Lorde 1984). Understanding what we are standing on and in relation to is necessary to undertake the "deliberate and thoughtful actions" (Blackstock 2019) needed in seeking equity as balance. Historicizing not only provides context to our lives, our relationships, and our goals, it is also a form of truth telling, particularly for those whose histories have been scattered, buried or otherwise sentenced to erasure. But truth telling must also extend into the present — the temporal context in which speaking the truth of one's experience, particularly as a BIPOC person, is likely to met with the most vibrant forms of dismissal, denial, and deflection. The truth of our experiences ought not to be reduced to the "bad feelings" that they cause institutions of whiteness (Ahmed 2009, 47) nor a pathologization of righteous anger in response to racism (Ahmed 2009; Lorde 1984; Williams 2001), both of which conveniently serve what Dr. Graham Hingangaroa Smith (2003, para 2) has named the "politics of distraction." The politics of distraction not only draw attention away from the responsibility of institutions to confront colonial violence and the failings of equity imagined through empire, they also serve to drain the collective energy needed to propel life giving work in service of the well-being of our families, communities, future generations, the earth, and our more-than-human relations.

Coyote was rather pleased with themselves for re-envisioning equity as water, ready to regale their human academic colleagues with their theoretical posturing on the ways in which "aqua-equity" would far outpace their previous imaginings. After all, Coyote thought, water was the lifeblood of Mother Earth and therefore the lifeblood of all humans; they do not live without her. In fact, Coyote noted, even when human beings travelled away from Mother Earth to visit Grandmother Moon or their strange outhouse in the sky (also known as the International Space Station), they remained tethered to the lifegiving energy of Mother Earth by carrying water and nourishment from her body in their own bodies and in their travel bags. Little humans came through the waters of their lifegivers, and humans themselves were mostly made of water. Coyote became increasingly self-satisfied with their theorizing.

Coyote was not wrong; their idea was rather clever. Anishinaabe-Métis legal scholar, Aimée Craft (2016,109) states that "water sustains all life." She also describes water as "our collective responsibility" (118). Equity, like water, is everyone's responsibility; however, the responsibility or burden of equity is not evenly shared. Motivation to attend to or attempt to achieve equity is not necessarily as interesting to those on the escalator of opportunity within universities as it is to those left climbing the stairs or searching for accessible entry and transit. If you have clean, running water in your home that can be heated or cooled at a moment's notice, then advocating for protection of and right relationship with the water may not feel as urgent or practical. However, if you cannot drink water from your tap nor safely wash your body with it, the urgency of respectful relationships with the water is undeniable. For equity-seeking employees of the university, these dynamics are reflected in critically needing but not experiencing conditions that support equity, or — drawing back to Dr. Blackstock's theorizing — the conditions that support balance.

A JOB YOU GET WITHOUT EVEN APPLYING: IN/EQUITY AND "DIVERSITY WORK"

BIPOC employees are frequently co-opted into the role of what Dr. Ahmed (2012, 59) refers to as "diversity practitioners" or "diversity workers," despite having never applied for, or perhaps even desired, such a role. For BIPOC faculty members, this may mean gathering or generating BIPOC -specific content to inform curriculum development and revision work, serving on equity, admissions and/or search committees to try to support equitable access to the university for students, staff, and faculty from BIPOC communities, or facing expectations of being a spokesperson for all things related to racism, equity, diversity and inclusion (James 2017). Indigenous faculty are likely to find their energies directed to decolonizing, Indigenizing and reconciliation efforts but not necessarily in ways that attend to our individual and collective well-being and sustainability. Indeed, much effort may be spent explaining and justifying reconciliation, decolonization, and Indigenization, and navigating anti-Indigenous racism, and the guilt, shame, anger, fear, resistance, or fatigue of those who would rather not engage with these efforts or who are confused about how best to do so (Koleszar-Green 2019).

Inequity reveals itself in many ways in the university, including in recognition, outcomes, and opportunities. It reveals itself in the available energy one has to develop research grants, publications, or conference presentations; it reveals itself in the available time and energy to visit, build relationships with, and protect relational accountability to our communities. It reveals itself in much more basic metrics, including the time to see the faces of our children or our mothers, be on the land, find and secure access to healthcare, or move our bodies beyond the face-lock of our computers. Indeed, I imagine that a balance(d) approach to equity could mean a life in which "our feet are on the Earth longer than our eyes are on technology" (Minogiizhigokwe 2019b, 50).

In the meantime, as BIPOC scholars — as inadvertent diversity workers — take up the work of building toward equity, those who need not be occupied by such efforts are freed up to write more, research more, publish more, and advance further and faster through the university echelons (Ahmed 2019). While this not only deepens disparities in service workloads and opportunities for research and publication, it arguably robs us of opportunities for relationships and learning from each other. For example, James (2017, 164) notes that as "long as racialized faculty members are perceived as the ones to teach, supervise, and mentor marginalized-group students and new faculty, majority faculty members will never take responsibility for meeting the needs and interests of marginalized students." Likewise, James (2017, 164) notes that dominant-group students "may never have the benefit of broader, different, or even more comprehensive perspective that racialized faculty members" might lend to their educational experience. Well, Coyote? How does equity as water help to clarify and transform these challenges?

WISDOM AT THE SHORELINE

Coyote is bored. It turns out the okay suit they bought for their campus gig is made of itchy and uncomfortable material. Worse than the rash caused by synthetic and non-biodegradable fabric, Coyote has discovered the discomfort of sharing one's theorizing with academic colleagues who aren't really interested in what you have to say and instead spend their time silently speculating how a Coyote got a faculty position in the first place ("Were there even Coyotes with PhDs? What kind of topics did they study? Probably best to have them teach that Coyote practice class. Don't worry, they won't last. Coyotes aren't very reliable after all"). Despite the discouraging effect of hanging out with academics, Coyote knows there is something to the equity as water idea. They take it to the shoreline where they know they'll get some real feedback from the relatives who make their homes and families on and in the water.

Coyote digs out their best swim trunk-ini and takes the necessary deep dive to hear from the salmon, orcas, ducks, clams, and even the seaweed. Coyote is reminded of the sacredness of the water and of its most beautiful Anishinaabe name: *nibi*. The water-based families remind Coyote that water gives, renews, and replenishes life; water heals, cleanses, and transforms. Snow, ice, mist, rain, salted, fresh, birth; the waters of life are necessary to ensure balance, cycles of rest and renewal, birth and rebirth. Understanding equity as *nibi* means restoring or renewing human understanding of our undeniable interconnectedness and interrelatedness that no amount of capitalist-driven, ad-filled, desire-based, purchased amnesia could forget. Coyote is so moved by this act of remembering that *nibi* even breaks free from their eyes, carrying away the toxins of their pent-up grief and frustration.

The beauty of equity as *nibi*, or viewing equity through the lens of *nibi*, is that equity can move from something needed, demanded or expected by "diverse" others, to something needed by everyone in order to sustain a meaningful balance among us and to renew our rightful relationships with Mother Earth and All Our Relations. It invites a rupture of practices of resource management, and in the case of the university, the management of diverse bodies as human resources to meet its image maintenance needs or to (voluntarily or not) form a body of diversity workers needed to free up those who ought not to be delayed in their ride up the academic escalator (Ahmed 2009; 2019). Equity as *nibi* ties discussions of "fairness" and "social justice" to local Indigenous Peoples and territories, and propels us away from equity pie politics which, for Indigenous Peoples, sounds altogether too much like the parcelling up and out of homelands.

Decolonizing equity aims to rematriate social justice on Turtle Island to the Indigenous ontologies of this place; it is an ancestral homecoming of what it means to be a good relative, to practice relational accountability, to live, give, and receive in balance. It requires dialogues and practices of relationality that emphasize the stewardship of equity and which rightfully re-root traditions and practices of redistribution so painstakingly protected by Indigenous Peoples despite generations of colonial assault. These practices of redistribution serve to maintain memory, renew relationships, and foster futurities that account for the well-being and balance of All Our Relations. Decolonizing equity resists and refuses pathways to equity founded in fear, scarcity, and fragmentation and instead emphasizes that which is generative and life giving. It invites us all, but especially those seeking equity, to see our needs in relation rather than in competition. Necessarily, decolonizing equity confronts the epistemic racism that continues to iterate the presumed inferiority of Indigenous ways of knowing, being, and doing; to be clear, epistemic racism remains one of the most critical linchpins in the colonial machinery of universities and the nation-states built atop Turtle Island.

Coyote pondered a career change. After only days in the academe, Coyote was already exhausted. So many meetings, so much talking. SO. MUCH. EMAIL. Coyote longed for the days when humans still remembered how to communicate without electronic devices and even without words. Besides, Coyote was also highly suspicious of the "Team Diversity" t-shirt that had been slipped under the doorway of their office; were they becoming a diversity worker? Aside from the confusing social climate of the academic workplace, Coyote found their heart deeply full from their visit to the shoreline, where equity as *nibi* was so beautiful and so obvious. They wanted to take up their role as a caretaker to *nibi* and therefore as a good relative to All Their Relations; they wanted to put their good trickster gifts toward dealing with those who would try to buy, sell, dominate, and poison *nibi*, those who would engage *nibi* without conversation or consent. This seemed easier and less taxing than spending their savvy trickster gifts dealing with academic administrators who sought to buy, sell, dominate, and poison equity efforts within the university and those who engaged with the fates of those in need of equity without conversation or consent. Coyote's work was done here for now. At least until a management position opened up. What good was an okay suit without a corner office to air it out in?

I am so grateful to Coyote who has travelled with me (or at least dropped by) on many legs of my journey to this point in my life. Coyote's mischief and joy, and their readiness to make fun of humans for the purposes of fostering growth always renews and sustains me. I am particularly grateful for Coyote's theoretical posturing and the opportunity to reconsider equity through the lens of *nibi* and to Dr. Blackstock (2019) for the opportunity to know equity as balance. Before concluding, I will briefly return to my intention of sharing some examples of what I have witnessed and contributed toward in terms of decolonial equity policies and practices.

DECOLONIAL EQUITY IN ACTION

I currently have the profound privilege of residing on the unceded homelands of the ləkʷəŋən peoples, the Songhees and Esquimalt Nations, and learning, working, and moving across the territories of both the ləkʷəŋən and W̱SÁNEĆ peoples in my role as an Assistant Professor in the School of Social Work at the University of Victoria. It is a deeply humbling experience to be an Indigenous person living on the territories of other Indigenous Peoples and striving to be a good relative through the lens of both my teachings and theirs. I want to be recognizable as a good relative through the eyes of both their Ancestors and my own. As an employee of an institution built upon unceded land, I am invested in what decolonizing can look like and mean when it is accountable to the local First Nations and their histories, teachings, and practices. How do, or would, these local Nations recognize the university as a meaningful, safe, and worthwhile space to engage? How might our university so deeply embed and embody our respect of local Indigenous laws and lifeways that the belongingness of the physical and psychospiritual space of the university to the local nations would become recognizable to all?

In thinking about this, I understand that part of my learning as a visitor here is to understand what equity looks like, means, and feels like through the lens of local teachings and through learning from the land. This is work that can only take place by being a very careful listener, by being a witness. While my own learning as a relative from away is necessarily ongoing, what I have witnessed on these territories is a kind of generosity that refuses the fear of scarcity, and a kind of intentionality that reflects relational accountability beyond the limits of Western time and space and includes more-than-human relations. I have experienced the opportunity to stand in the light of the teachings of local Indigenous Peoples — not only from ləkʷəŋən and WSÁNEĆ territories, but from territories spread across the island and onto the mainland. Standing in the light of these teachings has emphasized that equity must be generous, lifegiving, and accountable to more-than-human relations. While my learning as a relative from away will be lifelong, I name these examples here to articulate that my vision of decolonial equity includes relational accountability at the local level.

My treasured colleague and co-editor, Dr. Hackett, and I have spent several years walking with this notion of decolonizing equity alongside our relatives (faculty, staff, and students) in the School of Social Work. Within our School, decolonizing equity has been employed as a framework for admissions that centres intersectionality and currently aims to prioritize Indigenous Peoples, Black peoples, and other peoples of colour. Specifically, the School's current admission policy is described as such:

> The School welcomes and is actively recruiting applicants from communities that experience historical and present-day systemic discrimination and marginalization, and who are committed to social justice, equity, anti-racism and decolonization. In our admissions decisions, we will apply a decolonial equity framework which includes an intersectional lens and will prioritize applicants who are Indigenous, Black and people of colour. (University of Victoria School of Social Work, 2021, n.p.)

A decolonial equity approach recognizes the need for a body of social workers that is reflective not simply of the society we live in, but of those who are overrepresented in engagement (voluntary or mandated) with social work services. It further recognizes that inequity — as an outcome of historic and continuing colonization — will not be resolved by good intentions nor what Ahmed (2009) calls the "good feelings" work of diversity, and that it must be proactively addressed through action. Utilizing a decolonial equity approach invites a shift in equity work in admissions from conversations based in pie politics to generative dialogue and decision making about our responsibilities to redress the underrepresentation of BIPOC relatives and other equity-seeking groups in social work student, staff, and faculty bodies despite their overrepresentation in the teeth of social work services. Like equity as *nibi*, this approach leaves room for fluidity, recognizing that over time, conditions of in/equity will shift and transform. Decolonial equity has also become embedded more broadly in our School, including as part of our Unit Standards that are used to assess faculty performance and provide the criteria by which faculty members are appraised for merit, re-appointment, tenure and promotion, and as a fundamental framework for reimagining our curriculum.

Decolonial equity holds promise in helping to see urgent and poignant issues of inequity as interconnected rather than in competition. Regardless of where one wishes to seed and grow decolonial equity efforts, relationship and relational accountability are critical to building the trust needed to stretch beyond our equity needs to witness those of others and to find ways forward together that require neither fragmentation nor destruction (Alexander 2005; Lorde 1984). I would argue that decolonial equity functions on a desire for non-disposability, meaning a sense of trust that we won't, as relatives, throw each other away on the long and bramble-filled pathway to revisioning and realizing equity.

At its core, decolonial equity requires all parties involved to have some foundational understanding of and agreement about the realities of colonialism and the colonial inequities we are seeking to undo. While this may sound obvious, in the context of longstanding state denial and minimalization of colonialism, the vast majority of leaders in academic environments are unlikely to have had access to a primary, secondary, or postsecondary education that actively addressed the colonial violence underpinning the founding of the Canadian nation-state and the subsequent inequities created and maintained by Canada. In some spaces, this means that the facts, impacts, and relative importance of addressing colonialism are vigorously contested, feeding politics of distraction (Smith 2003, para 2) and substantially draining the psychospiritual and relational energy needed to realize decolonial change.

CONCLUSION

Decolonial equity work has been a source of healing for me. In line with the theorizing of Ozioma Aloziem in Chapter 7 and Dr. Hackett in Chapter 8, I see healing as central to the learning and unlearning process, and as critical to transforming equity from something steeped in colonialism to something steeped in, and emerging from, decolonization. I am grateful to walk in the light of BIPOC scholars, Elders, academic aunties, community siblings, and students who have shaped and informed my knowing, being, and doing, especially in coming to focus on what it means to be a good relative. I am forever indebted to my co-editor, Dr. Hackett, who so generously shares from her wealth of knowledge and experience, and whose endurance for the processing work that decolonial equity requires is beyond fathomable.

I hope that the knowledge shared through this book, so carefully offered up by each author, can serve to upend, deepen, or otherwise transform EDI initiatives both within and beyond universities. As University of Victoria roots the groundbreaking Centre for Indigenous Laws and joint Indigenous and Canadian Laws program, I envision the emergence of ever-increasing understandings of equity grounded in the teachings and laws of various Nations across Turtle Island. Equity without decolonization voids pathways to reconciliation. Equity without decolonization simply finds new ways to divide the empire rather than to restore and reinvigorate our responsibilities to All Our Relations needed to ensure and protect the well-being of Mother Earth and of *nibi*, her lifeblood. Decolonizing equity offers us a way to care for the waters shared between us, both physical and metaphorical, and to remember our relationships. Decolonizing equity does not equivocate our respective equity needs, but it does demand serious efforts toward decolonial solidarity.

My own understandings of decolonial solidarity have been informed by the writings of Dr. Alexander (2005, 269) who describes the necessity of women of colour to

> become fluent in each others' histories, to resist and unlearn an impulse to claim first oppression, must-devastating oppression, one-of-a-kind oppression, defying-comparison oppression. We would have to unlearn an impulse that allows mythologies about each other to replace *knowing* about one another. We would need to cultivate a way of knowing in which we direct our social, cultural, psychic, and spiritually marked attention on each other. We cannot afford to cease yearning for each others' company. (original emphasis)

Finding common ground requires that we understand what we are standing on and in relation to as we take up this work. There are no shortcuts, no expensive but efficient toll roads on the way to decolonial solidarity. It is a journey that, to borrow the words of Dr. Shauneen Pete in Chapter 2, requires developing and maintaining our stamina for the work. Dr. Alexander (2005, 283) likewise describes the endurance needed for such efforts:

> When we have failed at solidarity work we often retreat, struggling to convince ourselves that this is indeed the work we've been called to do. The fact of the matter is that there is no other work but the work of creating and recreating ourselves within the context of community. Simply put, there is no other work. It took five hundred years, at least in this hemisphere, to solidify the division of things that belong together. But it need not take us another five hundred years

to move ourselves out of this existential impasse. Spirit work does not conform to the dictates of human time, but needs our courage, revolutionary patience and intentional shifts in consciousness...

In seeding decolonial dreams of new ways of taking up equity in the academy, I am hopeful to see EDI departments that refuse to continue to trot out Canadian multiculturalism, nationalism, and diversity discourses in what can only be understood as colonial landscaping and maintenance work. Instead, decolonization should be the foundation of reimagining equity and working more authentically toward reconciliation. Coyote is pretty sure we shouldn't have it any other way.

References

Ahmed, Sara. 2009. "Embodying Diversity: Problems and Paradoxes for Black Feminists." *Race Ethnicity and Education* 12, 1.

___. 2012. *On Being Included*. Durham: Duke University Press.

___. 2019. *What's the Use? On the Uses of Use*. Durham: Duke University Press.

Alexander, M. Jacqui. 2005. *Pedagogies of Crossing: Meditations on Feminism, Sexual Politics, Memory and the Sacred*. Durham: Duke University Press.

Azhar, Sameena, and Kendra DeLoach McCutcheon. 2021. "How Racism Against BIPOC Women Faculty Operates in Social Work Academia." *Advances in Social Work* 21, 2/3.

Blackstock, Cindy. 2019. "Revisiting the Breath of Life Theory." *British Journal of Social Work* 49, 4.

Corntassel, Jeff, and Cheryl Bryce. 2012. "Practicing Sustainable Self-Determination: Indigenous Approaches to Cultural Restoration and Revitalization." *Brown Journal of Social Issues* XVII, 11.

Craft, Aimée. 2016. "Giving and Receiving Life from Anishinaabe Nibi Inaakonigewin (Our Water Law) Research." In *Methodological Challenges in Nature-Culture and Environmental History Research*, edited by Jocelyn Thorpe, Stephanie Rutherford, and L. Anders Sandberg. London: Routledge.

Farrow, Jon. 2019. "A Bigger, Tastier, More Equitable Economic Pie Is Possible." *CIFAR*. cifar.ca/cifarnews/2019/09/03/a-bigger-tastier-more-equitable-economic-pie-is-possible/.

Gaudry, Adam, and Danielle Lorenz. 2018. "Indigenization as Inclusion, Reconciliation, and Decolonization: Navigating the Different Visions for

Indigenizing the Canadian Academy." *AlterNative: An International Journal of Indigenous Peoples* 14, 3.

Hackett, V.C. Rhonda. 2016. "Families Building Nations, or Nations Building on Families? An Exploration of How African Caribbean Immigrants (Re) Construct Family in the Context of Immigration and Oppression in Canada." Doctoral dissertation, University of Toronto.

James, Carl. 2017. "'You Know Why You Were Hired Don't You?' Expectations and Challenges in University Appointments." In *The Equity Myth: Racialization and Indigeneity at Canadian Universities*, edited by Frances Henry, Carl James, Peter Li, et al. Vancouver: UBC Press.

Kennedy-Kish (Bell), Banakonda, and Ben Carniol. 2019. "Vision and Belief within Indigenous and Jewish Spirituality." In *Spirituality and Social Justice*, edited by Norma Jean Profitt and Cyndy Baskin. Toronto: Canadian Scholars' Press.

Koleszar-Green, Ruth. 2019. "What Can I Do? Teaching Indigenous Content in an Era of 'Reconciliation.'" *Intersectionalities: A Global Journal of Social Work Analysis, Research, Polity, and Practice* 7, 1.

Lorde, Audre. 1984. *Sister Outsider: Essays and Speeches by Audre Lorde.* Trumansberg: Crossing Press.

Mediacorp Canada. 2021. "Canada's Best Diversity Employers (2021)." canadastop100.com/diversity/.

Minogiizhigokwe (Kathy Absolon). 2019a. "Decolonizing Education and Educators' Decolonizing." *Intersectionalities: A Global Journal of Social Work Analysis, Research, Polity and Practice* 7, 1.

___. 2019b. "Reconnecting to Creation: A Spirit of Decolonization." In *Spirituality and Social Justice* edited by Norma Jean Profitt and Cyndy Baskin. Toronto: Canadian Scholars' Press.

National Inquiry into Missing and Murdered Indigenous Women and Girls. 2019. *Calls for Justice*. Ottawa, ON. mmiwg-ffada.ca/wp-content/uploads/2019/06/Calls_for_Justice.pdf.

ross, annie. 2021. "Don't Cry, Fight! Vs. Deference to the Corporate State." In *Coloniality and Racial (In)Justice in the University: Counting for Nothing!* edited by Sunera Thobani. Toronto: Canadian Scholars' Press.

Royal Commission on Aboriginal Peoples. 1996. "Volume 1 Looking Forward, Looking Back." Ottawa: Canada Communication Group.

Smith, Graham Hingangaroa. 2003. "Indigenous Struggle for the Transformation of Education and Schooling." Keynote address to the Alaskan Federation of Natives (AFN) Convention, Anchorage, Alaska. ankn.uaf.edu/curriculum/Articles/GrahamSmith.

Thobani, Sunera. 2007. *Exalted Subjects: Studies in the Making of Race and Nation in Canada*. Toronto: University of Toronto Press.

___. (ed.). 2021. *Coloniality and Racial (In)Justice in the University: Counting for Nothing?* Toronto, ON: University of Toronto.

Truth and Reconciliation Commission of Canada. 2015. *Truth and Reconciliation of Canada: Calls to Action*. Winnipeg. gov.bc.ca/assets/gov/british-columbians-our-governments/indigenous-people/aboriginal-peoples-documents/calls_to_action_english2.pdf.

University of Victoria. 2021. *Future Students*. uvic.ca/hsd/socialwork/home/home/our-programs/index.php.

Williams, Charmaine. 2001. "The Angry Black Woman Scholar." *NWSA Journal* 13, 2.

2

DECOLONIZING EQUITY PRAXIS

Shauneen Pete

In 2018, following an extensive community consultation that included diverse members of the community, the university where I work — University of Victoria — introduced its newly revised Equity Statement. It states that the university

> is committed to upholding the values of equity, diversity, and inclusion in our living, learning and work environments. In pursuit of our values, we seek members who will work respectfully and constructively with differences and across levels of power. We actively encourage applications from members of groups who have experienced barriers to employment.

The Equity Statement is meant to guide the recruitment and retention of greater numbers of racialized, Indigenous, queer, and disabled individuals. In 2019, the university reported that they employed 57.9 percent women, 11.3 percent visible minorities, 4.5 percent people with disabilities, and 3.6 percent Indigenous Peoples (University of Victoria 2018–2019). Equity — defined as the recruitment of diverse peoples — offers an important step toward the university reflecting the local population. However, in our case, our city is predominantly white, with an Indigenous population of 4.6 percent and a visible minority population of 15.2 percent (Statistics Canada 2017a). Our province has a visible minority population of 30.3 percent while the Indigenous population is 5.9 percent (Statistics Canada 2017b). Reporting in this way offers us a baseline of data that can be useful toward an argument for increased hiring of racial minorities; however, without disaggregating the data by ethnicity in the case of visible minorities, or by nationhood in relation to Indigenous Peoples, we do not have an accurate picture of whether we have begun to reflect our local community.

Additionally, Indigenous Peoples are not just concerned about race-based recruitment in higher education. Indigenous Peoples are concerned about confronting settler colonialism. As an Indigenous person living in the unceded territory of the Songhees, Esquimalt, and WSÁNEĆ peoples, I recognize that I am an uninvited guest in these territories; and that these lands, like the rest of Canada, are shaped by ongoing settler colonialism. Settler colonialism is a structure that assumes the assimilation of Indigenous Peoples into mainstream society. Settler colonialism (not *just* race) shape my experiences with the university. Therefore, in my view, equity, diversity, and inclusion are projects that are both marked by and serve settler colonialism. To go further, I often work in relation with *settlers* within the context of the colonial structure of higher education. My understanding of the term settler is informed by the work of Battell Lowman and Barker (2015) who state that settler is a relational term (contested, misunderstood, and denied). I also include people of colour under the umbrella of settler, because people of colour continue to assert their desire to continue to live on these lands.

Because I view the university as a settler colonial structure, and I view my work in teacher education as essentially about settler decolonization, I recognize that my labour in the university is marked by my goals toward decolonization. I assert that my labour is not just about fitting into an already established institutional milieu, but about the dismantling of that institutional milieu through the process of decolonization. As an Indigenous person I wonder: is it enough to (just) recruit Indigenous Peoples as employees without understanding what their goals are? What do settlers want when they work toward greater levels of recruitment of Indigenous Peoples and how does that differ from what Indigenous Peoples want from the university? Do equity policies do the work that Indigenous Peoples need or want? Lastly, I wonder: Is a decolonial lens missing in equity policy and practices?

Before I take on those questions, I begin the chapter with self-locating and by sharing select personal reflections about my own experiences in the academy. Then, I outline the equity policies at the university where I work. I briefly explore some of the experiences I have had while exposing the "settler logics" that I recognize (Lloyd and Wolfe 2015). Through these stories I begin to expose what settlers want from their Indigenous colleagues. I experience these discourses in problematic ways, which I explore through story. I use a storytelling approach because this, too, is a decolonizing act; for me, storytelling speaks back to the dominant norms of knowledge transfer in the academy. Decolonizing equity calls on us to expose the settler logics related to equity discourses. Throughout the chapter, I reflect on our search for a new university president and how this process exposes some of the holes in our equity praxis. I consider key ideas from Indigenous scholars and offer some integrated approaches toward decolonizing equity praxis.

PERSONAL REFLECTION

Dr. Shauneen Pete nitsigowisin. Niya nehiyawin. I am from Little Pine First Nation in Treaty 6 territory (Saskatchewan, Canada). I began my career in Canadian higher education in 2001. I've worked as both the Vice-President (Academic) and Interim President at First Nations University of Canada and as the Executive Lead: Indigenization at the University of Regina where I earned a full professorship before taking a leave to pursue a business initiative. Since 2018, I have been working at the University of Victoria as the Indigenous Resurgence Coordinator in the Faculty of Education. I bring to the position my experience in higher education informed by my radical Indigeneity and my commitments toward Indigenous resurgence. I interpret my role in the faculty as helping my colleagues and students to gain stamina for the ambiguity they will experience as they engage more actively in Indigenization, reconciliation, and decolonization.

The University of Victoria has a reputation of attracting and retaining Indigenous staff and faculty. In 2019, eighty-five Indigenous people worked at the university in various capacities (University of Victoria 2018–2019). Indigenous Peoples make up 2.3 percent of all employees and 2.5 percent of all faculty on campus. The university has been ranked as one of Canada's Best Diversity Employers. It has a well-established reputation for its diversity of Indigenous programs, for example in Education, Social Work, and Law.

Now that I have worked here for a time, I have noticed settler logics (Lloyd and Wolfe 2015) that are tied to the university's articulation of their policies that support equity, inclusion, and diversity. In fact, I have experienced an uncomfortable over-reliance on equity policies as a sort of deflection (that is, "look we have a policy…look at us being equitable") to avoid a deeper examination of and the necessary relational work of listening to how the institution is experienced by Indigenous Peoples working on this campus.

This chapter explores the following question: if equity in higher education is centred on the recruitment and retention of diverse peoples, including Indigenous Peoples, how do Indigenous Peoples experience equity in higher education? After collaborating with other Indigenous colleagues to re-centre Indigenizing and decolonizing responsibilities during the search for a new president, I was asked by an Indigenous faculty colleague to submit a chapter for this book. I am grateful for the opportunity to wrestle with the ideas of equity, especially given the way the president search has unfolded. Let's begin with this story.

SEEKING THE LEADER WE NEED: BECAUSE DECOLONIZATION AND RESURGENCE MATTERS

This past year, a group of Indigenous staff met to offer a safe space to one another to explore our experiences of working at our university. We needed more opportunities to meet and offer support to one another because we identified that the normal channels (speaking to supervisors, or calling someone in/out) when addressing racist, colonial attitudes shut down the possibilities for resolution and discouraged us from speaking up any further. While many stories come to mind, the story that I will share here concerns the search for a new university president.

The search committee held several open engagement sessions with staff, faculty, students, alumni, and others to determine the qualifications and experiences of potential candidates. Several Indigenous faculty and staff collaborated on a written submission for the search committee. We identified the skills, knowledge, experience, and attitudes that we felt were needed to advance Indigenization, reconciliation, and decolonization. We grounded our submission within the national policy framework of Universities Canada/Universités Canada; the provincial policy frameworks toward the United Nations Declaration of the Rights of Indigenous Peoples; the Truth and Reconciliation Commission of Canada; and the Tsilhqot'in Supreme Court Decision (Ministry of Indigenous Relations and Reconciliation Service Plan). We expressed the need to attract candidates who had a demonstrated track record of naming and addressing white supremacy and racism. We asked that candidates address how they have addressed racism in their past work. We wanted to hear how candidates understood colonization, settler colonialism, and decolonization. We wanted candidates to identify how they intended to drive change from inclusion toward meaningful reconciliation. Our written submission also addressed our desire to have candidates identify how they had dismantled institutional barriers for Indigenous learners, staff, and faculty, as well as how they had supported environmental and climate change concerns. In support of the application, we suggested that candidates should submit letters of recommendation from an Indigenous community leader, elder, organization, or band council. We also suggested the names of nine Indigenous and settler leaders who we felt could take up the work. We shared the written submission drafts with one another so that when we spoke at the public engagement sessions, we offered a consistent message. We informally confirmed with one another which of the consultation sessions we would attend; in this way we could ensure that every session included at least a couple of Indigenous Peoples. During the in-person consultation sessions we acknowledged that the scholarship on the retention of Indigenous Peoples in higher education focused on their experiences with racism and settler colonialism in these institutions. We also spoke to some of the ideas presented in our draft written submission; specifically, we addressed the need for candidates to demonstrate anti-racism and decolonizing praxis in their experience.

During the engagement sessions, a person of colour asked the search firm representative about the diversity of the search committee; in particular, they asked how Indigenous Peoples were represented on the committee. This was an important question, as it attempted to address our collective concern for Indigenous representation on all aspects of the search. The representative of the search firm could not answer the question. The person of colour asked whether the search committee could post a photo of the committee members on the university website — an attempt, I imagine, to get a clearer picture of diverse representation on the committee. No photo was provided; however, the list of names of the search committee were posted instead.

Following up from these sessions, several Indigenous staff and faculty joined with peoples of colour to draft a second letter to the search committee raising our concerns about the diversity of the committee itself. We were informed that the twenty-two committee members were selected following university policy and that they would be taking anti-bias training. We expressed our concern that the anti-bias training did not fill in for actual diverse representation on the committee. I wondered how many other Indigenous colleagues experienced the lack of representation on the committee as another example of the settler logic of "erasure and elimination" (Lloyd and Wolfe 2015). Merely inviting Indigenous Peoples to partake in the community consultation does not replace our full participation in the decision making processes. To our credit, we Indigenous staff and faculty remained hopeful that some members of the search committee would speak up for anti-racism, eco-justice, and reconciliation. But who on the search committee would speak authoritatively toward decolonization? How would a decolonizing equity praxis have offered us a different experience in relation to this search? What would decolonizing equity praxis look like within the search process? To answer those questions, I turn to our current policy environment to confirm how the university equity policies are framed. I suggest we need to interrogate settler colonialism in equity praxis because the experiences of Indigenous Peoples are not only about racism; they are also about ongoing colonialism.

EQUITY POLICY FRAMEWORKS

The University of Victoria has several policies related to equity, including the Policy on Human Rights, Equity, and Fairness that is aimed at the prevention of discrimination and providing procedures to resolve complaints. This policy is meant to be "an overarching policy that applies to all activities, initiatives and policies of the University" (University Policy NO: GV0200, effective May 2005, 2), and further states that:

> The University promotes a safe, respectful and supportive learning and working environment for all members of the university community. The University fosters an environment characterized by fairness, openness, equity, and respect for the dignity and diversity of its members. The University strives to be a place that is free from discrimination and harassment, injustice and violence.

The university also has an *Employment Equity Policy* (University of Victoria 2015–2020). The aim of this policy is to remove barriers to employment and create an inclusive and welcoming environment for members of designated groups. The policy states: "the university's goals of a diversified workforce across all ranks, job levels and classifications will be achieved within a framework of merit, inclusion, respect and a climate free of discriminatory barriers" (University Policy NO: HR6100, effective Sept. 2011). These policies also work in alignment with the university Equity Statement which I introduced earlier. The Equity Policy aims to recruit more diverse peoples to promote "a rich environment enlivened by the experiences, approaches, and ideas of people…" (University of Victoria n.d.). I can't help but wonder: do these policies simply offer up the appearance or illusion of being good at equity? I think the proof is in the storying of minoritized peoples. We need to ask, once we attract diverse peoples, what are the realities of our experiences in the university?

INDIGENOUS EXPERIENCE IN EQUITY LANDSCAPES

As a new faculty member (some twenty years ago), I was approached by a tenured faculty member. He added that I was offered a faculty role (albeit a term position) because I had two of the four equity bases covered. His comments implied that I had it made because of my gender and, of course, my Indigenous identity. The message was clear: he viewed my hiring as token, to fill a gap. I did not *earn* my position, I was handed it. Unfortunately, twenty years later, some Indigenous and racial minority peoples still experience this type of thinking from our colleagues.

In my view, the way that equity policy has been written is framed by dominant forms of feel-good multiculturalism that do not account for the experiences of minoritized peoples in the university. Minority employees report a range of racist microaggressions (Crandall and Garcia 2016; Johnson and Joseph-Salisbury 2018; Rollock 2018). They also report experiences with institutionalized racism (Ahmed 2012). While the scholarship of racial minority peoples exposes frequent experiences with racism, a closer look at Indigenous Peoples' experiences in higher education exposes both racism and colonialism. Grande and Anderson (2017, 139) assert that "unlike other minoritized groups, the political project of Indigenous Peoples is not one of inclusion, equality, or even equity (what does the equitable distribution of stolen land look like?) rather it is about decolonization, a political project that begins and ends with land and its return." I understand that colonialism led to the removal of Indigenous Peoples from their traditional territories by the state. The state facilitated this removal (erasure) to gain greater access to lands and resources. I also recognize that settler colonialism is ongoing and that it continues to shape the Canadian identity. Settler colonialism shapes our understanding of our histories, and the social constructions of race, difference, and power (Wolfe 2006). I recognize that settler colonialism enacts racism to dehumanize, and to justify the eradication of Indigenous Peoples. Settler colonialism establishes a settler society to replace Indigenous Peoples, and dominant norms and values are institutionalized into laws, education, governance, and other structures. Settler colonialism persists through the values and organizational norms of these institutions. I understand that even policies meant to advance equity and diversity may be constructed in ways that reflect settler colonialism. Can my workplace that wants to achieve the inclusion of Indigenous Peoples at higher levels through equity and diversity policies also contribute to decolonization? Again, I ask, can equity be decolonized?

What would a decolonial turn on equity look like? To explore this question, I turn to Lawrence and Dua (2005) who call for a decolonizing anti-racism praxis. Lawrence and Dua (2005, 127) assert that anti-racism is "constructed on a colonizing framework." These authors noted the absence of Indigenous Peoples from anti-racism theory and practice, including in their own earlier work. They agree that this absence "distorts our understanding of 'race' and racism" (132). I am guided by these scholars to likewise consider how equity frameworks are colonial, and to proceed with imagining decolonial equity by "talking on Indigenous terms" and beginning with "the realities of contemporary colonization and resistance" (Lawrence and Dua 2005, 137). I do so by exposing Indigenous experiences within the equity landscape in which I work. I share a collection of personal stories and I expose the settler logics within equity discourses, beginning with the settler logic of elimination.

SETTLER LOGIC OF ELIMINATION

I once served as a witness/ally for an undergraduate student. During their first class (Canadian Poetry), the student asked why there was no content by Indigenous Peoples. The instructor responded that there were no Canadian Indigenous poets. The student met with the instructor after the class. She told the instructor that there were two Indigenous poets who worked *on campus*. The instructor dismissed her comments and walked away. The student came to see me, in my capacity as Executive Lead: Indigenization. Together, we strategized some approaches for addressing her concerns with her instructor and the English department. I requested a meeting with the department head, and we were informed the instructor did not agree to attend. Our conversation with the department head was a disappointment and the student decided to drop the class. On the one hand, the instructor was not held accountable within the department and simply denied wrongdoing and then chose not to participate in attempts to resolve the issue. On the other hand, the Indigenous student invested her time and emotional labour into trying to resolve the matter, to no avail. Later, I experienced microaggression when I was advised to not overstep my bounds by interfering in another faculty (even when my role was to provide leadership across every faculty). I now understand this lack of responsiveness as intentional, in the same way that I see the lack of Indigenous content as intentional. Kuokkanen (2008, 68) explains that acts of ignorance like that expressed by the instructor are not just individual expressions but are rooted in epistemic ignorance: "the systemic exclusion and inequality of Indigenous epistemes, philosophies, and intellectual traditions in the academy." Epistemic ignorance serves as a control mechanism designed to naturalize the settler colonial goals of elimination and assimilation of Indigenous Peoples. In this case, it was the erasure of Indigenous Peoples from the Canadian poetry landscape. Tied to the settler logic of elimination is the assumption of assimilation.

I believe the goal of assimilation is central to the recruitment and retention strategies of the university. The control mechanisms in place to ensure an assimilative agenda include the expectation that we should be grateful for access (Gause 2011), while at the same time contending with the experiences of "cultural taxation" and "contractual benevolence" (Gause 2011) of the university that racialized peoples feel when we are hired to serve the needs of the dominant group. I explore these control mechanisms in the following sections.

THE CONTRACTUAL BENEVOLENCE OF THE ACADEMY

The recruitment and retention of Indigenous students, staff, and faculty has been a priority for many Canadian universities in recent years, especially following the release of the Truth and Reconciliation Commission of Canada's Final Report (2015). Many institutions developed senior administrative positions to advance Indigenization including Vice-Provost, Special Advisor, and other roles. I've wondered: how have these roles been perceived by members of the university community?

When I was appointed to serve as the Executive Lead: Indigenization I was invited to speak at the Executive Team Fall Retreat. I was asked to introduce our newly developed definition of Indigenization and the work plan that was co-developed by members of the Indigenous Advisory Circle. I projected the definition onto the screen and read it aloud. I was deliberate with my delivery, speaking slowly to emphasize phrases — Indigenization is the transformation of the existing academy…the establishment of physical and epistemic spaces that facilitate the ethical stewardship of a plurality of Indigenous knowledges…an essential element of the university…I followed up with a description of what the inclusion of Indigenous content could look like, citing examples from other institutions. I described the need to anticipate racism as students were exposed to the violent, racist history of our country, and I introduced the topic of decolonization. As I concluded my presentation, a hand went up in the audience. My colleague was aghast: "Dr. Pete, are you saying you want to change the university? You talk of racism… decolonization. Don't you think you would get more buy-in if you used language that was — well, less political?" In this example, I understood that there was a desire on the part of my colleague for my presentation to be — well, palatable, or at least comforting for him. But I did not believe that my responsibilities as an Indigenous administrative colleague were primarily to be non-confrontational or non-political; in fact, to do so would serve settler status quo. I am here with a very different agenda in mind: to disrupt and transform the colonial university. If you think I am working here to serve the status quo, then I am not the Indian you thought you hired! A decolonial turn on equity discourses requires a critical examination of what settlers want from equity, and thus what they want from their Indigenous colleagues.

I appreciate Gause's (2011, 6) reference to the experience of contractual benevolence: "you are welcome to come to dinner at my house and sit at my table; but you better behave while at the table." He further states that "members of the white dominant culture extend an invitation to a person of color...but with limitations. They must adhere to all 'codes' and not question or critique inequities" (8). In subtle and not so subtle ways, Indigenous faculty and staff are very quickly conditioned to use caution when they speak and respond to settlers. Yet, Stein (2017) asks, "When non-Indigenous scholars engage Indigenous thinkers, we need to ask ourselves: What are we expecting to hear when Indigenous people speak, and are we able to hear them when they deviate from that script?"

In a committee meeting where we were discussing the leadership qualities for a position, I suggested that we include a statement about the candidate demonstrating experience in reducing racism. A colleague responded, "I am very uncomfortable about the word racism." I responded, "I am very uncomfortable with the experience of racism." Not long after this meeting, the members were informed that the department voted to disband the committee. A new search committee was created, and I was not invited to participate. These experiences of feeling like I've broken the social codes about naming racism are real and all too common. First, Indigenous Peoples are already code switching — choosing our words wisely so as not to startle or offend. And yet, we can't assume that settlers share the same (academic) language as us. Kuokkanen (2008, 76) states that "when Indigenous Peoples seek to express themselves and their perspectives in a way that is grounded in their own epistemes and discursive practices...is when they are most likely to be miscomprehended or misinterpreted." So, we often go to great lengths to select the right words so as to avoid being perceived as hostile (there's an old settler trope).

Indigenous Peoples understand that settlers want us to be grateful to be here in the university, because they created equity policies that allowed more of us to attend and we are not supposed to expose the inequalities of the institution. When we name the kinds of racial microaggressions that are all too common for us, there are few institutional mechanisms to address them. Colleagues quickly point to the equity policy and the equity committee and respond, "but don't you see we are doing equity?" Kuokkanen (2008, 74) states that "Indigenous Peoples can't speak in the academy." She continues: "the discourses that control what can be said and what is understood are set to function only within certain parameters" (74). These parameters include using language in ways that comforts settlers — welcome to the table, but you better behave! On top of contractual benevolence, Indigenous Peoples are expected to pay a cultural tax.

THE PRICE OF (INDIGENOUS) ACCESS: PAYING THE CULTURAL TAX

Universities expect a lot from Indigenous scholars. When we are hired, they hold up the numbers of Indigenous faculty as a measure of institutional success — "See, we are inclusive." We are hired to fill the diversity gap in ways that fail to recognize that we do not merely align ourselves politically within a racially diverse stakeholder group; for our work, we insist on our inherent right to Indigenous sovereignty and self-determination. We set ourselves clearly beyond the boundaries of racial diversity in ways that also implicate racially minoritized peoples under the rubric of settler, a term that moves beyond whiteness. Those politicized distinctions are rarely understood by our white and/or settler colleagues.

Gause (2011, 6) describes cultural taxation as the "additional work expectations that do not boost their [people of colour] chances of earning tenure and/or promotion." This extra labour includes serving as the minority representative on committees, responding to all racial issues, and supporting all minoritized students and other (race) tasks. When I think back to my work as a full professor, I remember that in one of my annual reviews I reported that I had, for example, offered twenty-four hours of individual student contact hours (both with students in my faculty and outside of my faculty/university); seventeen hours of faculty mentorship and coaching (on topics concerning anti-racism, Indigenization, working with Elders, and so on) and that few of these acts of (race-based) service offered any forms of reciprocity. My additional labours were the assumed cultural tax that my participation in the workforce required.

There is an assumption that we bring to the academy our "perspectives" and that this will reform pedagogy and course and program design, and that we will help to retain Indigenous learners. We are hired to be change agents, and our numbers are usually small, so we carry the unfair burden of responsibility to fulfil the needs of settlers. But what roles do settlers (really) want from their Indigenous colleagues? We are consistently asked: Can you come into my class to give the land acknowledgement? Can you share traditional stories, invite an elder to come to my class? Can you come speak to my social work students about the First Nations child welfare system? Can you speak to my Education students and speak about residential schools? ...my Physical Education students to speak about traditional games? ...my Art students to speak about traditional crafts? ...my research methods graduate students to speak about Indigenous research? ...my music students to speak about Indigenous music? Contributions like these are the cultural tax Indigenous scholars pay for the price of access. We are often expected to be Indigenous experts, or knowledge brokers on all things Indigenous. The problem with this orientation to our work is that the learning outcome is predetermined by members of the dominant group (and their focus is often limited/ing) — we are expected to respond to what settlers want (usually without reciprocity). So, what happens when we are simply unavailable?

When Indigenous scholars are unavailable then these learning opportunities become optional or, worse, are eliminated completely. These one-off approaches do little to achieve anything close to the decolonial pedagogy that I seek to engage in. While they are easy, comfortable, and safe for settlers, they expose Indigenous leaders to a variety of hostilities (anger, denial, minimization, and rejection, among others) because we are taking up space from what some learners view as "the real curriculum." Because the focus has been predetermined by settlers, they often do little to deepen the settler gaze; yet, settlers often express their discomfort with these troubling knowledges, though I haven't even had a chance to get into the heavy stuff (the violence of colonization for example). The more impactful work is the messy stuff — where we must unpack colonization and its ongoing benefits which flow to members of the dominant group, because — get this — settler colonialism is not just about the oppression of Indigenous Peoples; it's about the maintenance and enforcement of white superiority.

This description often makes white/settler colleagues uncomfortable, which is a signal that they are experiencing cognitive dissonance and that the decolonial learning opportunity is in front of them. Too often I hear students ask, "But I thought I was going to learn about Indigenous people's cultures ..." as if learning about our cultures would be enough to create change. Settlers need to ask themselves what they would do with Indigenous people's cultures anyway. This, right here, exposes another settler contradiction — they want to experience and access our culture to protect their innocence from the violence of ongoing colonialism; at the same time, they participate in upholding the assumption that we should be grateful for gaining access.

THE ASSUMPTIONS OF ACCESS: PRESUMING ASSIMILATION

While speaking at an international conference where I co-presented a paper that explored decolonizing environmental education, a participant exclaimed, "Dr. Pete! How is it that you can even think about decolonizing the university — when it has privileged you with a professorial role?" Ask Indigenous Peoples in your institution why they were motivated to seek access in university or college — they will almost always respond that they want to gain the skills and knowledge that will help them to transform Indigenous communities, families, and individual lived experiences. Our intention is not assimilative but transformative.

Indigenous Peoples intend to serve their communities of origin through their leadership in ways that will support Indigenous sovereignty. We desire to be more powerful Indigenous Peoples and Nations. We remain steadfast in our assertion of our radical Indigeneity and our Indigenous futurity. Corntassel (2012, 88) asserts, "in order to live in a responsible way as self-determining Nations, Indigenous Peoples must confront existing colonial institutions, structures, and policies that attempt to displace us from our homelands and relationships...Indigenous resurgence means having the courage and imagination to envision life beyond the state."

Here's the thing that some settlers do not understand — we have an intimate knowledge of the system of ongoing colonialism, and as such we know the inner workings of the university. We are not strangers in it; we are savvy navigators and negotiators within the structure. Assimilation to dominant ways was never our goal — rejection, reconstruction, and resurgence are our aims. Given that, we require more than policies and statements toward equality — we want and deserve a decolonizing equity praxis.

DREAMING: THE POSSIBILITIES
OF DECOLONIZING EQUITY PRAXIS

As I begin this final section, I turn to the scholarship of Tuck and Yang (2012). Their article, "Decolonization is not a Metaphor" is one of those must-read articles. It offers an essential reading for any decolonizing considerations because it exposes how problematic this work can be. I do not want to fall into the trap of making decolonization a metaphor by "grafting it onto pre-existing discourses/framework" because, "decolonization is not a swappable term for other things we want to do to improve our societies" (Tuck and Yang 2012, 3). Tuck and Yang (2012, 2) state that "decolonization, which we assert is a distinct project from other civil and human rights-based social justice projects, is far too often subsumed into the directives of these projects, with no regard for how decolonization wants something different than those forms of justice." They further state that "decolonization is ultimately about the repatriation of Indigenous land and life." Given this stance, what does this mean for a decolonizing equity praxis?

Equity has limited opportunities for Indigenous Peoples in higher education. By that I mean that equity policies have certainly allowed some/more of us a place at the table, but the expectations for our ways of knowing and being are carefully controlled once we arrive and take a seat. The common control mechanisms include having low recruitment targets, expecting the adoption or assimilation toward the dominant norms, paying the cultural tax, and expecting contractual benevolence. These control mechanisms maintain settler status quo. Equity needs to be decolonized.

For me, the decolonization of the university is not just about altering academic programs to reflect decolonial epistemes and pedagogies; I want to decolonize the whole system of higher education including its policies. I recognize that for me, this desire reflects the "dreaming" phase of decolonization (Laenui 2006). Laenui writes,

> True decolonization is more than simply replacing Indigenous or previously colonized people into the positions held by colonizers. Decolonization includes the reevaluation of the political, social, economic, and judicial structures themselves, and the development, if appropriate, of new structures which can

> hold and house the values and aspirations of the colonized peoples. (4)

Decolonizing equity, then, is but one small step in a much larger project. Kuokkanen (2008, 143) states that decolonization is "the ongoing process of dismantling colonial regimes, structures, practices, and discourses." She continues: "decolonization refers to the present struggle for political but also intellectual, economic, and cultural self-determination; it includes reclaiming their rights to autonomy, land, identity, language, and worldviews" (143). As part of the dreaming, I return to the idea that decolonization is about the rematriation of Indigenous land and life (Tuck and Yang 2012) and I wonder how that relates to issues of equity in higher education; I remind myself that decolonization is not meant to be "swappable with other things we want to do" (Tuck and Yang 2012, 3). How, then, do we engage in the conversation of decolonizing equity?

Let's return to the story of the search for a new president. As I described earlier, Indigenous faculty and staff joined together to collaborate on and vision for the leader that we needed ––one who understood that decolonization and resurgence matter. We submitted our written document to the search committee, and we used it to send a consistent message during community engagement sessions. Several of us also collaborated on a written submission organized by the people of colour on campus, because we recognized the power of working in solidarity. Our collective response raised questions about the composition of the search committee and their ability to hear and act on our concerns for decolonization, anti-racism, eco-justice, and reconciliation. During the community engagement sessions, an Indigenous person suggested that the search process itself needed to be decolonized. The respondent suggested that the search committee needed to begin by meeting with local First Nations to hear from them what their priorities were for a leader at the university. The respondent stated that as an institution we are comfortable naming these local Nations in the university land acknowledgement and they need to consult with these local First Nations. The committee needed to honour Indigenous sovereignty. The respondent and I spoke following the meeting and they voiced their concerns that when the search firm itself lacks diversity and the search committee can't disclose its representation, then why should we believe that the process could be equitable? We couldn't help but wonder if the lack of representation on the committee and in the community engagement sessions was reflective of a much more insidious plan — the maintenance of settler dominance.

The University of Victoria is in a unique policy environment. British Columbia (BC) is the only province to have a Ministry of Indigenous Relationships and Reconciliation and the province recently adopted the UN Declaration of the Rights of Indigenous Peoples as a guiding framework for all its work. This is the first time in Canada that a provincial government has done so. This means that every provincial ministry, including the Ministry of Advanced Education, will report on how they are advancing reconciliation in their own areas. I think, as a university, we should be working in alignment with these provincial priorities and report on our reconciliation actions. For that to happen, I want settlers in senior administrative positions within the university to consider not only reporting on decolonial and reconciliation actions but to consider who they report to. I want university administrators to take seriously their relationships with local Indigenous communities. I want them to consider creating local advisory boards, or representative seats on the Board of Governors for local Indigenous leaders and to recognize their authorities in these territories.

In line with the aspirational goal of reconciliation, decolonizing equity praxis must reject the settler logic of elimination and must recognize Indigenous people's sovereignty. As a starting point, we must move beyond the land acknowledgement and toward authentic engagement within the local community. If we truly believe that "we are privileged to live, learn and play on the traditional lands of the…" then we Indigenous Peoples must be at every table! We must be at every table because it's our kitchen! The recognition of Indigenous sovereignty offers a starting point to decolonizing equity. This form of recognition would entail specific forms of relational accountabilities, including the responsibility of settlers to show up ready for the relationship. Showing up ready means that settlers have done their work of building an understanding of colonization, settler colonialism, decolonization, and resurgence. Settlers must actively engage in the work of settler decolonization. They can support developments in this area by taking up the study of settler decolonization with their colleagues. Settlers will need to demonstrate that they are ready for a new relationship with Indigenous Peoples by practising the deep listening necessary to move through their discomfort when we expose the maintenance of settler superiority. Instead of turning away from these truths, settlers must do their own emotional heavy lifting so that they can really hear what Indigenous Peoples say.

Indigenous Peoples are talking about settler colonialism, and we need settlers to stop denying ongoing settler colonialism. Settlers must work in solidarity with Indigenous Peoples. Battell Lowman and Barker (2015, 120) call on settlers to "mitigate the harm of ongoing colonialism, support Indigenous efforts, and dismantle colonial structures of invasion." White settlers can use their positions of authority in the university to ensure that settler labour includes anti-oppression and decolonizing work. Settlers of colour can invite solidarity with Indigenous Peoples when they continue to insist on our place at the table where decisions are made, when they promote Indigenous Peoples' leadership at all levels, and when they tie their struggles with our own. Settler decolonization aims to change relationships with Indigenous Peoples from one of erasure and assimilation to that of genuine respect for Indigenous nationhood. Settler decolonization calls on all settlers — white and people of colour — to replace narrow notions of equity as mere recruitment and move toward a new kind of relationality. When we sit at the table together as equals, then we have truly achieved the dream of decolonizing equity praxis.

References

Ahmed, Sara. 2012. *On Being Included: Racism and Diversity in Institutional Life*. Durham: Duke University Press.

Battel Lowman, Emma, and Adam Barker. 2015. *Settler: Identity and Colonialism in 21st Century Canada*. Black Point/Winnipeg: Fernwood.

Corntassel, Jeff. 2012. "Re-Envisioning Resurgence: Indigenous Pathways to Decolonization and Sustainable Self-Determination." *Decolonization: Indigeneity, Education & Society* 1, 1.

Crandall, Jennifer, and Gina Garcia. 2016. "Am I Overreacting? Understanding and Combating Microaggressions." *Higher Education Today* July 27, 2016. higheredtoday.org/2016/07/27/understanding-and-combatting-microaggressions-in-postsecondary-education/.

Gause, C. P. 2011. *Diversity, Equity and Inclusive Education: A Voice from the Margins*. Rotterdam: Sense.

Grande, Sandy, and Lauren Anderson. 2017. "Un-Settling Multicultural

Erasures." *Multicultural Perspectives* 19, 3.

Johnson, Azeezat, and Remi Joseph-Salisbury. 2018. "Are You Supposed to Be in Here? Racial Microaggressions and Knowledge Production in Higher Education." In *Dismantling Race in Higher Education: Racism, Whiteness and Decolonising the Academy*, edited by Jason Arday and Heidi Safia Mirza. Cham: Palgrave.

Kuokkanen, Rauna. 2008. *Reshaping the University: Responsibility, Indigenous Epistemes, and the Logic of the Gift.* Vancouver: UBC Press.

Laenui, Poka. 2006. *Processes of Decolonization. Multiworld.* sjsu.edu/people/marcos.pizarro/courses/maestros/s0/Laenui.pdf.

Lawrence, Bonita, and Enakshi Dua. 2005. "Decolonizing Antiracism." *Social Justice* 32, 4.

Lloyd, David, and Patrick Wolfe. 2015. "Settler Colonial Logics and the Neoliberal Regime." *Settler Colonial Studies* 6, 2.

Rollock, Nicola. 2018. "The Heart of Whiteness: Racial Gesture Politics, Equity and Higher Education." In *Dismantling Race in Higher Education: Racism, Whiteness and Decolonising the Academy*, edited by Jason Arday and Heidi Safia Mirza. Cham: Palgrave.

Statistics Canada. 2017a. *Victoria, CY [Census subdivision], British Columbia and Capital, RD [Census division], British Columbia* (table). *Census Profile. 2016 Census.* Statistics Canada Catalogue no. 98-316-X2016001. Ottawa. www12.statcan.gc.ca/census-recensement/2016/dp-pd/prof/index.cfm?Lang=E.

___. 2017b. *Canada [Country] and British Columbia [Province]* (table). *Census Profile. 2016 Census.* Statistics Canada Catalogue no. 98-316-X2016001. Ottawa. https://www12.statcan.gc.ca/census-recensement/2016/dp-pd/prof/details/page.cfm?Lang=E&Geo1=PR&Code1=01&Geo2=PR&Code2=59&SearchText=Canada&SearchType=Begins&SearchPR=01&B1=All&TABID=1&type=1.

Stein, Sharon. 2017. "So, You Want to Decolonize Higher Education? Necessary Conversations for Non-Indigenous People." Blog, December 5, 2017. medium.com/@educationotherwise/https-medium-com-educationotherwise-so-you-want-to-decolonize-higher-education-4a7370d64955.

TRC (Truth and Reconciliation Commission of Canada). 2015. *Canada's Residential Schools: The Final Report of the Truth and Reconciliation Commission of Canada.* Winnipeg.

Tuck, Eve and K. Wayne Yang. 2012. "Decolonization is Not a Metaphor." *Decolonization: Indigeneity, Education & Society* 1, 1.

United Nations. 2007. *United Nations Declaration of the Rights of Indigenous Peoples.* <un.org/esa/socdev/unpfii/documents/DRIPS_en.pdf>.

University of Victoria. 2005. *Policy on Human Rights, Equity and Fairness, Policy No. GV0200.* <https://www.uvic.ca/universitysecretary/assets/docs/policies/GV0200_1105_.pdf>.

___. 2011. *Employment Equity, Policy No. HR6100.* <https://www.uvic.ca/universitysecretary/assets/docs/policies/HR6100_1100_.pdf>.

___. 2015. *University of Vicotira Employment Equity Plan 2015-2020.* <uvic.ca./equity/assets/docs/eep2015.pdf>.

___. 2018a. *Employment Equity Statement.* <uvic.ca/equity/employment-equity/statement/index.php>.

___. 2018–2019. *Equity and Human Rights Annual Report 2018-2019.* <uvic.ca/equity/assets/docs/annualreport.pdf>.

___. n.d. *Employment Equity.* https://www.uvic.ca/equity/employment-equity/index.php.

Wolfe, Patrick. 2006. "Settler Colonialism and the Elimination of the Native." *Journal of Genocide Research* 8, 4.

3

A THEORIZING OF DE-COLONIALIZING EQUITY AND THE NATION-STATE

Kathy Hogarth

In 2015, the Truth and Reconciliation Commission of Canada (TRC) issued its final report raising some critical issues and concerns related to the histories and realities of Indigenous Peoples in Canada. As a result of the TRC's report, many sectors of society began to chart a renewed course of decolonization. However, decolonization efforts in Canada (and abroad) predated the TRC, although it often occurred and continues to occur in silos, focusing on singular, theoretical aspects of decolonization such as decolonizing curriculum, decolonizing education/pedagogy, or decolonizing social work (Donald 2009; Tamburro 2013; Wildcat et al. 2014). Many Indigenous scholars were at the forefront of decolonizing efforts (Battiste, Bell, and Findley 2002; Logan 2015; Smith 2021; Tuck and Yang 2012; Wildcat et al. 2014), which initially prompted the TRC, and this continues to give hope to the future of who will truly benefit from a decolonized nation-state.

What exactly does decolonization in the context of the nation mean, and is this even a feasible endeavour? When the nation-state is built on colonialism, and the subjugation of Brown and Black bodies (Cooper 2007; Tobias 1983; Vowel 2016) how do we begin the work of meaningful and sustainable decolonization? Attempts at decolonization within the nation-state have taken place within a very small, siloed vacuum and much of that work is focused on "Indigenization" (Gaudry and Lorenz 2018). Given that the TRC was the driver for many of these decolonial discourses, much of the decolonizing mission has adopted a somewhat narrow preoccupation that focuses on Indigeneity and makes invisible the histories and realities of non-Indigenous racialized bodies and colonial subjects. Yet, even within this narrow frame, decolonization remains a challenge. Often the work of decolonization remains depoliticized and dehistoricized which means that many realities and histories of colonialism, including those of Black peoples, are left out of the official decolonial discourse.

This chapter engages with an expansion of the decolonial discourse and practice and argues that the need for an equity lens in decolonization is not only desired but imperative if the decolonial mission is to achieve any success. At the same time however, this chapter questions the notion of equity itself as colonized and the need for it to be taken up through a decolonial frame.

Theorizing allows us to imagine a reality that is not yet lived. It creates an ideological and dialogical space for the possibility of transformation. Theorizing decolonization and theorizing decolonizing equity is apt, given that much of decolonizing has not been translated to the realm of reality, and even less so, through an equity frame. Even so, a critical question arises: is an equity frame sufficient to hold decolonization or instead, should equity be looked at through a decolonizing frame? The three main constructs under examination in this chapter are decolonization, equity, and the nation-state. In examining these constructs, key questions are considered, including: what is decolonization and decolonizing equity? Can decolonization effectively take place outside of an equity frame? How is nation-state–ness implicated in decolonizing equity? How is "settler" taken up in the decolonial discourse? The answers to these questions are intricately linked and could help in shaping our understanding of decolonizing equity.

The decolonization with which this chapter, and largely this book, is taken up goes well beyond the un-nuanced colonial delinking from the crown and a move to self governance of Nations as in Bonn's 1930s construction. It is important to note that the word "decolonization" is often attributed to the German scholar, Moritz Julius Bonn who is said to have coined the word in 1932 (Gordon 2013). This kind of geopolitical decolonization is terminal. It provides us with tidied boxes wherein colonization can be charted from beginning to end. However, in a more nuanced way, the insidiousness of colonization necessitates a consideration of cultural and psychological dimensions. From this perspective, colonization has not ended. In fact, the colonial machinery is always engaged. Whereas colonies may have been relinquished to self governance, new colonial relationships are constantly being negotiated and the impact of colonization marches on in steady motion. Decolonization involves the complex process of identifying and dismantling structures and systems of oppression that are both historical and constantly in the making.

Equity involves fair treatment and is often used as a synonym for justice; it occurs when resources, punishments, and rewards are allocated based upon one's contributions or need (Espinoza 2007). Though often conflated, equity is not equality because it goes beyond notions of equal distribution. The notion of decolonizing equity necessarily extends the concept of decolonizing, which, in and of itself, seems intuitively grounded in equity but, without making equity explicit, results in significant gaps in its material form. Decolonizing without equity runs the risk of becoming part of the very colonial machinery it aims to redress. Likewise, equity without decolonization becomes part of the colonial machinery it seeks to address.

Given that the decolonizing endeavour is potentially fraught with inequities, there is a need to establish linkages between decolonization and equity. Without troubling these concepts and how they inform each other, decolonization is problematic. The challenge in this regard is: should decolonization be viewed through an equity lens or should equity be viewed through a decolonization lens? One of the grounding principles of decolonization is that decolonizing and equity are not synonymous and, in fact, decolonizing does not necessarily lead to equity. Similarly, our historical practice in equity provides a cogent argument that equity can, and often completely obfuscates, decolonization.

Decolonizing equity requires an explicit distinction between decolonization and Indigenization. These two concepts are diametrically different yet often conflated because there is a general lack of understanding of either. Where decolonization is engaged, it is often interchanged with Indigenizing efforts and tied to Indigenous/colonizer/settler relationships. The concepts of equity, diversity, and inclusion often fall outside of the realm of the "decolonization/Indigenization" matrix, and these concepts are often linked to racialized bodies and their engagement in and with the structures of nation-state. Indigenization involves Indigenous ways of knowing and being. Decolonization looks at dismantling the broader colonial framework that has undoubtedly impacted Indigenous Peoples but encompasses more than the Indigenous. If Indigeneity is the only frame through which decolonization is approached, the decolonizing endeavour becomes inequitable and is doomed to fail.

Conversations about decolonizing nationhood in the absence of an intersecting frame of equity provides a less than complete imagining of decolonization. However, the very notion of equity must be scrutinized. Raising the question "equity for whom?" is essential. Not all colonized subjects are treated equitably in the decolonizing discourse. For example, much of the decolonizing literature focuses on principles surrounding Indigeneity (Gaudry and Lorenz 2018; Louie et al. 2017; Tuck and Yang 2012), thus "othering" communities of newcomers, Black people, migrant workers, and other subjugated bodies that may benefit from a decolonized nation-state. If all subjects are not treated equitably — and this is a clear distinction and departure from equality arguments (equity centres on justice while equality focuses on equal shares divided among the masses) — then, have we decolonized or have we in fact re-inscribed another version of colonization? A theorizing of decolonization without requisite attention to equity engages in the necropolitics of determining what is just and what is justifiable, who lives and who dies, who is heard and who is silenced.

My approach to decolonization and equity is informed by my situatedness as a colonial body and is deeply impacted by its legacy. I am of an enslaved generation. African slavery was a function of colonialism that resulted in my absolute disconnection from my deep ancestral roots. For my ancestors, the forced journey across the Atlantic meant being taken from their connections, displacement, and passing on a legacy of unknown-ness. As a colonial subject of an enslaved generation, I am a Trinidadian Canadian woman who lives with the pain of not knowing; I live with the pain of not being able to trace. I live with the pain of a very complicated generational history, the trauma of which is etched into my psyche.

However, African enslavement is not the only linkage to colonialism that informs my present. Until my maternal grandfather's death a few years ago, his "difference" was attributed to being Hispanic. Never, in my life with my grandparents or in any family relations was his Indigeneity spoken of. The erasing of his Indigenous identity was another element of colonialism that continues to impact my identity today. I approach this chapter as a body displaced and disconnected, as one forced to bear the legacy of being taken and of things being taken away. And, yet I survive. I therefore situate myself in this work as one deeply impacted by colonialism and amid an unknown making and remaking.

FRAMING DECOLONIZATION WITHIN THE NATION

Canada. A huge expanse of land that is reflective of its motto *A Mari usque ad Mare* which translates "from Sea to Sea." Embedded in this motto were both a proclamation of Canada's colonial mission and a signal of its future multicultural ideal. During the time of Confederation, when this phrase came into being in Canada, "from Sea to Sea" only existed as a dream of geographical domination. At the time, the Dominion of Canada consisted only of Ontario, Québec, Nova Scotia, and New Brunswick. "From Sea to Sea" did not geographically apply to Canada until 1871, when British Columbia joined Confederation and the Dominion extended from the Atlantic to the Pacific. The project of colonization carried ideological norms on the back of economic expansion. The goal of economic expansion led to the expropriation of land for new raw materials and transportation access points. The expropriation of land and raw materials generated the need for "management" of peoples, including the traditional caretakers and those already in residence in the newly assumed land and those expropriated from other lands. Race enters the story as a central pillar of the people management strategy of colonial powers.

In decolonizing theorizing, we must theorize first at the foundation of nation. I write from the premise that the systems in which we exist in Canada are not broken. Thobani (2007) offers great insight into the making of nationhood in her examination of how processes of racialization contribute to sustaining and replenishing the politics of nation formation and national subjectivity. In fact, these systems are working exactly the way they were designed to work by white supremacists. The task, then, of dismantling systems built and upheld by white supremacy is not an easy one. The unravelling of a supremist nation will be met with great resistance. Central to decolonizing is contesting the foundation of nationhood. Our foundations of nationhood are not merely historical. Those early foundations largely inform current sociopolitical relations with the bodies that occupy the nation-state.

The nation-state we know as Canada is "founded" on the premise of two (French and British), and when challenged, three (First Nations, Métis and Inuit; FNMI) founding Nations. In reality, the narrative of "founding" and "nation" is really that of a remaking because both founders and Nations existed prior to the Act that declared nationhood. The British North America Act of 1867, that affirmed and declared nationhood, also reaffirmed white supremacy implicit in the two solitudes of French and British foundations. These two solitudes of nationhood have been replicated over the past century and a half in the affirming of English and French as official languages, in the requirement for the leader of the nation, and notably, the justices of the Supreme Court, to be fluent in these languages, and in the explicit exclusion of Indigenous languages (Haque and Patrick 2015). These language policies in Canada have "functioned to manage racial difference through processes of erasure, forced assimilation and exclusion through the technology of language" (Haque and Patrick 2015, 27), maintaining a white settler nation. The two solitudes of French and British foundations continue to inform the manner in which Indigenous Peoples are absorbed into or left out of nationhood.

Multiculturalism, in some ways, lends further complication to colonialism. The multicultural ideal was also part of the colonial framing of nation-state. From the multicultural ideal set out during Confederation through to the official policy of the Multiculturalism Act, there was an intent to enshrine the two solitudes of French and English thereby reifying colonial power. The offshoot reality of multiculturalism is that it introduced a cultural diversity into the Canadian nation-state that must be implicated and addressed in the colonial–decolonial matrix. Yet, even within Canadian multiculturalism, whiteness reigns supreme (Carr 2008).

In theorizing decolonization and decolonizing equity, whiteness is inescapable. Theorizing decolonization cannot be successful without an interrogation and problematization of whiteness and practising decolonization cannot be successful without a disrupting and decentring of whiteness. Interrogating whiteness lays bare the racist underpinning of the colonial machinery. Within the nation-state, and indeed beyond, whiteness stands as a proxy for all that is good, and Others are constructed on a continuum that runs the gamut from less good to evil and grotesque depending on how those constructed identities support and affirm whiteness. Whiteness works through processes of normalization by silently imposing itself as the standard by which social differences come to be known. In as much as the Canadian demographic landscape is changing, whiteness remains an essential feature of "Canadian-ness." Our institutions educate for whiteness; therefore, part of the work of decolonizing is a necessary disruption of self in process. As Smith (2021) notes, it is the necessary work of recognizing that colonization operated and continues to operate at the level of the land where we see an immense impact for Indigenous Peoples; at the level of the body, giving rise to the enslavement of Black and other enslaved peoples; and at the ideological level, which largely operates throughout schools and other institutions. In theorizing whiteness, it is necessary to address the social, political, and economic constructs that uphold the nation-state, and that situate whiteness as the conveyor of power, authority, and privilege.

The normalizing of whiteness, however, is not a benign activity that occurs without thought or reason. Whiteness, like other ideologies, has been, and continues to be, carefully constructed and curated, in part, through institutional arrangements. The structures that underpin society are not merely managing racial ideologies; they are creating and enforcing racial meanings, ascribing power and privilege to one, while at the same time forcibly holding others in the margins. There is a relationality of whiteness to Otherness — one finds its meaning in the other. As such, both colonialism and decolonialism are cloaked in power and associated with whiteness. Critical whiteness takes note that the ideologies, norms, and practices of whiteness and the accompanying "white race" were invented as part of a system of racial oppression designed to solve a particular problem of colonialism. The work of critical whiteness theorists like Allen (1994) and Helfand (2011) clearly outlines the links to whiteness as ideology and the practice of colonialism.

Also tied to the notion of whiteness is the politics of representation. Who speaks for whom, and who produces knowledge about whom becomes one of the replicating colonial features of decolonial theorizing. Racial or white ventriloquism occurs when white scholars or white people in general speak for a non-white community, effectively silencing the voices of those people (Martínez Novo 2018). White ventriloquism continues to dominate discourses in such a way that it has reinvented colonialism, constructing knowledge of the colonized and determining whose histories, and how those histories and realities get written into the dialogue (Martínez Novo 2018). The projection of white ventriloquism in the decolonial discourse has created a form of colonial universalism. It is a mode of structural domination that suppresses the heterogeneity of colonized bodies without taking into consideration the wide-ranging variety of histories and realities of those indelibly marked by the colonial endeavour. Theorizing decolonization has largely been a form of discursive colonization. While there is a universality about colonial subordination, decolonization cannot be based on a rigid concept of universality that negates the wide variation of colonized experiences.

In theorizing decolonization then, there is a necessary urgency to develop a perspective that is committed to anti-essentialism about the multiple and, at times intersecting, colonized histories, realities, and cultures. There is no equalization of power when the marginalization of colour is pitted against whiteness. Whether that power is real or imagined, it induces a type of immobility that is a necessary element for the continued subjugation of the Other in white space (Said 1978). The production of stereotypical and antithetical knowledge that often compares the Other (read: undesirable) against the West (read: desirable) is a strategy through which colonial discourse gets its authority and is being used to regulate, discipline, and keep the colonized Other in their debased place (Chakrabarti 2012; Hamadi 2014; Said 1978).

CHALLENGES TO DECOLONIZING EQUITY

Decolonization will not take place in a vacuum. The threads of colonialism have been carefully and indiscriminately woven throughout the fabric of society. It touches everything. To meaningfully engage in the decolonial pursuit means attention is given to how colonialism was enforced and continues to be reinforced in and through societal structures. To equitably decolonize, fundamental concepts must be troubled. Decolonizing equity within the borders of nationhood requires contesting the accounting of history and — in light of the earlier discussion on the founding of the nation — the notion of the settler.

One of the greatest challenges to decolonizing nation-state lies in the inaccuracies of our historical accounts that serve as pillars of nation-state–ness. There are many historical records that need closer scrutiny; however, there are two that will be taken up here because of the ways in which they were engaged prior to the "duly constituted" nation we know today as Canada. These are historical records relating to Indigenous and Black Peoples.

On the history of racism in Canada, only recently have efforts to redress violence toward Black and Indigenous bodies been addressed. Utilizing a provincial case study, the Ontario Human Rights Commission (OHRC; 2018) published an education tool titled "Call It Out: Racism, Racial Discrimination and Human Rights." In this resource, they provided a historical account of racism in Canada. From their accounts, racism started in 1628 with slavery (OHRC 2018). The challenge here is that many view the OHRC as a credible source of information for learning. However, to start Canada's historical engagement with racism at 1628 is a complete erasure of Indigenous history and reality; it is a sanitized version of history that wipes Indigenous Peoples off their own landscape at worst, and at best, denies that the engagement with Indigenous Peoples post "discovery" was racist. Today's perpetuation of an inaccurate history is a continuation of yesterday's mandate to eradicate the "Indian" — a mandate for which the former Canadian Prime Minster, Stephen Harper, apologized but an apology that continues to be questioned as the mission of eradicating the "Indian" moves ahead. Our national education, of which the OHRC is but a mere example, continues to serve as a remaking, and masking, of colonialism.

Furthermore, the historical recording of Black peoples' presence and contributions in the "making" of Canada also suffers the ubiquitous fate of mis-accounting. Since 2017 there has been much movement in the acknowledgement of Black enslavement in Canada (Cohen 2019; Maynard 2017; Nelson 2017) but previously, Canada's engagement with slavery had been often linked to the Underground Railroad. In this account by the Canadian Government, it is noted that:

> Slavery has existed all over the world, from Asia, Africa and the Middle East to the Americas. The first movement to abolish the transatlantic slave trade emerged in the British Parliament in the late 1700s. In 1793, Upper Canada, led by Lieutenant Governor John Graves Simcoe, a Loyalist military officer, became the first province in the Empire to move toward abolition. In 1807, the British Parliament prohibited the buying and selling of slaves, and in 1833 abolished slavery throughout the Empire. Thousands of slaves escaped from the United States, followed

restrictive nature of the classification of Status Indians was necessary because Indigenous Peoples obstructed settlers' access to land and, as a result, their increase was counterproductive. Indigenous Peoples were a problem to be dealt with by subtractive measures, and therefore the most Indigenous of whites lost status as an Indigenous person. This restrictive racial classification of "Indians" played a crucial role in cultural genocide and the logic of elimination, a cultural genocide firmly supported by the Indian Act of 1876 which governed every aspect of Indigenous life in Canada (Wolfe 2006).

Amid the historical mis-accounting is the factor of constructed white ignorance. The challenge is that Black, Brown, and Indigenous bodies are still expected to bridge the gap of constructed white ignorance and resistance. The colonized are still being asked to educate the colonizer as to their very existence and needs. This pattern of engagement has long since been identified as a primary tool of all oppressors to keep the oppressed occupied with the concerns of the empire. That the oppressed must continue to not only endure the blows levelled by colonialism but must simultaneously inform the nation of their pain as it witnesses them bleed. In so doing, inequity continues to be inscribed as we build bridges to address it.

While the historical accounting in Canada presents a challenge to decolonization, one of the major concepts on which decolonization hinges is that of the settler. Deconstructing settler is also a challenge that must be reconciled. Who is the colonial settler and how does the construction of settler need to be disrupted? Many, within both Indigenous and non-Indigenous communities, have identified the settler as anyone that does not fall within the national designation of First Nations, Métis, or Inuit, or FNMI (Steinman 2016; Wildcat et al. 2014). Some have expanded the construction of Indigenous in Canada to include any Indigenous body from Turtle Island, and therefore, settler would come to encompass anyone not originating from Turtle Island. For the purposes of status and benefits, these constructions are worthwhile. However, for the purposes of understanding decolonization, these binary constructions fail. They obscure the histories of bodies colonized that fall outside of FNMI classification. It also hides the fact that bodies outside of the geographical domains have been simultaneously colonized and oppressed (Dotson 2018; Hogarth and Fletcher 2018; Tuck and Yang 2012). Decolonization cannot be based on a rigid concept of Indigenization that negates the wide variation of colonized experiences. The colonized framing of decolonization shows its limitation in its understanding of the depth and reach of the colonial machinery.

The "non-Indigenous" — and by this I have come to mean those who do not fit into the narrowly defined box of FNMI — cannot be all painted with the same "settler" brush. To do so ties decolonization to land and land only. The politics of land-based decolonization is that it obfuscates the messiness of colonized bodies. As I mentioned previously, colonialism reiteratively operates at the level of land, body, and ideology. However, it is important to highlight the fact that part of the colonial machinery involved, and continues to involve, the movement of bodies across continents to fulfill production needs on colonized lands. For slaves, that movement was not voluntary. To ascribe settler identity to the enslaved and their descendants gives them ownership over the process of resettlement — an ownership they never truly had. Vowel (2016, 17) asserts that "Black people, removed and cut off from their own indigenous lands — literally stripped of their humanity and redefined legally as property — could not be agents of settlement. The fact that slavery has been abolished does not change this history." Bodies have been settled in a very unsettling kind of way that needs to be acknowledged and tended to. These unsettled settlers cannot be rendered colonial settler (Vowel 2016). Such a rendering itself constitutes violence — the same kind of violence that forced them onto the landscape to begin with; the same kind of violence that continues to erase Canada's engagement with slavery. The concept of settler and, hence, that of decolonization is not simply metaphorical as noted by Tuck and Yang (2012), though their conception of the non-metaphorical nature of settler and decolonization did not encompass the enslaved.

The attempt to unsettle notions of the settler by the non-Indigenous has been argued as a move toward reconciling settler guilt and relieving settler responsibility for complicity in the marginalization and destruction of Indigenous Peoples. Tuck and Yang (2012, 9) refer to this as "settler moves to innocence." Such arguments fail to account for the fact that colonization — both in the global and national context — was not enacted solely on Indigenous bodies and its objective was not only, or primarily, displacement from lands. Further, such argumentation attempts to dissolve other colonial bodies and histories, and particularly Black enslaved histories, into the politics of the Indigenous (Byrd 2011).

There is a necessary caution in framing the non-white, non-Indigenous as from somewhere else but never here, excluding them from the Canadian decolonial project or, conversely, implicating them in the same way as the non-Indigenous white body. Even more challenging in this uneven decolonization is what Mbembé and Meintjes (2003) term necropolitics, or the determination of how some bodies may occupy space and are given voice in the decolonizing endeavour while others must die. The reality of colonialism is such that, as noted by Narayan (1997, 44), it "not only connects and divides Westerners from subjects in various Third-World nations in a series of complicated and unequal relationships. It also connects and divides mainstream Western subjects from Others in their *own* societies whose unequal relationships to the mainstream are themselves products of Western colonial history" (original emphasis).

RECOLONIZATION THROUGH DECOLONIZATION

Another significant challenge of decolonization —a fundamental challenge of decolonizing equity — is that the very concept of decolonization has been colonized. The very act of colonization stands in direct opposition to notions of principles of equity. If decolonization is another power grab — a recolonizing through decolonization — we continue along the path of structural inequity even in our decolonizing. The colonizer is often the one who gets to frame decolonization. The loudest calls for decolonization come from institutions that remain heavily guarded and routinely policed by "whiteness." Colonized ventriloquism has dominated notions of decolonization in such a way that it has silenced the voices of those colonized and serves as a mechanism of further oppression. Decolonization is in fact, another iteration of the colonizing endeavour producing another form of structural domination that suppresses the heterogeneity of colonized people. The place at which we necessarily start discussion on decolonization is also the site for deconstruction. Can the system change itself when the colonizer dominates the discourse of colonization? With a resounding "no" that echoes the voices of Third World Feminists, "the master's tools will never dismantle the master's house" (Lorde 2007, 112). Within this colonization of decolonization, knowledge has been monopolized and the monopolizer, in a modernist sense, holds the power. Knowledge is highly politicized and weaponized. Some knowledges are positioned as obsolete and others as advanced but often it is the knowledge of the subjugated that is repackaged and assembled as new.

Because a lot of institutional decolonization efforts have been taken up with an Indigenous focus, there is an acceptance of the conflation of Indigenization with decolonization. These two concepts are distinctly different; however, the conflation presents a real challenge to the decolonizing endeavour. One of the major tenets of Indigenization is the centring of Indigenous knowledges and practice, including Indigenous histories, teachings, languages, traditions, ceremonies, and practices. At the heart of Indigenization is the support of reconciliation. The Truth and Reconciliation (2015b) Calls to Action highlights in unambiguous ways the need for its operationalization as a necessary part of the process. It involves critical reflection on the impacts and legacy of colonialism on Indigenous Peoples. Indigenization involves affirming Indigenous sovereignty, valuing, and re-establishing Indigenous laws, values, and relationships (Roth 2019). Gaudry and Lorenz (2018) posit that Indigenization has three distinct meanings that are located on a continuum, marked on one end by Indigenous inclusion and reconciliation, with Indigenization in the centre, and decolonial Indigenization at the opposite end. It is important to note that even within Indigenization scholarship, there is a departure when it comes to decolonization. Yet, while Indigenization requires a critical examination of systems of domination and it is a decolonial process exposing where dominant structures must be dismantled and remade, it is not the totality of decolonization. The term Indigenization became part of the dialogue at the administrative level of academic institutions after the release of the TRC Calls to Action, where there was a commitment to begin a process of reconciliation and address historical wrongs. Prior to the TRC's (2015a) final report, there had been significant debate and scholarship on the need for institutions, and specifically Canadian academic institutions that have historically been complicit in assimilation education, to build policies of inclusion within the institutions. The debate centred a worldview that aimed to assimilate Indigenous Peoples and was presented as a "colonial benevolence" that continues to resonate today.

Decolonization requires a broader view. There are three fundamental aspects tied to colonialism that must be inextricably linked to decolonization. Colonialism is a structural reality. It was and is a machinery of the state to build empire. Colonialism is also a relational reality. It is an encounter between people and a process of conquest and domination through which power relations are inscribed with the colonizer on top and colonized under. The legacy of colonialism continues to operate through various forms of reproductions in a "postcolonial" era and the political and cultural interdependence of subjugated bodies. Such reproductions of colonialism are evident in the unequal relationships between racialized Others and the "rest."

The challenge of decolonization is that colonization is not fixed. There is no end period. The effort of decolonization is an effort in remaking while the thing being remade is still being made; by this I mean that Canada continues to be settled by settlers and exploited economically and politically. However, possibilities for decolonization to become equitable exist, by creating new structural frameworks to borrow from Zapatista principles that build a world in which many worlds fit (Holas Allimant and Demuro 2020). Additionally, to understand colonization as a structural and relational reality, it becomes necessary to approach decolonialization as a structural and relational undertaking. It is futile to think that we can have structural gain with a sole focus on individual interventions.

Roth (2019) argues that while colonialism and capitalism are deeply and historically enmeshed, and the global rise of capitalism and globalization has relied on colonial expansionist policy to support Eurocentric power, there is an opportunity to examine the possibilities, and limitations, of decolonizing capitalism. Battiste, Bell and Findlay (2002, 84) show that this is a process also of "animating sites of decolonization" and understanding the core tenets of colonialism including capitalism, racism, patriarchy, and domination, in order to transform "sites of colonial harm into sites of healing, and restoring community well-being" (Roth 2019, 308).

In its function, decolonizing is a form of resistance. Decolonizing is an explicit attempt at naming and resisting the colonial machinery and its machinations. Resistance, however, creates new dynamics. Resistance through decolonization is a disturbance to the status quo and a disturbance to white sensibilities and, in the midst of such resistance, counter-resistance seems inevitable.

A PATH FORWARD

Decolonialism finds its relevancy because colonialism existed, and the colonial machinery continues to be enacted. It stands to reason, then, that if we were to truly engage in the decolonial endeavour we must peel back the layers of the colonial endeavour. There is a necessary cautiousness in asserting with fixity any definition, as the concepts discussed here are fluid and constantly changing and, in many ways, still unknown and evolving. What is certain is that decolonization is a complex process that requires the identification, recognition, and understanding of the multi-faceted and multi-dimensional structures of colonialism, and then engaging in practices and processes that disrupt colonial power. The task of decolonizing requires a process of "unpacking the central assumptions of domination, patriarchy, racism, and ethnocentrisms that continue to glue…privileges in place" (Battiste, Bell, and Findlay 2002, 84). Colonization has been a successful endeavour, yet not fully. There has always been a resistance at some level to colonialism. It is this resistance that offers hope and a path forward.

Colonialism is an enactment of relationships of power. Conversely, decolonization requires a fundamental change in power relationships, with a move toward power sharing. It means shifting epistemes. It means decentring ideological whiteness. It is this fact that makes the work of decolonizing difficult if not near impossible. To borrow from the words of Fredrick Douglass written in 1857: "Power concedes nothing without a demand. It never did and it never will" (Blackpast 2007, n.p.).

For decolonization to be enacted there must be a willingness of the nation-state to relinquish its paternal role. There is an ongoing conflict between public interest, paternalism, and structural racism. Progress on implementation has been impacted by competing priorities for public funding where the broader public interest does not include the interests of the colonized. An example of note is the legal challenge by the Canadian Government to the Canadian Human Rights Tribunal ruling regarding the complicity of the federal government in the discrimination against First Nations children including family separations and deaths, as compensation to victims is considered not in the public interest due to the anticipated costs in the billions in restitution.

The decolonizing endeavour involves not only the decolonizing of lands but also the decolonizing of capitalism, of psyche, of bodies, and all the associated trappings. Such decolonizing will likely not mean a change in an entrenched, dominant model; it could mean that space is created for other models, models in which principles of those colonized are used to re-centre other ways of knowing and being with the explicit goal of advancing the ability of the once colonized to thrive. Equitably decolonizing means that we see each other, our multiplicities, as contributing to the life giving of the whole. Equitable decolonizing embraces the principle of Ubuntu in reflexively knowing that we are always in relation and dependent on each other. It is a stark contrast to the colonial paradigm of only the strong survive or the loudest voice gets heard. Such decolonizing requires a shift away from the exclusion that leads to a re-defining, re-identifying, or misidentifying those who are Indigenous from other lands as a colonial settler.

Delinking decolonization and Indigenization allows room for a more equitable decolonizing discourse that is more inclusive to subjugated bodies that continue to live with the legacy of colonialism. It allows for a theorizing of equity and decolonization that does not involve replicating oppressions while changing oppressors. The path to decolonizing equity considers the painful thread that binds the colonized. There is a shared history of being moved, removed, and moved again. It is a shared history of taken-ness — of things being taken from us and of us being taken from things. It is a shared history of violence, the kind of violence which gets inscribed and re-inscribed for generations. This is a shift away from the narrow preoccupation often taken up in the settler colonial discourse.

Decolonization cannot only exist in metaphorical and theoretical spaces. It must move toward action. It must inform national policy and everyday practice if it is to become a part of Canadian reality. Anything less than this is performative decolonization. Equitable decolonization or decolonizing equity will require considerably more than symbolic progress — it requires fundamental institutional change. It requires an acknowledgement and reckoning with our racist and colonial past and current realities and a preparedness to make amends. Equity decolonization or decolonizing equity comes with an explicit challenge to the notion of what is just for one and justifiable for the other, and must be addressed in a re-iterative fashion at the level of the land, body, and ideology.

References

Allen, Theodore. 1994. *The Invention of the White Race, Volume 2.* New York: Verso.

Battiste, Marie, Lynne Bell, and L.M. Findlay. 2002. "Decolonizing Education in Canadian Universities: An Interdisciplinary, International, Indigenous Research Project." *Canadian Journal of Native Education* 26, 2.

BlackPast. 2007. (1857) *Frederick Douglass, "If There Is No Struggle, There Is No Progress."* blackpast.org/african-american-history/1857-frederick-douglass-if-there-no-struggle-there-no-progress/.

Byrd, Jodi A. 2011. "'Been to the Nation, Lord, but I Couldn't Stay There': American Indian Sovereignty, Cherokee Freedmen and the Incommensurability of the Internal." *Interventions* 13, 1.

Carr, Paul. 2008. "'Equity Waltz' in Canada: Whiteness and the Informal Realities of Racism in Education." *Journal of Contemporary Issues in Education* 3, 2.

Chakrabarti, Sumit. 2012. "Moving Beyond Edward Said: Homi Bhabha and the Problem of Postcolonial Representation." *International Studies, Interdisciplinary Political and Cultural Journal* 14, 1.

Cohen, Amy. 2019. "'Slavery Hasn't Ended, It Has Just Become Modernized': Border Imperialism and the Lived Realities of Migrant Farmworkers in British Columbia, Canada." *ACME: An International Journal for Critical Geographies* 18, 1.

Cooper, Afua. 2007. "Acts of Resistance: Black Men and Women Engage Slavery in Upper Canada, 1793–1803." *Ontario History* 99, 1.

Donald, Dwayne. 2009. "Forts, Curriculum, and Indigenous Métissage: Imagining Decolonization of Aboriginal-Canadian Relations in Educational Contexts." *First Nations Perspectives* 2, 1.

Dotson, Kristie. 2018. "On the Way to Decolonization in a Settler Colony: Re-Introducing Black Feminist Identity Politics." *AlterNative: An International Journal of Indigenous Peoples* 14, 3.

Espinoza, Oscar. 2007. "Solving the Equity–Equality Conceptual Dilemma: A New Model for Analysis of the Educational Process." *Educational Research* 49, 4.

Gaudry, Adam, and Danielle Lorenz. 2018. "Indigenization as Inclusion, Reconciliation, and Decolonization: Navigating the Different Visions for Indigenizing the Canadian Academy." *AlterNative: An International Journal of Indigenous Peoples* 14, 3.

Gordon, Rob. 2013. "Moritz Bonn, Southern Africa and the Critique of Colonialism." *African Historical Review* 45, 2.

Government of Canada. 2017. "Discover Canada — Canada's History." canada.ca/en/immigration-refugees-citizenship/corporate/publications-manuals/discover-canada/read-online/canadas-history.html.

Hamadi, Lutfi. 2014. "Edward Said: The Postcolonial Theory and the Literature of Decolonization." *European Scientific Journal, Special Issue* 2.

Haque, Eve, and Donna Patrick. 2015. "Indigenous Languages and the Racial Hierarchisation of Language Policy in Canada." *Journal of Multilingual and Multicultural Development* 36, 1.

Helfand, Judy. 2011. "Constructing Whiteness." *Race, Racism and the Law.* racism.org/articles/race/66-defining-racial-groups/white-european-american/378-white11a2.

Hogarth, Kathy, and Wendy Fletcher. 2018. *Decoding Racism, Multiculturalism, and Post-Colonialism in the Quest for Belonging in Canada and Beyond.* New York: Oxford University Press.

Holas Allimant, Israel, and Eugenia Demuro. 2020. "Reading the World Anew: Zapatista Stories, the Denial of Singularity, and the Creation of a Plural World." *Journal of Postcolonial Writing* 56, 6.

Logan, Tricia. 2015. "Settler Colonialism in Canada and the Métis." *Journal of Genocide Research* 17, 4.

Lorde, Audre. 2007. "The Master's Tools Will Never Dismantle the Master's House." In *Sister Outsider: Essays and Speeches.* Berkeley: Crossing Press.

Louie, Dustin, Yvonne Poitras-Pratt, Aubrey Hanson, and Jacqueline Ottmann. 2017. "Applying Indigenizing Principles of Decolonizing Methodologies in University Classrooms." *Canadian Journal of Higher Education/Revue canadienne d'enseignement supérieur* 47, 3.

Martínez Novo, Carmen. 2018. "Ventriloquism, Racism and the Politics of Decoloniality in Ecuador." *Cultural Studies* 32, 3.

Maynard, Robyn. 2017. *Policing Black Lives: State Violence in Canada from Slavery to the Present.* Black Point, NS/Winnipeg: Fernwood Publishing.

Mbembé, Achille, and Libby Meintjes (translator). 2003. "Necropolitics." *Public Culture* 15, 1.

Narayan, Uma. 1997. *Dislocating Cultures: Identities, Traditions, and Third-World Feminism.* New York: Routledge.

Nelson, Charmaine. 2017. *Slavery, Geography and Empire in Nineteenth-Century Marine Landscapes of Montréal and Jamaica.* London/New York: Routledge.

OHRC. 2018. *Call It Out: Racism, Racial Discrimination and Human Rights.* <ohrc.on.ca/en/learning/elearning/call-it-out>.

Roth, Solen. 2019. "Can Capitalism Be Decolonized? Recentering Indigenous Peoples, Values, and Ways of Life in the Canadian Art Market." *American Indian Quarterly* 43, 3.

Said, Edward. 1978. *Orientalism.* London: Penguin Books.

Smith, Linda Tuhiwai. 2021. *Decolonizing Methodologies: Research and Indigenous Peoples.* London: Zed Books.

Steinman, Erich. 2016. "Decolonization Not Inclusion: Indigenous Resistance to American Settler Colonialism." *Sociology of Race and Ethnicity* 2, 2.

Tamburro, Andrea. 2013. "Including Decolonization in Social Work Education and Practice." *Journal of Indigenous Social Development* 2, 1.

Thobani, Sunera. 2007. *Exalted Subjects: Studies in the Making of Race and Nation in Canada.* Toronto: University of Toronto Press.

Tobias, John. 1983. "Canada's Subjugation of the Plains Cree, 1879–1885." *Canadian Historical Review* 64, 4.

Truth and Reconciliation Commission of Canada. 2015a. *Canada's Residential Schools: The Final Report of the Truth and Reconciliation Commission of Canada.* Winnipeg.

___. 2015b. *The Truth and Reconciliation Commission of Canada: Calls to Action.* Winnipeg.

Tuck, Eve, and Yang, K. Wayne. 2012. "Decolonization is Not a Metaphor." *Decolonization: Indigeneity, Education & Society* 1, 1.

Vowel, Chelsea, 2016. *Indigenous Writes: A Guide to First Nations, Métis, and Inuit Issues in Canada.* Winnipeg: Portage & Main Press.

Wildcat, Matthew, Mandee McDonald, Stephanie Irlbacher-Fox, and Glen Coulthard. 2014. "Learning from the Land: Indigenous Land Based Pedagogy and Decolonization." *Decolonization: Indigeneity, Education & Society* 3, 3.

Wolfe, Patrick. 2006. "Settler Colonialism and the Elimination of the Native." *Journal of Genocide Research* 8, 4.

Round 2

BEING AND DOING

Decolonial Equity in Practice

The chapters in this section offer examples of what decolonial equity does or can look like in practice, whether in community or in the classroom. Roberta Pike, along with contributors Cheryllee Bourgeois and Sara Booth, consider decolonial equity in the context of their work at the Toronto Birth Centre (TBC) — a community-based, Indigenous-governed health centre that serves midwifery clients in the city of Toronto. Presenting an analysis largely grounded in the Anishinaabe teachings of the lead author and contextualized in the history of the TBC, Pike et al. articulate how principles of decolonial equity are integrated in the TBC governance model, leadership, and relational practices. This chapter is significant in representing practice-based knowledge from an urban Indigenous perspective in a community-driven health care setting and extending our discussions of decolonizing equity beyond educational settings.

In Chapter 5, Terry Gardiner reflects on efforts to decolonize equity in the context of supporting pathways to postsecondary education for Black and Indigenous students through a Summer Mentorship Program (SMP). Emphasizing the importance of the students feeling seen and heard, Gardiner's chapter highlights several key practices including contextualization, representation, relationship building, collaboration, and process-orientation. He also speaks to the importance of decolonizing curriculum and creating space for stories, culture, and connection.

Similarly, Dr. Roland Sintos Coloma's chapter serves to contextualize, historicize, and politicize efforts to decolonize urban education with the aim of redressing the gross inequities embedded in it. Dr. Coloma outlines what readers might understand as important tenets for decolonial equity work, including the refusal to erase or subsume Indigenous presence and knowledges, the importance of decolonizing affect(ive knowledge) and the necessity of (decolonial) structural analysis that can draw on the deep wells of knowledge held in Ethnic Studies, Indigenous Studies, and in the embodied knowledge of Black, Indigenous, and people of colour (BIPOC) scholars and communities. Integrating wisdoms from across critical disciplines, Indigenous communities, and communities of colour — locally, nationally, and globally — reminds us that we are not alone and further, that our struggles are not disconnected.

These three chapters collectively centre practices for decolonizing equity in urban spaces and consider pathways to equitable access to, on one hand, birthing (Pike et al.), and on the other, education (Gardiner; Coloma).

4

TKARANTO ONDAADIZI-GAMIG

Birth Is a Ceremony

Roberta Pike

with contributors Cheryllee Bourgeois and Sara Booth

Working toward decolonial equity is a daunting challenge, one which must begin at birth. Tkaranto Onddaazi-Gamig or The Toronto Birth Centre (TBC) was envisioned as a culturally safe place for Indigenous families to give birth in a self-determined way. At its foundation is an Indigenous Framework rooted in *Itapisinowin* — a Cree/ Nehiyo concept shared by Maria Campbell during the visioning of the Birth Centre, which brought together Elders, Knowledge keepers, parents, community members, and midwives, and was documented in the birth centre visioning report by Smylie, Wolfe, and Senese (2016). This concept centres Indigenous ways of knowing and seeing; this framework guides the TBC's governance and operations, placing the building of cultural integrity for all peoples at the centre of its activities: from teaching to governance to clinical care.

Tkaranto has always been a place of convergence for a diversity of peoples who belong to one or more equity-seeking communities whose experiences of health and well-being reflect the entrenched colonial bias, racism, and inequity that pervades the health care system. By building and nurturing relationships within a larger web of community connections, the TBC asserts space for resurgence of each person's cultural and personal connections to their family, lineage, and history. Every infant born at the TBC and their family is part of the ceremony of birth and it is our goal that they have the full experience of what it means to "do" equity in a good way.

This chapter introduces the author and contributors who share the story of how TBC was born and examine the governance and leadership structures, key principles, and Indigenous knowledge that supports our Indigenous Framework. Next, we share stories, knowledge, and examples to illustrate our understanding of decolonial equity in practice followed by a recommendation for the next generations of Indigenous and non-Indigenous Peoples taking up the work of seeking decolonial equity.

SELF-LOCATION/INTRODUCTION OF AUTHOR AND CONTRIBUTORS

AANIIN! BOOZHOO! Nawh'odae'geezhigo'kwe dezhnikaaz. Anishaabekwe endow. Bekanon ndoonjibaa. Waubizhaysii endodem. My English name is Roberta (my pronouns are she/her) and I am Anishinabek (Ojibwe) and a proud member of the Henvey Inlet First Nation. I am Marten clan. I come from a lineage of patriarchal leaders; my great great-grandfather Chief Wagamake signed the Robinson-Huron Treaty in 1850 with his clan mark, a drawing of Amik or Beaver — I am from the people of the Beaver. Half of my ancestry and blood is tied to the rugged land around Georgian Bay in Ontario and my other half to Newfoundland, another chiselled land, where my white father was born. I have three brothers, two Indigenous and one non-Indigenous who found me in the last year. I was cross-trained in psychology and social work and worked within Indigenous health care and government for many years with a focus on the health and well-being of the Indigenous community; I am now a leader of a non-profit organization. I am a partner to an Anishnaabeinini from Wikwemikong Unceded Territory, and we created a beautiful son who, at the time of the writing of this chapter, was thirteen years old. I am fortunate to have been blessed by parents who understood the racism that exists in society and took the care to ground and encourage me in my identity as an Indigenous woman. It has helped me in my journey in being and becoming a leader. I feel honoured to be the Executive Director of the TBC and hope that everyone who has a connection with us feels all the good energies and life flowing all around us.

I want to acknowledge my colleagues who have contributed wisdom and guidance in the preparation of this chapter: Cheryllee Bourgeois and Sara (Sadie) Booth. Cheryllee is an Exemption Métis Midwife, with connection to home territories in Red River of Southern Manitoba and North Dakota; she was one of two Indigenous Midwife Co-Leads who proposed and pushed forward to develop and operationalize the TBC. Cheryllee is also Past President of the Board of Directors of the TBC. Sara (Sadie) Booth is a white settler Registered Midwife, and Clinical Director of the TBC. Both Cheryllee and Sadie have contributed their experience and knowledge by way of content and examples highlighted within this chapter.

INDIGENOUS WAYS OF SEEING, KNOWING, RELATING, AND DOING AS FOUNDATIONS OF DECOLONIAL EQUITY

We are writing this chapter in the time of the Seventh Fire of Creation. In the past six months, we have experienced some very rapid times of change with Wet'suwet'en political sovereignty being boldly asserted and solidarity actions that have had very "inconvenient" impacts on Canadians. We are going through the experience of a global pandemic in which all of us humans are being forced to rethink the meaning and value of life in the face of huge rates of infection, illness, and death, interruption of the fabric of our familial and social structures and physical, mental, emotional, or physical health, alongside "emergency orders" in the legal, health, education, economic, and justice systems. We are also witnessing the Black Lives Matter movement on Turtle Island demanding a reckoning for long ignored historical abuses and oppression that continue to play out today and that require us to critically self-examine how we uphold these legacies of a colonial system. Are we on the cusp of the lighting of the Eighth Fire? The Eighth Fire of creation is said to be an eternal fire that represents the shift away from all that is wrong with society to create a world founded on peace, love, friendship, and respect for all. Is there more we must endure and survive? Those who have inherited the benefits of the colonizers have two paths before them. The first is to continue on the dark road to destruction to grow their own empires on the backs of, and to the detriment of, peoples on the basis of Indigeneity, race, gender, class, sexuality, and disability visible in the inequitable burden of colonial harms such as violence, poverty, illness, and social exclusion. Or they can take the more difficult road to acknowledge and learn about their implication in the colonial systems and racist and oppressive attitudes that have become so entrenched in our systems and failed so many people, and then actively seek to end the harm and to live in peace.

Commitments to "decolonize this" or "Indigenize that" are thrown around very loosely these days, seeming to serve as more of a rallying cry than a genuine commitment marked by learning and deep understanding, action, and change. Indigenous knowledge exists within all Indigenous Peoples, in our teachings, social structures, myths and legends, relationships, creation stories, and in our systems of justice, health, and well-being. Decolonial equity from an Indigenous perspective is unapologetic; it does not ask for permission, seek power or control over others, or covet economic, social or political gain, and it does not try to make us all "equal." It is a process of reclaiming, recovering, reviving, and living our ways. We need to go back to our teachings and cultures as distinct Indigenous Peoples, develop a critical awareness of how we have been affected by colonialism and embrace our identities as Indigenous Peoples, recognizing and resisting efforts of indoctrination, acculturation, and all forms of colonial brainwashing, and calling out white supremacy culture's "moves to innocence" (Fellows and Razack 1998; Tuck and Yang 2012) when we see them. Let there be no mistake: we as Indigenous people have *all* suffered from and felt the repercussions of the colonizer/colonial system that is so deeply entrenched in society, even to this day. We are Indigenous Peoples of this land; our creation stories do not tell us that our origins began from the Bering Strait — they tell us we have been here on Turtle Island since the beginning of creation and that the Creator gifted us with this land and all of life on this land. We are the original inhabitants and as its stewards, we see and understand the world (worldview) wholistically, think (Indigenous knowledge, values, principles, and epistemologies), relate (how we feel, connect, demonstrate support, and live in harmony and balance in relation to creation) and do (our practices, policies and strategies to get action) things very differently from those with a Eurocentric worldview.

As a place with diverse Indigenous Peoples, Tkaranto presents the reality of working across different Indigenous Nations' ways of seeing, being, knowing, and moving in the world, requiring that we critically think about, articulate, and interpret intentions, meaning, and action. This is especially true in our experience at TBC in our commitment to cultural integrity. Equity in Indigenous communities means that every human being has intrinsic worth. We have differences in ability, character, gifts, and talents that are to be celebrated — no one is greater or less than the other because of these — likewise each of us have needs that are different — no greater or less than those of others but may require different approaches in order to be met. As each spirit comes through the eastern doorway it is born into a physical body and has been gifted with unique roles and responsibilities. Each is entitled to their fair share of resources and benefits in the community. Equity means that the community looks out for and provides for those with unfulfilled needs, which may be due to barriers of their own making or those that are out of their control.

Anishinaabe trickster stories were often told in the long nights of winter when we had more time to rest and socialize. These stories are full of examples that explain why things are the way they are in the natural world; they exaggerate negative behaviours and emotions — vanity, anger, lust, coveting, jealousy, stealing, and laziness — and provide a moral for each that was meant to teach and instruct our children. They teach about sexuality, the rewards of being a hard worker, and of being happy with what you have to avoid pitfalls later in life. There are many Indigenous people who escape from their trauma through substance use. These folks do not need to be judged for being weak or for having some other defect of character; instead, substance use needs to be recognized as a symptom of the deeper trauma and pain. Alcoholism, substance use, violence, and gambling does result in many negative consequences for families involved, but this is not a reason to ever deny someone assistance. Compassion for others and belief in everyone's potential can be life changing.

Many urban Indigenous people may not be members of a First Nation and may not have grown up with a strong relationship to the land. Many don't own a rifle, or hunt, and don't have much, if any, experience in skinning and butchering wild game. There is a myth that urban Indigenous people fare better than those on First Nations reserves or that they have access to more and better services. This is simply not true. The costs of living in urban environments are relatively higher than on some reserves, and the racism and lack of culturally safe services is greater. Equity at the TBC is about being prepared to provide diapers and other basic clothing supplies and other supports for those who do not have much. Equity is also about anticipating needs before they happen and making provisions for the future. We will talk more about the specifics of this later when we discuss policy development.

VISIONING FOR A BIRTH CENTRE

The Indigenous community in Toronto has been very active since the 1960s with friendship centres, social clubs, and other Indigenous-led agencies that have evolved over time. Throughout this time, the community was aware that we as Indigenous people were leading the way, statistically speaking, with the worst health disparities and outcomes, poverty, discrimination, racism, incarceration rates, and education completion. Access to Indigenous health and social services grew rapidly in the city; however, there was no place to give birth other than in hospital. Moreover, Indigenous people of child-bearing age were conditioned to believe that there was no other choice but to go to the hospital to give birth. Hospital usage for Indigenous Peoples continues to be a contentious experience, and many Indigenous Peoples delay seeking care as a result of terrible racist encounters, stereotyping, and attitudinal responses in the health care system (Allan and Smylie 2015). The practice of midwifery — expertise that used to be abundant in our communities — was almost stamped out by colonialization. Midwifery was (and is still perceived as) a mostly middle-class white woman's birthing "experience." Those Indigenous community members who were concerned with maternal and child health, including the few Indigenous midwives, dreamed of the day when Indigenous Peoples (and other peoples of priority communities) could have a respectful, culturally safe, and loving place in which to birth. In 2012, a community visioning gathering was held at the local friendship centre that brought together a broad range of community members and key stakeholders; from this gathering the dream of opening an Indigenous birth centre in Toronto became a reality. This process is documented in *For Seven Generations: Visioning for a Toronto Aboriginal Birth Centre,* a key resource that outlines the context for the birth visioning process (Smylie, Wolfe, and Senese 2016). A funding call from Ontario came available in early 2012 for the building of birth centres. Two Indigenous midwives from Seventh Generation Midwives Toronto, Sara Wolfe and Cheryllee Bourgeois, who would become the Indigenous co-leads of the Birth Centre, developed a proposal with the overwhelming support of the Toronto midwifery community and were awarded funding to build and operate the Toronto Birth Centre. We could not write this chapter without a special mention and honouring of Sara Wolfe, who, alongside Cheryllee and others, worked to articulate and document how Indigenous ways are built into an organization, and its policies and processes. G'Chi-Miigwetch Sara!

Many layers to the planning and built design of the Birth Centre make it highly relevant to the people using the space, enable it to support ceremony, and identify with culture overtly and through the subconscious through symbolism and Indigenous design. There is deep meaning for the location of the Birth Centre and positioning in the community, especially the framework on which the Birth Centre was built, to which we turn next.

INDIGENOUS FRAMEWORK

The TBC was founded based on a conceptual structure that is reflective of many cultures and teachings of the peoples who are Indigenous to Turtle Island (both the Anishinaabek and Haudenosaunee creation stories refer to the creation of the continent of North America upon the back of the turtle). This framework is based on the diversity of the First Peoples on Turtle Island and the worldviews that we hold. Resurgence for Indigenous Peoples is an active, conscious commitment to live life according to our worldviews as Indigenous Peoples. *Itapisinowin*, a Cree/Nehiyo word that represents an Indigenous worldview, reminds us that the way we see and know the world can vary from community to community, nation to nation, and person to person.

Despite their multitude and diversity, the worldviews of the various Indigenous Nations who call Turtle Island home have some common big picture elements or principles. At the core of these worldviews is the acknowledgement that we are "relational" spiritual beings. Human beings exist on the earth as spiritual beings in physical form; our spirits exist in relation to the world around them, thus, the Anishnaabemowin term *Indinawe maaganidog* or "all my relations" refers to relations with other humans, insect and plant life, non-human beings (beaver, muskrat, buffalo, seals, fish and so on) and other-than-human beings or spirits. Our creation stories, legends, and trickster stories teach us about the

"the North Star" and settled in Canada via the Underground
Railroad, a Christian anti-slavery network. (Government of
Canada 2017)

Such a rendering of history completely obfuscates Canada's 200 years of
engagement in the active slave trade of Black bodies and the enslavement
of Indigenous Peoples. Indeed, such a rendering indicates that education still operates as an assimilationist tool to absorb the Other into the
body politic of the nation-state and in so doing, continues the colonial
mandate. The task and challenge then in decolonizing is in de-schooling
and re-schooling the nation. Recent moves like the 2015 TRC and the
2021 Declaration of Emancipation Day in Canada, though significant in
their official acknowledgement of the violent colonial processes of the
Canadian Government on Black and Indigenous bodies, may be much
too late, considering that this violence is central to the creation of the
Canadian nation-state.

The nation-state in its interactions with bodies of difference became
the colonizer. It is vitally important that we understand a central principle of colonial functioning that governs both historical and current
engagements. This principle simply is that policies were designed to best
serve the needs of the colonial master and not the needs of the colonial subjects from the point of encounter to today. Colonial subjects are
clearly defined, and the colonial masters continue to reify their presence
in the continued making of nation-state. The use of policies to manage
Indigenous and Black Peoples to meet the needs of the settler colonist
(the elimination of the Indigenous Peoples and the capture and containment of the slave) is an enactment of this principle. Through the one
drop rule, the whitest of Black people were bound to slavery because
the policy ensured that the offspring of their slaves and any other parent with any African ancestry, no matter the distance, and regardless of
the physical characteristics or appearance, would be enslaved, thereby
increasing the number of slaves who could serve the colonist's interests. The opposite was true for Indigenous Peoples. Where one drop of
Black blood forever tied Black people to the land as slaves, one drop
of white blood forever separated Indigenous Peoples from the land as
Indigenous. Wolfe (2006) notes that for Indigenous Peoples, non-Indigenous ancestry compromised their Indigeneity, producing "half-breeds"
in a regime that persists in the form of blood quantum regulations. The

interconnectedness and interdependencies of all of creation. We are taught from an early age to have respect for the sacredness of all of life, our roles and responsibility to the natural world, the laws of nature, and what happens if we do not keep harmony and balance with the natural world. We are taught about our kinship relations (biological, customary, clan, chosen). Our relations with others are focused on nurturing healthy relationships of respect and reciprocity. An example of the reciprocity relationships can bring is detailed in the document entitled "Three Sisters Accord" that TBC has co-created with Women's College Hospital and Seventh Generations Midwives Toronto (SGMT). The document outlines the details of our relationships, shared values and common goals, and how we work together. We have a close relationship to Seventh Generations Midwives as a co-located midwifery practice, and TBC and SGMT often assist and support each other's organizational endeavours that have benefit to the Indigenous community. In the face of the COVID-19 pandemic, TBC was able to ask our "eldest sister," Women's College Hospital, for Personal Protective Equipment (PPE) supplies when we were at risk of closing due to shortages in the market. We experienced a very positive response to our request once we explained our longstanding relationship with the hospital to folks that were new to their jobs and unfamiliar with the Accord.

TBC services are all grounded in the Indigenous Framework from governance to operations. Indigeneity is both very personal and very political, evoking strong reactions and emotions. Indigenous identity in a city such as Toronto has many expressions. There is a growing Indigenous community in Toronto and high levels of movement back and forth from First Nation reserves and/or urban to urban communities across the country. There are Indigenous people residing in Toronto that are isolated from the urban Indigenous community and those that choose to walk around anonymously and prefer to keep it that way. There are generations of folks that know they are Indigenous and haven't explored what that means, and there are those who were adopted out to non-Indigenous families and are in the process of repatriation. There are people who left their First Nation when they were younger because it was not safe to express their sexual identity, or adoptees who have been rejected when they tried to make connections to their relatives on reserve. Indigenous people that are part of the TBC family are First Nations, Métis, and Inuit, status, non-status, are two-spirited, trans, urban, lesbian, queer, and gay; we are of all sorts of mixed ancestry, bi-racial, and tri-racial. Our identities have been affected by, challenged by, called into question by, colonizers to the point that many are still on a journey of seeking their identity, coming to understand who they are, and establishing a sense of belonging. The very worst expression of colonization is when we allow ourselves as Indigenous people to be seduced by the colonizer's definitions of Indigeneity and become pitted against one another. To respect this, the TBC has developed a statement on Indigenous identity as part of its governance policies that succinctly seeks to educate and allow for self-determination (one of our core organizational values) and self-identification to unfold without assault or question. As an organization, we ensure that the Board of Directors positions are held by midwives and an Indigenous majority. Executive leadership of the Birth Centre has always been Indigenous, and for the past two years, over half of our staff are Indigenous.

Debwewin, or "truth" in Anishnaabemowin, is reflected in our organizational belief that we have a responsibility to bring an awareness and acknowledgement of the true histories of Indigenous Peoples in Canada. We recognize the intergenerational impacts/legacies of colonization, and we support Indigenous reclamation of culture and identity and political resurgence. We support efforts to resist colonization; we require that all people involved with the Birth Centre, especially the non-Indigenous midwives who use the Birth Centre and non-Indigenous Board and Committee members, educate themselves, self-locate, and make connections between their own power and privilege. We ask that they critically reflect upon different narratives of history, society, and health, and make a commitment to not perpetuate false narratives; we ask that they develop skills which enable them to provide culturally safer care not only for Indigenous people but for all priority communities who we hope to serve. Facing the attitudinal bias and systemic racism within oneself is difficult; working to change these is the epitome of bravery or, what we call in Anishnaabemowin, *Aakwa'ode'ewin.*

Rights of Indigenous Peoples

The TBC supports the rights of Indigenous Peoples; these rights are clearly entrenched in the United Nations Declaration of the Rights of Indigenous Peoples (UNDRIP) and legally through the Constitution of

Canada and the Ontario Human Rights Code. There is a difference between self-government for First Nations (which often ties nationhood to decision making by the people tied to a land base) and self-determination (which is also about a nation's decision making but more from a community, family, and personal perspective) for all Indigenous Peoples including urban Indigenous Peoples. We at the TBC feel strongly that everyone has the right to determine what their future will look like, beginning with those decisions involving birth.

One of those rights is the right to practice Indigenous midwifery in the ways of our ancestors, without regulation, interference, and judgment by outside colonized institutions and ways of thinking. The Board of Directors had articulated a stand early in the Birth Centre's development to support this right, and just last year were able to credential the first midwife working under the Aboriginal exemption at the Birth Centre! This was a significant milestone for the Birth Centre, one which we are yet to celebrate. We also have cultural teachings that speak to our collective roles and responsibilities to every member of the community. Indigenous people can have their whole family and extended family members and friends at their birth if they want; they can conduct ceremonies during their stay; they can drum, sing, pray, and have multiple helpers present at their birth including cultural knowledge keepers and doulas. This stands in stark contrast to the hospital environment, which seeks to limit Indigenous Peoples in what they can do and who can be present. Having culturally safe places to give birth, without having to make all sorts of arrangements ahead of time and where one feels at home, is amazing!

Cultural Safety

The concept of cultural safety was first introduced by Irihapeti Ramsden, a Maori nurse in Aotearoa (New Zealand), in 1989 (Ramsden 1989, 1990; Ramsden and Spoonley 1994). Her description of the term explained that cultural safety moves beyond cultural sensitivity and cultural competence in that it analyzes power imbalances in society, as well as political ideals of self-determination and decolonization (Ramsden and Spoonley 1994).

The TBC has been working on cultural safety for many years. All Board members, staff, and students are required to complete cultural safety training, and to continue to update their knowledge and skills by seeking and creating further opportunities. As cultural safety also differs from cultural competence models by incorporating specifically anti-racist content (Churchill, Parent-Bergeron, and Smylie 2017), this training is particularly important for non-Indigenous people. The Board has also made it a mandatory requirement for credentialling and to continue to be part of the midwifery staff at TBC that midwives attend educational and training sessions approved by the Board. Midwives must also provide evidence of mandatory ongoing learning within regular timeframes. The TBC accesses training seats through online and in-person trainings and provides updated opportunities. These opportunities have become a baseline for cultural safety within the TBC and we look forward to beginning new rounds and endeavours to further our learning.

Everything that is done at the TBC is guided by the organization's four core values: Self-determination, Equity, Justice, and Dignity. Self-determination means that all persons involved with the Birth Centre are recognized as doing so of their own free will. We acknowledge and remember we are all responsible to ourselves, to our families, and to our community. Equity means that the TBC is committed to establishing policy, procedure, and guidelines that promote equity among all peoples. Dignity means that we aim to conduct all our relationships and interactions with the utmost dignity; this includes acting in a manner that builds trust, creating an environment free of judgment, being honest and direct in all our dealings, acknowledging power differentials, and being open to discussion. Justice means that we work to create an environment and practice that resists false narratives of history, society, and health while actively addressing health disparities both in voice and in action. Value-based work is front and centre in everything that goes on at TBC; in everything we do and in every decision that we make, the core values are always guiding us.

Decolonial practice for Indigenous allies is about the process of examining beliefs about Indigenous Peoples and cultures by learning about one's self in relationship to the communities where one lives and the people with whom one interacts. We all have deep-seated impressions, assumptions, or things we have learned as children and in society; some of this bias is very much conscious, and some bias is unconscious. It is the role of the ally to work hard to uncover those beliefs and work toward correcting them through education, awareness, and a commitment to critically consider their behaviour in relation to the systems they move in.

Many of our peoples have gone through very dark days of self-loathing, hate, and discrimination by enduring racist or abusive comments, attitudes and experiences, and have internalized these things in thoughts and behaviours that are self-destructive. Many Indigenous people are learning how to reclaim their voices and to not feel ashamed to ask for what they need, even if they continue to be in the spotlight when they do assert their rights. In one's practice, having compassion and respect for Indigenous Peoples as human beings and the strength that they must have to survive is a wonderful place to start. But we also must be clear and deliberate in our expectations of relationship with non-Indigenous people, in being able to speak freely and truthfully about their motivation and intent working with and supporting Indigenous communities.

Indigenous Governance

The TBC works within a mainstream view of organizational structure for non-profit corporations. It is operated based on principles of Indigenous governance. There are differences in procedure versus process versus product. For us, the procedures are about the non-profit organizational entity and the rules that apply for operating it. These procedures are externally imposed via bylaw, letters patent, minutes, funding agreements, and other guidelines. Process refers to the ways in which leadership is chosen, the ways in which discussion leads to decision making, and how decisions are made. The product is about the decisions that lead to the services provided and ultimately the outcomes we are striving for.

The TBC operates within a mainstream structure; we do not receive government funding specifically designated for Indigenous organizations. We are uniquely positioned in that any community accountability mechanism is co-created by the organization, leadership, staff, clients, and larger community without imposed criteria. We take this responsibility and relationship very seriously. Our vision is to build a space where people, families, and communities can access culturally safe birthing care. Our objectives are to achieve optimal health and wellness for the whole community through culturally centred care, education, and research that supports the practice of Indigenous midwifery in its fullest scope, both culturally and professionally. The TBC was "gifted" with the corporation from a group who had wanted long ago to build a multi-purpose maternal and child organization incorporating a place for births to happen in the community. The group was non-Indigenous and had bylaws that needed to be changed to meet the needs of the Indigenous community. The governance structure of the Board and how the Birth Centre operated also needed to be outlined. The new Board was created with nine Directors, composed of two-thirds midwives and with the majority also/or being Indigenous. The TBC was set up with two main advisory committees to represent and balance the work needed to be endorsed by both midwifery practice and the Indigenous community. Other committees such as the Quality Advisory Committee, Credentialing Committee, Quality of Care Committee, and ad hoc committees were established at the same time or would come later. One of the principles of governance was to ensure that no one person would sit on multiple governance structures to distribute responsibility widely rather than to the same people in multiple contexts. This is not to say that Board members cannot sit on committees, or that they are not welcome to provide context; rather, they do not participate in the committee's voting processes.

Elements of Indigenous Governance and Leadership

Equity for Indigenous Peoples is the freedom from bias or favouritism originating in white supremacist culture, as well as the freedom to do what needs to be done to meet the needs of our people. Equity for Indigenous Peoples is hard to realize in greater society, so we strive to ensure we are doing our best to ensure our internal structures, processes, and products are based on Indigenous knowledge which is the basis of decolonial equity.

Decolonial equity begins with an understanding of colonialism, the different worldviews of Indigenous people and white supremacy culture, and how systems have developed all around us rampant with injustice, prejudice, racism, and oppression. The real histories of Indigenous Peoples and their experiences in the evolution of these systems provide a context for understanding all the health and psychosocial challenges and barriers that exist for Indigenous Peoples. As mentioned earlier, our organization expects all Board members, volunteers, staff, and midwives to participate in Indigenous cultural safety training to be provided with a baseline understanding of what colonization has done and to begin the personal exploration of what each individual can do to be an ally to Indigenous people, Black people, People of Colour, 2SLBGTQIA+ and marginalized groups that experience inequity in white supremacist culture.

Relationships

As mentioned earlier, Indigenous worldviews are all about "all my relations." We all have a purpose on the earth and a journey to fulfill. Healthy and reciprocal relations with other humans and other-than-humans are needed for us to do our work and to survive as a people. We know the importance of taking the time to build good relations and honour those that assist us or contribute to the work that is birth, including but not limited to midwives, volunteers, individuals, clients, families, medicines, ancestors, spirits, and our bundles. We do this through ceremony, solstice and equinox gatherings, our Annual General Meeting (AGM), special events, and by recognizing and supporting midwives working with priority populations.

The TBC takes up the careful work of questioning and challenging the teachings we hear. We invite the involvement of Knowledge Keepers and Elders who have a heightened awareness of and experience with resistance to colonial ways, and who know how to create an environment where the circle feels as safe as possible. Gender-based teachings and protocols, heavily influenced by the church and state, had led to the near obliteration of teachings surrounding Two Spirit, contrary, or queer peoples, and severely impacted and undermined our understanding of healthy relationships, Indigenous family, and community.

Our leadership try to role model for each other and our community(ies) the best of our teachings. Our leadership navigates many worlds, and we continue to address disparities, seek remedy, and collaborate on solutions to further issues of social justice facing Indigenous Peoples, Black people, People of Colour, and other priority communities.

Meeting Local, Indigenous, and Cultural Needs

Decolonial equity means that we need to develop and offer programs that meet local needs, share Indigenous knowledge and cultural needs, and find funding to support this. The Birth Centre partnered with SGMT for their Generations Group on Mondays. The group is open for anyone in the community to attend and is meant to provide a fun and relaxing atmosphere to connect with others across the generations (aunties, grandparents, Elders, families and so on) who are interested in learning more about all things birth-related and Indigenous culture. The program is positioned within the larger Baby Bundle program that is targeted to reach Indigenous families by providing practical, wrap around support to Indigenous pregnant people and families in Toronto through community education and outreach, integrated Indigenous midwifery care, resource creation, and to participate in the ongoing resurgence of Indigenous Birth Work.

The TBC also provides meaningful engagement of midwives and Indigenous community not only in its governance structure but in strategic planning and ongoing work plans to support the Birth Centre. We try to bring everyone together annually to review our intentions and successes, and to plan for outward years.

The TBC is also keenly aware that it is not just the responsibility of one organization or person in the community to continue addressing health issues and social determinants of health for Indigenous Peoples. It is a huge undertaking that will not be addressed overnight. As we have become aware of the circumstances confronting families, we have developed relevant policies that enable equitable access to baby clothing, taxis to and from the Birth Centre, meals and snacks, and lending of infant car seats. We look at issues of food sovereignty/security and provide access to resources in the community that can assist in addressing issues such as housing, child care, and employment. We have also tried to build community by hosting soup drop-ins, inviting community to our celebrations, becoming involved in the local community garden, connecting with local programs, hosting tours, doing outreach to community organizations, sharing resources with Indigenous community, and opening our doors to grassroots groups to use space.

The transmission of Traditional Knowledge and Ceremony is part of our culture and a highly personal experience that occurs at the Birth Centre, in hospitals, outside, and in the community. They are not commodities. It is not unusual to see folks steeplechasing Indigenous people to try and insert themselves in ceremonies and circles that have nothing to do with them and to which they have not been invited. Anyone who charges for traditional knowledge or is in the line of work to regularly give a "ceremonial experience" in exchange for money is not safe.

Leadership

At the TBC, the Board of Directors are the ultimate leaders of the organ-ization. The organization places the majority of the decision making at the Board level. The Board was established to strike a balance between midwifery and Indigenous perspectives. In addition to these voting seats, the community council also nominates a Knowledge Keeper to the Board and a youth member; neither hold voting powers but can be very influential in the discussion and decision making of the Board.

The best decision making is informed by many perspectives. There was a reason why we always have seasonal meetings in our societies to allow for long discussions of the problems and consulting widely with all members affected. Working within a Eurocentric structure of a "Board of Directors" does not allow for long and lengthy meetings. Sometimes staff are frustrated by the number of times items go before the Board be-fore they are addressed — because it is not the right time, because there are other priorities and, sometimes, because in their wise opinion, we (the staff or the community) are just not ready or adequately prepared to address issues. This leads us into a quick note on the dichotomy of time — mainstream society demands quick decisions in a short timeframe or decisions to make the work move along. Decision making in Indigenous governance can be slow, sometimes deferred, and always at the pace of leadership and community readiness. Consulting widely with advisory groups slows the process, and while the process in and of itself is slow, it has a lot of intrinsic learning and value.

There are always power differentials that exist: between leadership and staff, Board and staff, staff and staff, midwife and midwife, midwives and clients, midwives and students, staff and students. Each person involved with the TBC is encouraged to examine their own power and understand how in different circumstances it may be misused or abused, and to be cognizant of this in their interactions. This is emphasized in HR policies and credentialling systems designed to address issues related to pow-er differentials to allow a mechanism to address issues of concern for everyone involved at the Birth Centre. The TBC has developed a Code of Conduct for all staff, midwifery staff, clients and visitors, Board mem-bers, volunteers who are affiliated with the Birth Centre; this code also overlaps with other policies related to discrimination and harassment. The TBC expects that each person involved with the TBC will respect our core values and will uphold their responsibility for their own words and actions, including participating with others in aiming to address any entrenched conflicts or disputes. Our policy outlines what is acceptable and unacceptable conduct and behaviour and what the TBC will do to address the issue.

We believe that in the absence of a power differential affecting people's ability to advocate for themselves, direct communication between the parties involved in a conflict is the best approach to resolution. When direct address of the conflict is perceived to be ineffective, or unsafe for some of the parties involved, the TBC is committed to supporting conflict resolution by other means.

Indigenous societies have always had means by which to resolve disputes that were based on the specifics of each culture but almost always involved a council of Elders, community members or other representatives that would hear disputes and make recommendations. The consequences were often in line with the nature of the behaviour and specifics of the incident requiring correction. The offending individual could be requested to issue a public apology and/or make reparation to the person harmed. One of the worst consequences that anyone in such a society could be given is to be ignored and made "invisible" for a period of time or outright banned forever from participating in the life of the community. Modern day community councils for alternative sentencing try to seek assistance for the individual and order them to make reparation through community service and apology to the person wronged.

In the context of the TBC, we have used individual coaching with each party to a dispute to see if they could (with support) work through the issues on their own. We have used the advice of an HR committee (members of the Board), talking circles, sharing/healing circles, and sought external mediation for other HR issues to different degrees of effectiveness. We have had a few incidents at TBC which have resulted in poor and unacceptable behaviour by visitors to the TBC which made us revisit our policy and build ways in which to make it more evident to visitors, through tours and by posting clear signage of our Code of Conduct and expectations. Decisions to ban certain individuals are exceedingly rare and not taken lightly, and are only taken when the safety of those in our space is at risk. Asking someone to leave, calling the police and/or banning them from participating in a birth/future births is one of the most serious consequences that can be levied. We have only ever banned one person from the Birth Centre but even then, the period during which they were banned was not set. Indigenous cultures have a strong belief in the ability of people to learn and grow. It is possible that we would consider ending this person's ban in the future if circumstances were to change.

Decision Making

Our organization bridges both Indigenous and Eurocentric worldviews. Decision making at the TBC makes use of evidence-based information and conducting risk analyses using standard matrices. The primary decision making strategy for the TBC is consensus. Many people think that consensus means everyone must agree to the decision as presented. Our policy and procedure manual outlines the decision making framework of the TBC and provides helpful guidance as to the ground rules, process, and how you know when consensus has been achieved:

For TBC, the process of consensus involves checking for agreement among all participants and coming to a decision when all participants agree. Members contribute to the process of decision making by holding robust discussion: they may add to or improve upon the suggestion at hand, consider alternatives and rationales, or they may simply agree to it. Members who disagree with a decision have a responsibility to explain their dissent and the reasons for it, so that their viewpoints may inform the rest of the group's approach to the decision at hand. Ideally, all dissenting viewpoints will be incorporated in shaping the best possible decision unanimously. The TBC's approach to consensus is that a decision can be reached when 75 percent or more of participants agree. However, we recognize that dissent may become entrenched at times, with no agreement to change. For issues that are challenging or contentious, the TBC is encouraged to use its decision making tool which can be a useful aid in helping to work through a decision based on our organization's core values, and thinking about the potential impacts to communities, and the development of mitigation strategies.

The TBC decision making tool considers the seventh-generation principle such that any decisions/actions that are taken today should be made based on the best interests of our people and should be sustainable seven generations into the future.

WEAVING DECOLONIAL EQUITY IN LEADERSHIP: ROBERTA'S STORY AND REFLECTIONS

When I first started at the TBC, Sadie, the TBC Clinical Director, asked me to describe my leadership model. I was taken aback at this because I had never analyzed my leadership style or spoken to anyone about it. I had taken numerous management courses and have had lots of opportunity to read books about various types of "Eurocentric" leadership models and learning about the qualities of "emotionally intelligent" leaders. As the daily operational leader for the organization, I like to lead with a shared or collaborative style. I have no issue delegating the lead to others as needed. I know when I am out of my area of expertise and when to hand over navigation to someone else. I dislike being in the spotlight unless the spotlight requires my representation as a leader. I understand many things about my culture as an Anishnaabekwe and always look to understand the world from this perspective. I want others to get recognition for their talents and what they do. When posed with a problem, my preferred method is to seek understanding via many different viewpoints and sharing problems for group solutions. Many minds lead to a better resolution/outcome/product. While responsible for the overall daily operations, I do not "run" the organization by myself; from the beginning, the co-leads, the Board, the midwives of TBC, the Executive and Clinical Directors, and our frontline staff have all been responsible for the operation of various parts of the Birth Centre and as such have all contributed to and have pride in the shared "ownership" of its success as a community.

As a leader, over the years I have made some amazing decisions and I have also made mistakes (big, small, and silly), but I have learned from each of these. I don't feel guilt, shame, or humiliation in making mistakes and having them become known. Strong leadership does not mean that you are right all the time; it means that you are not afraid to make decisions and be wrong. Leaders take responsibility for actions or decisions and when wrong, apologize with a sincere heart, make whatever amends/reparation that can be made and move forward. We must never become complacent in what we know, and we must humbly admit that we are all lifelong learners.

Indigenous leadership is a role and responsibility that not many people need or want. Indigenous cultures raise up their leaders, those who have had a calling, that is, whose life journey is meant to lead others and having a positive impact on something in the world. Indigenous leadership requires that leaders look to those who hold them up (the community) for advice and guidance. In this case, TBC Board members individually and as a collective, the Indigenous communities I have been a part of and those that hired me have been my rock. I am eternally thankful and grateful for our Clinical Director being there to support me in wading through my (mis)perceptions and (mis)interpretations and to be my sounding board in understanding the context and meaning in things. I trust her completely with all things to do with the organization and the Indigenous Framework, but it has taken a long time to get to know her and know where her heart lies as a true ally to Indigenous people.

Boundaries are both real and imagined, and always fluid in Indigenous leadership. When I first started at TBC, I was pretty sure that maintaining solid boundaries between my work and personal life with staff and Board members was a healthy and good thing. This is what Western society teaches us through our educational system, through our professional colleges, through our workplaces, and through media of all sorts. At each opening of the Board meeting, we often begin with a smudge, a teaching/ a prayer and do a go around the circle to check in with one another. At one particular meeting in the fall, one of our non-Indigenous Board members began to cry talking about her week at work, her stress with an aging parent, and her homelife balancing being a mother of young and active children while also holding a challenging career. After letting go of all that stress and having a good cry, she apologized to those present for crying and somewhat embarrassedly said, "I really don't know what came over me." Not one of us present would ever have thought that she was inappropriate or that she lost her boundaries by disclosing such personal stuff. We are all people; we feel, we hurt, we laugh, and we also have the capacity for empathy.

Using medicine to open meetings is a tool. It is a simple, very powerful, and very effective ceremony on its own. We know that the spirit of the medicine works to loosen blockages, open us up, and provide release so that the cleaning and healing energies of the world may do its work. Being real, voicing our truths and emotions is not a loss of personal or professional boundaries; in the Indigenous community, it would never result in a loss of faith in leadership. I am constantly in awe of how all these wonderful Board members navigate through layers of relationship, history, and time to work together in such a good way.

Each of us spend time as leaders coaching and mentoring our employees, not only because we would do so as the employer but because we want to. Being a leader does not mean that you are going to be friends with those you have responsibility for, but it does not exclude you from being a friend when a friend is needed and disclosing relevant personal experiences that validate another's feelings.

Decolonial equity is about leadership that is trusted, not feared. Leaders that reign with an iron fist expect everyone to bend to their will. This encourages a workplace culture rampant with lateral violence. In this environment, individuals will decimate anyone standing in their way and do whatever needs to be done to serve their self-interests: feed misinformation, refuse to help a colleague, encourage misdirection and lies, gossip about someone or their abilities, steal ideas, and take credit for the work of others. I have seen this in many organizations but nowhere near as perfected as in government, where the colonial structure has been built upon position and power. The execution is perfected — the smiling, friendly face of the person in front of you is highly skilled at stabbing you/poisoning you when you least expect it, or when you are most vulnerable.

Decolonial Indigenous leadership is the antithesis of this; it is relational. It fosters an environment of trust, deep and abiding respect for the individual and their safety, and communicates care for everyone as a person. Decolonial leadership builds a foundational support that encourages individuals to help one another, learn together, and share their lives in a meaningful way; it provides opportunities for individuals to pursue their dreams and talents and know they always have a voice and that they are always welcome in the circle. In this environment, the work becomes much more than just another job. This kind of leadership results in a cohesive team where commitment, dedication, and loyalty to the organization and communities served far surpasses anything else. Decolonial leadership sees the value and potential in people and has respect for the roles and responsibilities each of us has on this earth and is supportive in this journey. Non-interference in the pull that people experience to follow their dreams, goals, and so on (self-determination) and not holding people back from pursuing their dreams and supporting them in learning and development is decolonial equity in practice.

ALLIES IN DECOLONIAL EQUITY

Over the past five years, the focus on the outcomes of the National Inquiry for Missing and Murdered Indigenous Women and Girls (NIMMIWG) and the work of the Truth and Reconciliation Commission (TRC) have highlighted many things that can be done to break the chains of colonization. Organizations and individuals respond to the TRC (2015) Calls to Action and the NIMMIWG (2019) Calls for Justice like they are checking off a list of things to do to address equity. But simply going through the motions of what is recommended is empty and meaningless; the real learning begins when individuals and organizations can explain what they are doing and why and establish a deeper emotional connection to the work. For example, land acknowledgements at local schools and in mainstream spaces in the urban community are often monotone and devoid of heart. The education systems in Ontario and the City of Toronto use these land acknowledgements because someone somewhere has mandated them to do so. I like the fact that someone somewhere may hear the message and it will spark their interest in knowing more about Indigenous Peoples and our unique worldviews. The optic of going through the motions, however, is clearly visible to the Indigenous community in the efforts of those who do not bother learning how to pronounce the words in Indigenous languages or speaking about one's learning in relationship to the statement. Decolonial equity and the work of allies need to be congruent — both in words and in actions.

A white settler midwife was once struggling with her hospital's policies and its relationship with Indigenous people. I and many others in the community had felt frustrated by the amount of energy that had been poured into the same issue for the last thirty years with not much improvement. The midwife heard about various issues arising from a policy from several sources in the community and tried to gain some traction for the Indigenous community by very politely calling out the hospital on its colonial attitudes and oppressive behaviours, and trying to find out where the matter was stalled in the hierarchy of the hospital. It was incredible to witness the speed at which some of the institution's employees who felt threatened by her call to action started work to discredit her professionalism and threaten actions which would endanger her livelihood. This is an example of how being an ally and calling out organizations for their racist and oppressive operations can have material consequences.

Allyship in decolonial equity is about having the courage to fight and stand up to the systems, people, policies, and practices that oppress others. It is also about having our backs and being trusted to have those courageous conversations with the bigots, racists, and oppressors in the world. It is having the influence on others to grab these teachable moments to educate about how colonization has had an impact on Indigenous Peoples and why it is important to support self-determination.

DECOLONIAL EQUITY: LOOKING AHEAD

In response to the Black Lives Matter movement's visibility in 2020, many organizations were jumping on the equity bandwagon and scrambling to see what they could implement to alleviate their fears that they will be viewed as racist and oppressive. The Indigenous community experienced a similar response in the wake of the final report of the TRC. Tokenism — for example, a white organization hiring one non-white part-time person, or providing one-time/piecemeal equity training, or relying on a single person to speak on behalf of an equity-seeking group — is not right and it is downright exhausting. While professional development related to anti-colonial health care practice is a growing area of interest and there are more options for this kind of learning, it is not the terminus of equity work — it is just the beginning. Embedding equity work in the strategic planning of an organization is fruitless unless there is support from a senior champion who is both committed to working long-term in this area and has unfettered access to resources to back the work.

The voices and vision of the people who are affected is what needs to be placed at the forefront of all equity work. All organizations need to expect much more from themselves, and they need to evaluate how their structures, processes, and policies keep people oppressed. They need to uncover where bias is hidden in their organization and plan to address it instead of half-heartedly skating on the surface of narratives of equity discourses. Workers and organizations need to understand that as non-dominant people and groups identify their needs, those in power need to be highly attuned to recognizing (hearing/seeing/feeling) these sometimes subtle and sometimes overt messages, attributing value to them, and exploring what can be done to make things better. Inviting communities to engage in equity discourse is nice, but only action shifts the power balance.

In the work of decolonizing equity, organizations and practitioners need not be afraid to sit in their discomfort. Moving awkwardly through new language, issues, and concerns of a specific community, intersectionality, or identity is a common experience to navigate and should be approached with intention and kindness. Part of that is getting used to using words in the correct context and having enough real practice so that language use becomes second nature. The part that is often the most anxiety provoking is confronting the fear that we as humans and our policies and practices may be biased in ways we never knew were possible. This is the starting place that reminds us we should always be willing to engage with discussion, criticism, and feedback in thoughtful and meaningful ways if we are truthfully committed to evolve and grow.

I feel that this discussion is not over without some homework for the reader. A highly recommended reading by Jones and Okun (2001) was shared with the Board and staff by Sadie through her learnings in this area. One of the strengths of this work is its reminder that systemic racism does not require intent to exist and prevail, and that unexamined organizational culture can support white supremacy. It also provides a toolkit to generate awareness, intentional reflection, and discussion so that activities and dynamics steeped in racism can be challenged and replaced. I think many of us will be reading and rereading it for many years to come.

CLOSING WORDS

Each of us are born into the world with gifts and purpose. At Tkaranto Ondaadizi-Gamig, Birth is a Ceremony. We create a space where babies can be welcomed and their role and purpose honoured through care and ceremony. One of the goals of our work at TBC is to actively decolonize birth, and one of the ways we do that is to share Indigenous knowledge of decolonial equity. We invite everyone who is willing to come and sit with us in the circle, to learn what it is like to provide/experience equity in a way that honours and values each individual and strives to fulfill our basic human need to connect with one another and be wrapped in the care and love of All Our Relations. *Gawaabamin Miinwaa!*

References

Allan, Billie, and Janet Smylie. 2015. *First Peoples, Second Class Treatment: The Role of Racism in the Health and Well-Being of Indigenous Peoples in Canada*. Toronto, ON: Well Living House/Wellesley Institute.

Churchill, Mackenzie, Michèle Parent-Bergeron, and Janet Smylie. 2017. *Evidence Brief: Wise Practices for Indigenous-Specific Cultural Safety Training Programs*. Toronto: Well Living House.

Fellows, Mary-Louise, and Sherene Razack. 1998. "The Race to Innocence: Confronting Hierarchical Relations among Women." *The Journal of Gender, Race & Justice* 1, 4.

Jones, Kenneth, and Tema Okun. 2001. "White Supremacy Culture." From *Dismantling Racism: A Workbook for Social Change Groups*. Portland, OR: ChangeWorks. cwsworkshop.org/PARC_site_B/dr-culture.html.

Ramsden, Irihapeti. 1989. *A Model for Negotiated and Equal Partnership*. Wellington: Author.

___. 1990. *Kawa whakaruruhau: Cultural Safety in Nursing Education in Aotearoa*. https://www.moh.govt.nz/NoteBook/nbbooks.nsf/0/707224B-C1D4953C14C2565D700190AD9/$file/kawa-whakaruruhau.pdf.

Ramsden, Irihapeti, and Paul Spoonley. 1994. "The Cultural Safety Debate in Nursing Education in Aotearoa." *New Zealand Annual Review of Education* 3.

Smylie, Janet, Sara Wolfe, and Laura Senese. 2016. *For Seven Generations: Visioning for a Toronto Aboriginal Birth Centre*. Toronto: Seventh Generation Midwives Toronto/The Well Living House. welllivinghouse.com/wp-content/uploads/2018/09/Visioning-For-a-Toronto-Aboriginal-Birth Centre-Report.pdf.

Tuck, Eve, and K. Wayne Yang, 2012. "Decolonization is Not a Metaphor." *Decolonization: Indigeneity, Education & Society* 1, 1.

5

INTRODUCING INDIGENOUS AND BLACK YOUTH TO A NEW VISION OF SOCIAL WORK

Terry Gardiner

The social work profession has engaged in conversation and theorizing exercises on equity and decolonization for several decades. Many social workers, however, have not been as active or clear on the application of theory to practice in ways that reduce the impact of existing trauma and that don't cause more harm. This chapter reflects on the development and implementation of programming in a Faculty of Social Work to introduce Black and Indigenous high school students to social work as a profession and area of postsecondary education. I discuss the skills, practices, collaborations, and partnerships that supported this work and the decolonial lens that informed it, with the intention of focusing on the *doing* informed by the *seeing* and ongoing openness to expansive ways of knowing. I will highlight examples from the social work module within the Summer Mentorship Program (SMP) for Black and Indigenous high school students and my process of coming to understand that supporting youth from colonized communities required a new framework, specific content, different process, and facilitators from outside of the dominant academic and professional pool. Concrete examples include: 1) expecting and acknowledging the particular needs and lived experiences of Indigenous and Black youth, including historical and contemporary experiences; 2) prioritizing instructors and facilitators who identify as Indigenous and Black; and 3) shaping physical spaces and interactional modalities to engage and hold cultures, including using oral tradition and personal sharing to affirm youth and community experience. I conclude with reflections on how this vision of positively engaging youth has been shared with educators, social workers, and social service community partners and how it illustrates a decolonial approach to equity practices.

LOCATING MYSELF IN THE CONTEXT OF CANADIAN COLONIZATION

I am called to position myself and to articulate that positionality as I start to share my experiences and thoughts. I am not separate from the work. My lived experience has shaped the lens through which I see and experience the world, and the ways in which it is possible for me to engage with others. I exist in relationship to others and to the world.

I situate myself as a Black Canadian born in Montréal who grew up on a tiny island in the Caribbean which, today, is still a British colony. I know colonialism to be complicated. I was raised to be Black in a society where the overwhelming majority of citizens identified as Black, where my teachers, public officials, and those in positions of power looked like me. I have studied and worked as a Black man in the United States and then back in Canada as a Black educator and social worker. I have come to see that being Black has a situational meaning and differential experience depending on geographic context. My experiences of Blackness in the Caribbean, the United States, and Canada have had similarities and have all also been very different. I have been welcomed in many spaces and locations and been taught by many who came before me to care about the people around me and their experiences, regardless of our similarities and our differences. This intentional seeing and caring is what I aim to bring to the work.

BLACK AND INDIGENOUS PRESENCE

The underrepresentation of Black and Indigenous students in institutions of postsecondary education has been noted and explored for many years. James (2019) suggests a pipeline theory referencing data which indicates that Indigenous and Black students are less likely to succeed

through primary education. Black and Indigenous students are dispro-
portionately affected by structural adversity (for example, racism, un-
stable housing, and poverty) which negatively influence the opportunity
to access education and succeed in school. Children's coping responses to structural issues are often interpreted within the education system as threatening (Sanders et al. 2021). Black students are four times
more likely, and Indigenous students over three times more likely, to
be expelled from school than white students (James and Turner 2017).
Students with academic challenges are also more likely to be referred to,
and experience ongoing interactions and involvement with, the child
welfare system (Sanders and Fallon 2018). Robyn Maynard (2017) highlights Black students' experience of being labelled as violent and ultimately criminalized as yet another product of systemic racism and colonialism. Additionally, social work as a profession has been identified by
Bergen and Abji (2020) as a link in another pipeline, funnelling racialized youth from child protection systems to the prison system, and for
those who are noncitizens, into a deportation or "crimmigration system"
(Stumpf qtd in Bergen and Abji 2020).

The confluence of these structural factors leads to fewer Black students
in the pool eligible for secondary and postsecondary studies (James and
Turner 2017). In particular, the paucity of Black and Indigenous individuals in pre-service programs for helping professions such as medicine (Vogel 2019), nursing (Flynn 2008) and social work has been a
concern as these are areas where Black and Indigenous communities
are overrepresented as service users (Boatswain-Kyte 2018; Pon, Gosine,
and Phillips 2011). This overrepresentation is but one legacy of anti-Indigenous colonialism, for example, residential schools, the sixties scoop
and others (Sinclair 2004) and anti-Black racism, for example, housing,
employment and policing (Maynard 2017). Understanding how this
disparity developed and is maintained is important to shift the balance
toward greater representation of Black and Indigenous people as service
providers in the helping professions. Alongside this underrepresentation of Black and Indigenous student presence within predominantly
white universities, European narratives and discourses subsume and
leave little room in the curriculum for the history, knowledge, and experience of racialized peoples (Dei 1999; Hackett 2019).

Social work education has been a colonial practice because what has
been considered education in Canada sprang from European colonial

foundations. Sheila Cote-Meek (2014) conceives colonization as a dominating ideology connected to control over the land that is violent, traumatic, and ongoing for Indigenous Peoples in Canada. Colonization has also been visited on the continent of Africa and the impact of the transatlantic slave trade on Black people across the diaspora continues in contemporary times. I, myself, was educated in a secondary school system that implemented a British curriculum for a majority Black student population in the Caribbean. Many students today are still faced with learning concepts and principles through a European Western lens and via examples that are overwhelmingly, if not completely, centred on white experience and sensibilities. Within postsecondary social work education programs, theory and practice developed by and for Black, Indigenous, and people of colour (BIPOC) remain the exception rather than the norm (Magalang and Rao 2021). This exclusion of Black and Indigenous knowledge, experience, and leadership calls for decolonial equity approaches which centre Black and Indigenous voices, expectations, and needs (Hackett 2019) and returns sovereignty to Black and Indigenous people.

THE SUMMER MENTORSHIP PROGRAM

Shortly after graduating with my Master of Social Work (MSW) degree in Toronto, I was hired to engage in outreach activities at the Faculty of Social Work where I had earned the professional degree. In many ways, I understood the mandate of the role as informing the public about social work and about what social work education looked like at our faculty. Professional responsibilities included presenting to undergraduate students considering a master's program. I also soon learned that the university had a Summer Mentorship Program (SMP) that was designed to introduce postsecondary education to Black and Indigenous high school students. These high school students were invited to campus for a month in the summer to see and experience university first-hand. I learned that the Faculty of Social Work had been part of this program, but due to funding cuts, there was no plan to participate in the upcoming year. "This is social work," I thought. Making space to include individuals and communities who have been kept to the margins is central to the Faculty's and profession's core mission and values. How could the faculty not be a part of this effort? Taking a pass on participating in the

SMP seemed to me a betrayal of a key professional and institutional commitment. Thus began a ten-year experience of engaging in learning and building skills in equity programming through my experiences with the SMP social work days.

The SMP was developed to address the underrepresentation of Black and Indigenous students in postsecondary education and has evolved to focus on the lack of ethno-racial representation in the health sciences. Initial attempts by the university to understand the experience of Black and Indigenous high school students and their presumed lack of interest in higher education suggested that many had never visited a university campus. Black and Indigenous high school students indicated to both high school and university administrators that they were less likely to consider university because they did not see themselves represented within postsecondary education in the faculty or staff complements or in the student body. High school students have shared with colleagues that they did not know anyone who identifies as Black or Indigenous at the university. In initial high school student consultations with Black and Indigenous students, the students' predominant perception was that Indigenous and Black people were not present on university campuses and did not belong in this setting. It appeared that university was a white space by and for white people. This perception fed a self-fulfilling prophecy whereby individuals with potential for educational success, when faced with a vision of university that did not include them, were far less likely to work toward being admitted to university because that outcome seemed unattainable and in fact, undesirable.

The focus of many who explore this issue has been on perception. Sara Ahmed (2012) has pointed out that the problem is that institutions of postsecondary education are not just seen as predominantly white, they are predominantly white. This isn't perception — it is a reality. The high school students don't just fail to "see" themselves within postsecondary educational institutions, they accurately assess that there is minimal space, if any at all, for members of Black and Indigenous communities within the hallowed halls of academia. High school students may also be taught and guided by few, if any, teachers who identify as Black or Indigenous or who acknowledge and validate their experiences as a racialized individual. This makes it doubly hard for them to learn to challenge the absence that exists in their potential educational futures when this gap is also present in their high school reality.

As with educational settings more broadly, this underrepresentation of Indigenous and Black people is true too of the helping professions. The SMP is coordinated by the Faculty of Medicine in collaboration with health science units including dentistry, kinesiology, nursing, pharmacy, and social work. Students spend a month in the summer at the university and, during that time, visit with each unit so that by the end of the program they have been exposed to and gained an introductory sense of the range of postsecondary health science educational options available to them. I focus on social work, as this is my sphere of practice. In Canada, the social work profession has struggled to recruit and engage students and future professionals beyond the stereotypical pool of white women with a determination to do good and "make a difference" in the world. This leads to a challenging spiral where people of colour (POC) don't see themselves as part of the institution, so they don't consider being a part of the institution, and the whiteness of the profession is reinforced and the cycle reified.

Intentional Representation

Since there was a lack of Indigenous and Black students in university and also within social work, addressing representation became an important equity aspect of the approach to the social work component of the SMP. To correct the absence of Black and Indigenous voices and presence, it was necessary to first envision a social work faculty that was representative of, and could authentically speak to, Black and Indigenous experiences. Then it became important to recruit Black and Indigenous masters and doctoral students, faculty, staff, and alumni to embody this intentional and specific social work community. One of the goals was to challenge the narrative high school students in previous years had reported, and replace it with incontrovertible evidence of Black and Indigenous people who were studying social work in graduate school, working and teaching at the university, and also practising as social workers in the community. We had to move from presenting a generic image of social work as multicultural and diverse, to actually being a social work team that reflected the specific ethno-racial communities from which the students hailed — also, we had to be a team that could speak to experiences and issues that would be relevant and meaningful to this specific group of learners. This intentionality was key. It was crucial to put the students first, assess their learning needs and then develop a team and a program that could reasonably support their needs.

Decolonizing the Program

Moving from a focus on the individual to a focus on the collective is one way that Indigenous and Black communities have weathered centuries of oppression. Shifting to a community approach or framework is one way to decolonize experiences of education. Building a community of educators involves inviting a range of knowledge and experiences. I came to appreciate that a village of Black and Indigenous social workers was indeed needed to effectively support Black and Indigenous high school students learning about social work.

Because of the limited number of Black and Indigenous social workers in the profession or training in graduate programs, building a community to develop and deliver intentional programming required targeted outreach and thoughtful recruitment. I was fortunate to work initially with another social worker of colour who had preceded me in my role and who had both the experience of coordinating the program and having been a participant in the SMP in years earlier. For my first year in the program, we facilitated together. It soon became clear that not only were more hands needed to effectively plan and implement engagement with up to forty high school students, but we would also need more diversity of experience, thought, and perspective. By stroke of luck, I happened to meet a Black doctoral student while we were both waiting for our shared supervisor to be available for a meeting. We struck up a conversation in the waiting area and I asked if we might schedule a meeting so I could tell her about the program and opportunities to become involved. She showed up at the meeting with two other doctoral students — one Black and the other Indigenous. These three women with years of social work practice in Black and Indigenous communities became my teachers in building a program that is responsive to participants' individual needs and, in particular, to community cultural considerations.

To effectively implement a community effort, one must be part of a community and have an authentic and working network within that community. I reached out to Black and Indigenous alumni of the faculty and communicated with colleagues to identify individuals who might be invited to participate in the program. Each year I took note of Indigenous and Black MSW students and shared information with them about the SMP's existence. Through specific and direct communication, a group of interested and committed individuals would be brought together each year; this coming together of social workers who identify as Indigenous and Black fostered the building of a community where shared connection unified us toward a common purpose. The intentional building of community fostered the experience of being in community.

When Indigenous and Black social workers were invited to participate, they would often respond along the lines of "This sounds like a fantastic program! I wish I had something like this when I was in high school." The opportunity to be of service was the most often heard incentive to participate. Encouraging and nourishing the next generation with their presence and experience seemed to give life to practising social workers. A secondary outcome of the invitation to participate in the program was the demonstration of the desperate need for Indigenous and Black role models. The program provided an opportunity and training ground to increase capacity for role modelling.

The opportunity to be at the front of the room or the centre of the circle in the spotlight was something I came to realize was not often afforded to Black and Indigenous social work students, practitioners, and staff. When it was offered within mainstream settings, the spotlight was not often perceived or experienced as a safe or supportive space. Within the social work SMP, the opportunity to lead, guide, and take on responsibility had a wider purpose in being a site of leadership development for graduate students and social work professionals. Positive outcomes were sustained by a supportive team working toward a common goal. Creating opportunity and a platform for Black and Indigenous social work students, staff, and alumni was one way to help build their capacity and experience in public speaking, group facilitation, and leadership skills. Team members shared that increased levels of personal confidence and cultural pride were often at the heart of the "good feelings" they took away from their participation in the program.

When these different community members — all at different stages in the profession — were brought together in collaborative practice, sharing the space led to an expansion of possibilities across the board. Black MSW students had the chance to observe Black doctoral students speak about their work and process, Indigenous masters students were able to hear Indigenous social workers in practice describe their work, philosophy, and interaction patterns and learning from clients. Doctoral students observed and heard from faculty creating new knowledge and paying attention to cultural values and norms as well as the expectations Black and Indigenous communities have of the social work profession. The narrative about who is a social work student/faculty/practitioner was being rewritten for all involved. Ultimately, everyone on the program team was also learning from the high school students and their younger, newer lens on their own lives, evolving society, and on the social work profession. This milieu supported a reciprocal and ongoing exchange where everyone present was able to interact with someone on a similar journey who was a few steps or maybe lengths further down the proverbial road. Everyone involved contributed to and received benefit from the experience of coming together to share knowledge and experience about social work as a profession and educational pathway. Over the years the program benefited from the knowledge and experience of many team members who generously contributed their time and their expertise to support the experience of those who would come after them.

Resistance to Resistance

Equity work involves making visible the power imbalances inherent in the structures and systems in our contemporary society. These structures have often worked hard to keep the imbalances obscured and out of sight. When doing equity work, it is not unheard of to come across resistance from the dominant group or individuals in positions of power (Massaquoi 2007). It is all too common that when those who have experienced marginalization seek to shift the status quo and alter the balance of power, those who have been in a privileged position resist, dig their heels in, or push back hard. So, I should not have been surprised when I encountered resistance to the equity focus of the social work SMP.

One particular year I reached out to a Black social work alumna in a health care setting to invite her participation in the program. We had taken undergraduate classes together and I knew her to be intelligent, innovative, and passionate in her area of the profession. I was excited by her initial enthusiasm and eagerness to participate in the program and share her knowledge and experience with the high school students. We reviewed the program's goals and objectives and discussed expectations for her participation. All seemed to be a perfect fit and she promised to get back to me once she had cleared the requisite morning off with her supervisor. The following week I received a phone call, without warning, from her white female supervisor inquiring about the program. I naively thought this supervisor actually desired more information about the program, so I launched into the background details on Black and Indigenous high school student perceptions, the goal of providing opportunity for youth to learn about and hopefully attend university, and feedback from previous student and professional participants. When I finally took a pause she asked, "Well, why wasn't I invited to participate in this program? I have been a mentor for many students over the years." I thought maybe I hadn't been clear about the program's intention, so I detailed for her the specific purpose of correcting the recognized lack of opportunity for Black and Indigenous high school students to interact with individuals in university and in the social work profession who identified as either Black or Indigenous and who could share lived experiences. I articulated the importance of the students meeting and engaging with people who looked like them and with whom they shared ethno-racial identity. Her response was that she was white but born in Africa and if the only reason she was ineligible for this experience was her race, then this sounded to her like reverse racism.

This woman was the social work lead at a major health care institution and sat in a position of power over social work policy and practice at that organization. She argued that the SMP, designed to give opportunity to students and social workers of colour, was racist if she couldn't access it. This was the person who contributed to and influenced major policy decisions for the health care institution and had oversight over not only the hiring of social workers, but supervision of and quality control for the service social workers provided to a wide and diverse ethno-racial community of clients. White women make up the overwhelming majority of the social work and education workforce. Their voices and perspective on the world overwhelmingly inform both high school and university classroom experience as well as client and social worker interactions. The SMP was designed explicitly to provide alternatives to that universally white lens. The Indigenous and Black students needed to hear from and engage with people who shared some of their lived experiences, which were structured through racial identity. I considered offering her the opportunity to have high school students visit her onsite but decided instead to suggest that if she was interested in mentoring, the faculty had a graduate student mentoring program and that I would be happy to send her information on opportunities to mentor MSW students. It is interesting to note that she never responded to three follow-up messages about the MSW student mentoring opportunities.

Debriefing with my manager was helpful in that I received validation that this social worker's request and approach had been inappropriate. This white social work supervisor did ultimately authorize the Black social worker's participation and I believe that being a role model for youth was a positive growth experience for that Black social worker.

Engaging and effectively navigating conversations like this one becomes a required skill for equity practitioners who are asked to be in open and constructive dialogue with individuals and institutions with access to power — who may have grown accustomed to wielding that power in ways that are oppressive and even harmful. Beyond tact and positive communication skills, social workers aiming to operate from a decolonial equity perspective, who also have experiences of marginalization connected to social location and/or identity (for example, race, gender, sexual orientation), are required to put aside their personal self so that their professional self can supportively guide someone with power whose words and actions may be offensive and even harmful to them personally. There is a rage that can build up in response to ongoing experiences of oppression that have no socially sanctioned outlet (Hardy 2013). The conundrum experienced by many equity-focused practitioners is developing the ability to monitor and manage that rage while working professionally with colleagues and senior leaders whose words and actions cause the very inequities that generate this individual and collective rage.

This experience highlighted that doing equity work requires its practitioners — who affirm ideas and practices outside the mainstream — to develop the ability "to push for, or drive forward, agendas" (Ahmed 2012, 140). I was also required to push myself beyond comfortable and polite space to resist acquiescing to a request generated out of racist entitlement. Decolonial equity work calls for going against the flow, an insistence that those in power see and hear experiences and perspectives other than their own. In doing equity work, I am called to push the boundaries of the status quo beyond what has already been deemed acceptable by the colonial structure. I have to find the strength to push back, to resist, when people with power use that power to marginalize and/or oppress — to resist when they insist on colonial thinking and practice, to resist when they resist change. This is when we move closer to becoming what Sara Ahmed (2012, 140) refers to as "the heart and mind of the institution." The mission and values are at the heart of any enterprise and those who feel and think and spotlight those values for the institution and mainstream leaders, "aim to transform what the institution is for" (Ahmed 2012, 140).

Decolonizing Course Content

Once a new vision was formed and a team assembled to enact that vision, it was important to look at the content that would be shared with the high school students. Black and Indigenous social work students have long complained that it was a struggle to connect to course content and materials that were all created by and for white experts. Even when content was not explicitly white, neutralizing specifics of social location and identity often had the same outcome in that information and examples did not resonate with or match the lived experience of Indigenous and Black pre-service social workers or the Indigenous and Black individuals, families, and communities they imagined they were preparing to work alongside. To authentically engage Black and Indigenous high school students, program content needed to be relatable and relevant.

In introducing high school students to social work as an academic and professional discipline, we as a team always understood that it would be important to include a history of social work to provide context for how the profession has arrived at contemporary perspectives and approaches, and to inform future directions for the field. In preparing the first version of the "condensed" history of social work, I scoured standard social work textbooks, searched peer-reviewed journals for articles and put together a timeline of the last one hundred years that spoke to the profession's roots in religious principles of love and care for our fellows and the early influence of economists and policy makers. The overall bent was aspirational, steeped in the social work maxim of positive change and "making a difference." It wasn't until PhD student colleagues began to add their critique highlighting the continuing overrepresentation of Indigenous and Black children in the care of state officials (Pon, Gosine, and Phillips 2011) that I began to have a sense that I might be presenting a history that was partial and reflecting back the dominant colonial white stance I had been taught and that I had very effectively absorbed. My colleagues and teammates injected their Indigenous knowledge of, for example, social work's implication in the residential school system and broader colonial practices, and it became obvious that I had left gaps in the original draft big enough to permit a significantly sized truck to drive through. Telling the story of social work's history through Black and Indigenous voices and from a Black and Indigenous perspective was crucial for the content to resonate and to be received as meaningful by Indigenous and Black high school students.

This also highlighted the challenge of locating Black and Indigenous contributions to social work practice. Often, the ways of knowing and doing from marginalized communities have been unrecognized and undocumented by mainstream record keepers and historians, offering the illusion that there has been little or no involvement or input to the profession by Indigenous (Sinclair 2004) and Black people other than as service recipients. Even when those narratives surface, the complexity and dynamic nature of interactions and relations between the multiplicity of communities and identities is unacknowledged (Hackett et al. 2020). Finding ways to weave multiple strands of many narratives into a tapestry of social work history became a task to ensure that our approach was more in line with principles of equity and decolonial practice. Acknowledging social work's failings and making explicit the harms done became a different way of telling the story of our profession beginning with the ways that social workers as agents of the state removed children from their families of origin, their community, and their culture, and contributed to cultural genocide of Indigenous Peoples in Canada. The lessons important to impart to young learners became more about awareness of mistakes and acknowledgement of harms committed by social work on Indigenous and Black communities as a way of ensuring that current and future social workers don't repeat those mistakes and harms.

Finding balance is the key. Social work's history is not all negative. It would not serve learners or the profession to tell only one aspect of what has gone before. Retaining aspirations and the positive contributions of the profession was critical through a relevant cultural perspective. This was embodied in the professional accomplishments of Canadian social work visionaries Senator Dr. Wanda Thomas Bernard (2015) and Dr. Cindy Blackstock. Introducing the high school students to these two leaders and citing some of their many contributions provided a way to demonstrate that the power to effect change exists already within Black and Indigenous communities. These two celebrated social workers have advanced the profession as a whole and specifically social work's awareness of and ability to effectively support Black and Indigenous communities. Their careers helped to set a standard of excellence in social work for the high school students.

Principles of equity suggest the importance of engaging individuals with content that is relevant and applicable to their context to invite interest and active participation. Equity also invites inclusion of the participant's preferences and voice wherever possible both in content and process. High school students' SMP feedback consistently affirmed that participants were particularly averse to didactic instructional methods that typically required them to sit still and listen to information delivered verbally or visually via text on a screen. Students year after year told organizers that they wanted learning that actively engaged them on several levels. The social work SMP team responded with the development of a case study that would involve a role play or a simulated social work interview intended to demonstrate core skills in action.

The original case study in the SMP was that of a young girl who had experienced bullying. It was reworked to reflect an eleven-year-old Indigenous girl whose experience reflected that of too many young Indigenous children and the influence of structural inequality and systemic racism inherent in a family becoming termed "child welfare involved." Having read a brief overview of the case, the students are guided in considering how they might prepare to understand the circumstances, feelings, and expectations of the child client, who was set to be just a little younger than the high school students, which would potentially allow them to situate themselves as close to her experience. Facilitators invite accessing empathy with prompts like "what do you think might be going on for her considering what has happened to her family?" and "do you remember what it was like to be eleven years old and how might you have reacted in that situation?" The students are supported in collectively developing questions they might ask to start a social work interview with the goal of better understanding the client by gathering information.

Facilitators also enacted a role play featuring a Black couple who are senior citizens that provided the opportunity to learn about engaging with folks at the other end of the lifespan. The issues include terminal illness, the challenges of working with a couple with different goals and expectations and navigating differences in age between social worker and client. The students are invited to consider how a young worker might respectfully question a senior and how the positioning of seniors or Elders in Indigenous and Black cultures might impact the approach. Prompts include: "think about how you might say that to your grandfather. What words might you use to find out that information?" and, "If this was someone in your family, how might you want the social worker to be with them?" Students are invited to consider the couple's history and potential prior interactions with the health care system.

These activities allowed high school students to observe and also to actively inform the flow and outcome of the scenario. Planners debated the propriety of including high school students in an actual role play and whether it was ethically responsible to put young people with minimal training or preparation into a situation that many graduate students and even some qualified professionals find stress inducing. Consideration was given to the feeling of responsibility that can arise when taking on the social worker role even in a simulated exercise. Additionally, attention was paid to the stress of saying and doing the "right" thing that is often described by social workers in training when a client's well-being is at stake — this is the case when the client is being portrayed by an actor or even a colleague pretending to be a client. Participants in the role play would be in a very real spotlight as they would be observed by a room full of their peers. This high level of scrutiny could be anxiety producing which is not conducive to learning. Further, the potential for a student participant to be triggered by language, the scenario, or even just being in the simulated social work setting was deemed too great a risk. To find openings for high school students' active participation, the role play was acted out by members of the SMP team (MSW and PhD students, and MSW alumni) who take on the roles of the client couple and of the social worker interviewer, with the high school students observing. At regular intervals, the role play pauses and the individual playing the social worker breaks the fourth wall to ask the student observers what they think is taking place and what she should say or do next. This device, in effect, provided the students with an ability to actively participate by directing the flow and outcome of the role play while not having to directly experience the challenge, responsibility, and stress of "client" response and reaction. In this way, the power imbalance inherent in traditional colonial approaches to education and teaching, where the knowledgeable expert dictates and controls both content and process, is upended by a sharing of power with the participant learners.

Decolonizing the Process

Decolonial equity practice invites us to consider our process and to do things in ways that acknowledge and celebrate participant culture and community. It is important to shift the balance of power to re-centre colonized — in this case Indigenous and Black — cultural practices and ways of being. In the following subsections, I highlight a number of the practical approaches the SMP takes to try to support an environment that supports decolonial equity.

One of the ways to decolonize the work of equity is to create an atmosphere that supports connection building between and among people — to find as many ways as possible to express that participants are seen as full and whole people. All humans have physical needs, and it is standard practice in many cultures that almost any coming together is assisted and supported by the presence of food and beverage. This is particularly so for Indigenous and Black communities. It is important to ensure that the food provided is culturally appropriate, at some level familiar, and likely to be pleasing to participants. Food is a way to extend welcome beyond words, to convey the message to participants that their wellness, their comfort, is important to the organizer and host. Offering coffee and snacks is considered standard social work practice but is not always engaged in academic settings where the focus is on the business of learning. Decolonial practice invites a philosophy of prioritizing people and the building of connections, making the work — in this case the learning — secondary to that human element. Seeing the people, expressing care for the people, engaging the people, becomes a prerequisite preparation before we can effectively get to the work of learning and cognitive development.

In addition to creating atmosphere, decolonial equity work also invites intentional attention to the physical space where the work is undertaken. This includes making every effort to engage participants in spaces that are bright and open to support feelings of comfort and positive regard. Feedback from high school students over the years indicated that the physical comfort afforded by the furniture made a difference to their experience. Ensuring that seating was comfortable and inviting was something we paid attention to with the seating arrangement changing from standard issue folding chairs to comfortable cushioned modular sofas.

The physical space also extends to the arrangement and positioning of learners. The standard colonial classroom reinforces a power dynamic where the teacher commands attention at the front of the room, sometimes elevated and sometimes positioned at a lectern which signals their higher status. Learners are spread around the room in orderly rows all facing the teacher who can easily command attention by wielding the power afforded by physical positioning. Learners at the front of the room may benefit in some ways from close proximity to power but have no access, without movement, to what everyone else situated behind them is doing. Shifting this configuration to a circle — a traditional Indigenous practice — serves to equalize power and allows everyone to see everyone else in the space and invites conversation and contributions that can be shared with everyone in a communal fashion. In standard practice, the teacher dictates from the front and students receive and absorb learning. In a circle, the engagement is multi-directional and the leader guides and facilitates, supporting the contributions of knowledge and experience from all points around the room.

Narratives and stories help to unveil the interpretive processes of cultural groups, explaining how group members view themselves, the world, and their collective selves in relation to the world (Freeman and Couchonnal 2006). Black and Indigenous communities have long histories of oral tradition, which is counter to the European dependence on the written word. Storytelling and narrative as a primary means of transmitting knowledge is well established in Indigenous and Black cultures in North America and across the globe. This became clear in the SMP social work sessions when students were demonstrably more engaged when group facilitators shared anecdotes from their professional or personal experience as opposed to when facilitators employed didactic teaching methods. The knowledge transmission modes are more effective when they are culturally appropriate and relatable for student participants.

The narrative approach highlights the value of people's unique stories of their lived experiences, amplifying subjugated narratives (Rockquemore and Laszloffy 2003). I first observed the power of personal narrative when a Black female social worker agreed to talk for five minutes about her experiences in high school and share an overview of her pathway from high school to university and then to the graduate social work program. She began by sharing with students that she had been a strong student with mostly A grades. Her mother had expressed expectations that she would attend university, so she made an appointment and visited the high school guidance counsellor to explore options available to her. The counsellor reviewed her transcript, looked up at her, and asked if she was sure about university. "Maybe you should consider beauty school," the social worker told the room she had been advised by the counsellor. As I looked around, I could see in the eyes and nodding heads of a majority of the young women in the room that they knew from experience what she was describing. This experience of their academic potential being devalued was all too familiar to them. By telling her story and sharing lived experience, she was allowing them to see themselves and their experience in her narrative.

She then went on to describe how she had sought other supports and had found her way to university where she completed an undergraduate degree in psychology before being admitted to social work as a graduate student. At the time of this interaction, she was a social worker in a major mental health hospital. She described her work, challenges, and triumphs and, without having to say it explicitly, demonstrated for these young people that this too could be their trajectory, their future if they were potentially interested in this path. The option of becoming a mental health social worker in a hospital became viable for them.

Story also became a tool for supporting the development of empathy. Hearing someone else's story invited the students to be witnesses to lived experiences that could be painful, celebratory, and everything in between. One doctoral student shared her experience of becoming a parent as a teenager and her subsequent efforts to complete high school, attend university while parenting a young child and then working professionally and completing a PhD. At the end of her narrative one young woman commented in awe "Can I just say that you are so beautiful!" The ability to focus less on adversity and more on the overcoming of it was organically engendered and supported through the sharing of the lived experiences of team members.

Telling the story of residential schools became an essential narrative as part of social work's history in Canada. It was likely that some students would be personally connected to this experience through relatives who attended the schools or through family members who were indirectly affected. Inviting consideration of historical and cultural trauma for a population of participants who may be affected by that trauma or may be triggered by linkage to other lived experiences of trauma required careful consideration of how that information would be presented through thoughtful and intentional planning (Cote-Meek 2014) to ensure that appropriate supports would be available to students if and when needed. Equity work requires seeing the whole individual and all the history they may bring to the interaction or experience. That also required the program to have team members trained and prepared to hold space for students who might need support to deal with emotional activation from exposure to challenging program content. This role was taken up by members of the team who were practising social workers, and who had experience working with clients in distress. It was built into the program introduction that these team members would be identified as being available at any time if a high school student wished to step away from the group to have a compassionate conversation or wished someone to sit with them as a supportive listener. While not shying away from hard truths, we, as practitioners, have to be prepared to support individuals through experiences of trauma and do everything in our power not to cause harm or further traumatize those who have already been harmed.

Ultimately, one of the things we may come to through equity work is a place of healing. In developing and building a space that is meant to support and affirm participants, we may create a healing space that allows Black and Indigenous people to breathe easier. Cote-Meek (2014) refers to healing as a lifelong process beginning with exposure and naming of colonial practices including racism that can assist individuals in understanding the pain and hurt they have experienced. Validation may be offered which can allow individuals to reclaim authorship and ownership of their own lived experiences. She describes an approach to healing that is not an "away" experience — not something that takes place outside of, or separate from everyday life, but is holistically incorporated into aspects of everyday living. As such, creating a space for stories that don't get told in mainstream classrooms, with peers who are often not encountered in typical learning environments, and led by people who are not the norm of dominant colonial educational spaces, can in itself affirm the Indigenous and Black learner in ways that are experienced as healing.

Being a part of this process can also be healing for Black and Indigenous MSW and PhD students who are often part of a small minority in their postsecondary classes, alone in experiencing content and processes that feel, and are, foreign to their cultural ways of being. It can also be healing for Indigenous and Black social workers to be part of re-authoring the experience of a next generation of learners and pre-service social workers. There is healing, too, for Black and Indigenous high school students in being validated, affirmed, and supported in bringing forward their knowledge and experiences and having them received positively. Building hope for a different future out of historically painful collective experiences offers a form of healing.

VISIONING THE FUTURE

Part of the implicit and explicit vision of the SMP social work session was to provide an alternate experience for young Black and Indigenous high school students on many levels. To be treated with dignity and respect in a learning process was key. As an alternative to the predominant POC student experience in traditional educational spaces of being exposed almost exclusively to white teachers, the SMP also provided an opportunity for high school students to be guided in shared knowledge production by individuals who look like them and share cultural and racial identity. Additionally, the chance to engage with content that explicitly reflected their lived experience and lens on the world was intended to invite new ways of considering and projecting their possibilities for the future. All of these were also intended to inspire the MSW and PhD students as well as social work practitioners to reconsider what is possible in their respective spheres of professional existence. If these methods can engage and inspire in a single session, what might be the outcomes of using these methods as part of ongoing social work practice both in academia and across the range of direct practice settings? Helping high school students to see others who look like themselves as effective contributors invites the visioning of a future where they too are active participants in a society where communities work collaboratively toward a common and decolonial future.

It is not possible or helpful in the long run to protect Black and Indigenous students with the creation of an artificially safe bubble before sending them out into a world that does not and will not maintain or reflect that sphere of safety. In fact, such a strategy could well be argued to be harmful if it gave a false impression of the social work profession and set inauthentic expectations for young learners. Taking a "both/and" approach, the SMP social work sessions aimed to support and affirm Indigenous and Black high school students while also introducing them to, and preparing them to, engage in a predominantly white professional environment.

Once the team had introduced students to this specific perspective of social work, the second half of the social work SMP module involved students visiting social workers onsite at their workplaces to get a more experiential sense of the work. We approached social service organizations and agencies whose stated mission and work aligned with the vision of social work introduced to the high school students in the morning. Social workers, social service workers, and allied professionals were invited to partner with the program to help students encounter what social work is like in their sector and who delivers social work services. Students were sent out in pairs to visit children's mental health centres, child welfare organizations, and HIV/AIDS-focused service providers, to identify a few. Some sites prioritized service to Indigenous and Black populations while others did not. All site hosts demonstrated commitment to support the learning and positive experience of the high school students and the mission of the program to encourage ongoing participation in education. This external collaboration with community partners was instrumental in expanding the opportunities available to the students. Students were encouraged to share information from their site with their peers and to actively support access to knowledge for one another.

Finally, students were invited to provide feedback on the morning program delivered at the faculty and their social work site visit via an anonymous survey. This was an effort to empower students to have their opinions and perspectives counted. It was explicitly articulated to the students that their feedback would be able to influence the evolution of the program and examples were given to them of how the comments of previous cohorts of students had informed shifts in what they experienced. Often students cited appreciation for the authenticity of the SMP experience using words like "real" to describe their perceptions. They also generally indicated that they had a new understanding of the complexity of social work as a profession and as a practice. Almost overwhelmingly, they highlighted the experience of the role play, often requesting that section be made longer so there could be more active interaction. They also generally expressed appreciation for the personal narratives which they experienced as compelling.

CONCLUSION

In this chapter, I have shared lessons learned on what decolonizing social work practice can look like in a program introducing Black and Indigenous high school students to the profession specifically and to postsecondary education in general. Building a team representative of the population of learners who can speak to relatable lived experience, developing content intentionally to be relevant to learners, and crafting processes that move away from traditional oppressive paradigms and seek to recalibrate the balance of power in ways that empower and uplift learners, are all key facets of what the students and the program taught me. Participating in developing dynamic reciprocal relationships — being open to inviting and listening to the experiences of others — are also core practices that support decolonial ways of being. I also understood how important it was to stand firm against the resistance that is to be expected when shifts in inequitable power distributions are implemented.

Ultimately, when we engage decolonial practice, we get closer to authenticity in seeing others and being with others (Pidgeon 2019). The ultimate sign of success for the SMP sessions was releasing any expectation of transactional benefit to the Faculty of Social Work and the social work profession that might be derived from expending resources to introduce high school students to social work. The students were encouraged to consider all their options for higher education. This is a vision of Indigenous and Black student success that works toward individual empowerment and community self-determination. In this way, the SMP social work module created an alternative to the colonized norm of the educational standard and embodied a decolonized "elsewhere" (Tuck and Yang 2012), a concrete space and place where Black and Indigenous experience and futurity are affirmed and secure. My hope is that those Black and Indigenous youth who have experienced these sessions will move through the world expecting and creating spaces where they are seen, heard, and celebrated both inside and outside social work structures.

References

Ahmed, Sara. 2012. *On Being Included: Racism and Diversity in Institutional Life*. Durham: Duke University Press.

Bergen, Heather, and Salina Abji. 2020. "Facilitating the Carceral Pipeline: Social Work's Role in Funneling Newcomer Children from the Child Protection System to Jail and Deportation." *Affilia: Journal of Women and Social Work* 35, 1.

Boatswain-Kyte, Alicia. 2018. "Overrepresentation and Disparity of Black Children Reported Under the Child Protection System: The Need for Effective Cross-System Collaborations." Doctoral dissertation, Université de Montréal. quescren.concordia.ca/en/resource/NV8JLHJE.

Cote-Meek, Sheila. 2014. *Colonized Classrooms: Racism, Trauma and Resistance in Post-Secondary Education*. Black Point/Winnipeg: Fernwood Publishing.

Dei, George J. S. 1999. "Knowledge and Politics of Social Change: The Implication of Anti-Racism." *British Journal of Sociology of Education* 20, 3.

Flynn, Karen. 2008. "'I'm Glad That Someone Is Telling the Nursing Story': Writing Black Canadian Women's History." *Journal of Black Studies* 38, 3

Freeman, Edith and Graciela Couchonnal. 2006. "Narrative and Culturally Based Approaches in Practice with Families." *Families in Society: The Journal of Contemporary Social Services* 87, 2.

Hackett, V. C. Rhonda. 2019. "African Caribbean Presence: Decolonizing Social Work Education." *Intersectionalities: A Global Journal of Social Work Analysis, Research, Polity, and Practice* 7, 1.

Hackett, V. C. Rhonda, Amoaba Gooden, Billie Allan, and Devi Mucina. 2020. "Walking Together: Indigenous and Black Perspectives on Decolonizing Education." In *S'Tenistolw: Moving Indigenous Education Forward*, edited by Todd Ormiston, Jacquie Green, and Kelly Aguirre. Nanaimo: JCharlton Publishing.

Hardy, Kenneth V. 2013. "Healing the Hidden Wounds of Racial Trauma." *Reclaiming Children and Youth* 22, 1.

James, Carl. 2019. "Adapting, Disrupting, and Resisting: How Middle School Black Males Position Themselves in Response to Racialization in School." *Canadian Journal of Sociology* 44, 4.

James, Carl, and Tana Turner. 2017. *Towards Race Equity in Education: The Schooling of Black Students in the Greater Toronto Area*. Toronto: York University.

Maglalang, Dale, and Smitha Rao. 2021. "'Theory's Cool, but Theory with No Practice Ain't Shit…': Critical Theories and Frameworks to Dismantle Racism in Social Work Education and Practice." *Advances in Social Work* 21, 2/3.

Massaquoi, Notisha. 2007. "Crossing Boundaries — Radicalizing Social Work Practice and Education." In *Doing Anti-Oppressive Practice: Social Justice Social Work*, edited by Donna Baines. Black Point/Winnipeg: Fernwood Publishing.

Maynard, Robyn. 2017. *Policing Black Lives: State Violence in Canada from Slavery to the Present.* Black Point/Winnipeg: Fernwood Publishing.

Pidgeon, Michelle. 2019. "Contested Spaces of Indigenization in Canadian Higher Education." In *Indigenous Education: New Directions in Theory and Practice*, edited by Huia Tomlins-Jahnke, Sandra Styres, Spencer Lilley, and Dawn Zinga. Edmonton: University of Alberta Press.

Pon, Gordon, Kevin Gosine, and Doret Phillips. 2011. "Immediate Response: Addressing Anti-Native and Anti-Black Racism in Child Welfare." *International Journal of Child, Youth and Family Studies* 3/4.

Rockquemore, Kerry Ann, and Tracey A. Laszloffy. 2003. "Multiple Realities: A Relational Narrative Approach in Therapy with Black-White Mixed-Race Clients." *Family Relations* 52, 2.

Sanders, Jane, and Barbara Fallon. 2018. "Child Welfare Involvement and Academic Difficulties: Characteristics of Children, Families and Households Involved with Child Welfare and Experiencing Difficulties." *Children and Youth Services Review* 86.

Sanders, Jane, Faye Mishna, Lance McCready, and Barbara Fallon. 2021. "'You Don't Know What's Really Going on': Reducing the Discipline Gap by Addressing Adversity, Connection and Resources." *School Mental Health.* doi. org/10.1007/s12310-021-09481-3.

Sinclair, Raven. 2004. "Aboriginal Social Work Education in Canada: Decolonizing Pedagogy for the Seventh Generation." *First Peoples Child & Family Review* 1, 1.

Thomas Bernard, Wanda (ed.). 2015. *Still Fighting for Change: Black Social Workers in Canada.* East Lawrencetown: Pottersfield Press.

Tuck, Eve, and K. Wayne Yang. 2012. "Decolonization Is Not a Metaphor." *Decolonization: Indigeneity, Education & Society* 1, 1.

Vogel, Lauren. 2019. "Queen's to Redress Harms of Historic Ban on Black Medical Students." *CMAJ* 191, 26.

6

DECOLONIZING URBAN EDUCATION

Roland Sintos Coloma

My commitment to decolonizing urban education is not only intellectual and pedagogical; it is also deeply personal. I have been a student of empire, colonialism, and education, especially of the United States and its so-called manifest destiny within its geopolitical boundaries and beyond (Coloma 2009, 2012, 2013, 2017). I am also continuously involved in urban education where I have spent most of my professional career as a schoolteacher, and as a university faculty member and administrator. I am particularly interested in bringing to bear insights from studies of empire and decolonization to scrutinize a number of major prevailing views on urban education and, following Gloria Anzaldúa (2015, 90), "to cultivate nuestras facultades that rely on inner knowledges." This inner knowledge comes from embodied epistemology and deep engagement with "*el sitio y la lengua* [site and discourse]," in this case, of urban schools and communities (Pérez 1991). For Anzaldúa, *la facultad* is "anything that breaks into one's everyday mode of perception, that causes a break in one's defences and resistance, anything that takes one from one's habitual grounding, causes the depth to open up, causes a shift in perception" (Anzaldúa 1987, 39). Hence, my aim is to trouble what has become normalized and commonsensical in our theorizing and praxis of urban education to better serve students, families, and communities, especially those who experience historical and ongoing marginalization.

Toward this end, I draw heavily from the field of Ethnic Studies — a field that emerged out of revolutionary critiques of empire, colonialism, white supremacy, militarism, and labour exploitation; a field that emerged out of multi-racial and transnational solidarity, connecting local and global struggles for freedom, liberation, and self-determination (Butler 2001; Collins and Solomos 2010; Elia et al. 2016; Takaki 2008). This moment is especially significant since, when I gave the presidential address for the American Educational Studies Association in November 2019 — which served as the foundation of this essay — coincided with the fiftieth anniversary of the establishment of the first Ethnic Studies programs in the United States. In his book *Third World Studies: Theorizing Liberation*, Gary Okihiro (2016, 1) provides an intellectual history of "a revolutionary student movement led by the Third World Liberation Front" in San Francisco State College and the University of California, Berkeley, in the late 1960s. This coalition of Black, Latinx, Native American, and Asian American students led and organized a series of protests and actions from November 1968 to March 1969, the longest student strikes at any college or university in the United States. Among the student demands was the establishment of a "Third World curriculum," which was central to their vision of higher education reflecting the country's rich racial and cultural diversity and redressing the hegemonic racism impeding equitable access and opportunity. Like many social movements working against oppression, exclusion, violence, and genocide, self-determination was the hallmark of this student activism (Curley et al. 2018). Self-determination meant having a say and control over matters that impacted those historically excluded from decisions over power, representation, and materiality. Their demand was not merely about having a seat at the table; rather, it was rethinking the table and seats altogether to scrutinize oppression and complicity in systemic discrimination and explore possibilities for transformative change. In education, like in other aspects of life and politics, who controls what for which ends mattered then and continues to matter now.

Drawing insights primarily from Ethnic Studies, this essay is broken into the following components: outlining the elusive task of defining urban; delineating three decolonizing moves in relation to representation, structure, and affect; and ending with the ongoing struggles for Ethnic Studies in PK–12 schools and higher education. This essay is also driven by the following questions: What regimes of truth govern the legibility of certain statements and understandings, marking some as legitimate while others not, in urban schools and communities? How are subjects formed in these particular regimes? Who gets to be included, and who gets to be excluded? How does their inclusion or exclusion reveal dominant logics and rationalities in urban education? What technologies of power reflect and facilitate structural conditions of oppression or resistance? How do emotions produce labour rendered to particular individuals and collectives, thereby creating relations of affect and subjectivity? By pursuing these questions, my goal is to sharpen *nuestra facultad* and deeply engage with *el sitio y la lengua* of urban education. These questions serve to unpack what has been normalized, construed as common sense, and, therefore, taken for granted in urban schools and communities.

DEFINING "URBAN"

Defining the terms "urban" and "urban education" has been an elusive task, one that has challenged scholars and researchers in various academic fields such as education, design, geography, history, political science, and sociology (Carmona et al. 2010; Paddison 2001; Sayer 1984). In the *Handbook of Urban Education*, editors Rich Milner and Kofi Lomotey (2014, xix) suggest that there is a "definitional gap" because "research has failed to provide a comprehensive, uniform definition of urban education." An examination of various academic journals that focus on urban education reveals a rich array of topics pursued under the rubric of urban education, but they do not offer any singular definition of what urban education means. The *Urban Education* journal "publishes papers addressing urban issues related to those from birth through graduate school, from both a U.S. and an international perspective," and covers topical areas ranging from curriculum, instruction, and teacher education, to education policy and equity in urban education. The *Education and Urban Society* journal "examines the role of education as a social institution in an increasingly urban and multicultural society," and explores "the functions of educational institutions, policies, and processes in light of national concerns for improving the environment of urban schools that seek to provide equal educational opportunities for all students." The *Urban Review* journal "provides a forum for the presentation of original investigations, reviews, and essays which examine the issues basic to the improvement of urban schooling and education." The *National Journal of Urban Education & Practice* "contribute[s] to new knowledge and ideas in the quest for educating urban teachers and learners" and "to the building of urban professionals that are caring, committed and culturally responsive." Among the various journals reviewed, the *Journal of Urban Mathematics Education* perhaps offers the most clear and concise conceptualization of urban and urban education in its description: "the view of the urban domain extends beyond the geographical context, into the lives of people within the multitude of cultural, social, and political spaces in which mathematics teaching and learning takes place."

The term urban has generally been conceptualized in relation to geography and population. According to the US Census Bureau, an urban area is a "densely developed territory, and encompass[es] residential, commercial, and other nonresidential urban land uses" (Urban Area Criteria for the 2010 Census 2011, 53030). The Organisation for Economic Co-operation and Development (2013, 3) defines an urban core as "a high-density cluster of contiguous grid cells of 1 km2 with a density of at least 1,500 inhabitants per km2." Acknowledging that defining "urban" can vary from country to country, the United Nation's Children's Fund considers an urban area as constituting one or more of the following components: "administrative criteria or political boundaries, a threshold population size, population density, economic function, or the presence of urban characteristics" (UNICEF 2012, 10). Rich Milner (2012, 560) provides a helpful "evolving typology of urban education" under the three categories of "urban intensive," "urban emergent," and "urban characteristic." Defined by size and density, the urban intensive category represents "school contexts that are concentrated in large, metropolitan cities" such as Atlanta, Chicago, Los Angeles, and New York, with at least a million people (Milner 2012, 559). The urban emergent category describes school contexts located in large cities but not as large as those in the urban intensive category. These cities generally have fewer than a million people, with fewer people per capita, such as Austin, Texas; Columbus, Ohio, and Charlotte, North Carolina. The urban characteristics category describes school contexts that "are not located in big or midsized cities;" in fact, they "might be located in rural or even suburban districts" (Milner 2012, 559). However, what makes these school contexts "urban" is that they "may be starting to experience some of the challenges that are sometimes associated with urban school contexts" in major cities (Milner 2012, 559).

I argue that the notion of urban characteristics underpins the use of the term urban as a code or euphemism for students of colour, particularly African American and/or Latinx students from low-income or working-class backgrounds. The demographic marking of urban points to race and class as a pivotal grammar in this regime of truth. In other words, when some educators, parents, politicians, or philanthropists say urban — urban schools, or urban students — they usually refer to schools with a large-enough and visible proportion of Black and/or Latinx students from poor socioeconomic backgrounds.

According to the most recent available data from the National Center for Education Statistics (2013), there are just under fifty million students in public elementary and secondary schools in the United States in 2013 (see Table 1). The breakdown of public-school students in relation to geography is as follows: about 30 percent in urban schools, about 40 percent in suburban schools, and about 30 percent in rural and town schools. When we take a cross-categorical analysis of geography and race, the national data indicates that the majority of white students are not in urban public schools. Only 18 percent (or less than one out five) white students are in urban public schools; white students are about equally distributed across suburban and rural/town public schools. Black and Latinx students are generally more concentrated in urban public schools: 47 percent of Black students and 43 percent of Latinx students are in urban schools.

Out of the fifteen million students in urban public schools in 2013, the overwhelming majority or about 70 percent of the students are nonwhite (see Table 2). In fact, many urban schools already have what has been called "majority–minority" student bodies in which students of colour outnumber white students (Maxwell 2014). Across the country, Latinx students constitute 35 percent, while Black students constitute 24 percent of the urban public-school student population. One might say that Latinx and Black students are "overrepresented" in urban schools when they actually compose 25 percent and 16 percent of the general US population, respectively. However, these figures need to be understood within historical, legal, sociological, political, and economic frameworks that address the histories and legacies of racism, and white flight, as well as government disinvestment and neglect on the one hand, and of migration, community formation, and resilience on the other hand (Camarillo 2007; Powell 2002).

Table 1. *Number and percentage distribution of public elementary and secondary student enrolment by race/ethnicity and school location (Fall 2013) Source: National Center for Education Statistics (2013).*

Race / Ethnicity	United States		Urban		Suburban		Rural & Town	
	Number	% Over-all	Number	% Urban	Number	% Sub-ur-ban	Number	% Rural
White	24,689,060	50.15	4,475,771	18.13	10,085,508	40.85	10,127,781	41.02
Black	7,685,967	15.61	3,585,366	46.65	2,682,003	34.89	1,418,598	18.46
Lati-no	12,295,151	24.98	5,278,865	42.93	4,878,849	39.68	2,137,437	17.38
Asian	2,386,501	4.85	1,009,898	42.32	1,177,264	49.33	199,339	8.35
Pa-cific Is-lander	174,644	0.35	58,500	33.50	73,974	42.36	42,170	24.15
Amer-ican Indi-an / Alas-ka Na-tive	509,799	1.04	100,257	21.24	90,502	17.75	311,040	01.01
Two or more races	1,484,581	3.02	478,818	32.25	628,489	42.33	377,274	25.41
Total	49,225,703	100.00	14,995,475	30.46	19,616,589	39.85	14,613,639	29.69

When we analyze further the cross-categories of geography, race, and socioeconomic class, it becomes evident that poverty disproportionate-ly impacts students of colour in public schools (see Table 3). In urban public schools, 42 percent of white students are in schools where the majority (51 percent or more) of all students are eligible for free or re-duced-price lunch. Yet, 86 percent of Black students and 84 percent of Latinx students are in schools where the majority of all students are eli-

gible for free or reduced-price lunch. A similar pattern of disproportion-
ality prevails regarding race and poverty in suburban and rural/town
public-school contexts, in which greater percentages of Black and Latinx
students are in schools where the majority of students live in poverty. For
example, looking at the rural/town school data (see Table 1), 41 percent
of all white students in US public schools are in rural and town schools,
in comparison to 18.46 percent of all Black students and 17.38 percent
of all Latinx students. In rural/town public schools (see Table 3), 44 percent of white students are in schools where the majority of students are
eligible for free or reduced-price lunch. Yet 79 percent of Black students
and 73 percent of Latinx students are in rural/town schools where the
majority of students are eligible for free or reduced-price lunch. In other
words, even though Black and Latinx students are comparatively fewer
in numbers than white students in rural/town public schools, more sizable percentages of them are in schools with high poverty.

Table 2. *Number and percentage distribution of public elementary and
secondary student enrolment by race/ethnicity and urban location (Fall
2013). Source: National Center for Education Statistics (2013).*

	United States		Urban	
Race / Ethnicity	Number	% Overall	Number	% Within Urban
White	24,689,060	50.15	4,475,771	29.85
Black	7,685,967	15.61	3,585,366	23.91
Latino	12,295,151	24.98	5,278,865	35.20
Asian	2,386,501	4.85	1,009,898	6.73
Pacific Islander	174,644	0.35	58,500	0.39
American Indian / Alaska Native	509,799	1.04	108,257	0.72
Two or more races	1,484,581	3.02	478,818	3.19
Total	49,225,703	100.00	14,995,475	100.00

Interestingly, even though poverty exists in rural/town and even suburban school contexts, the term "urban" or, borrowing from Milner (2012), "urban characteristics," gets mobilized only when referring to people or contexts when a sizable number of Black and/or Latinx students appear as problems or challenges to address. The term urban is never used when referring to poor white students and families. The euphemism of urban gets invoked at the appearance of poor racialized minorities in suburban and rural/town contexts.

Table 3. *Number and percentage distribution of public elementary and secondary student enrolment by race/ethnicity, school location, and eligibility for free or reduced-price lunch (Fall 2013). Source: National Center for Education Statistics (2013).*

Race / Ethnicity	% US	% Urban	% Suburban	% Rural & Town
Total	52.21	68.62	39.30	52.70
White	34.13	41.76	20.69	44.14
Black	76.95	85.53	64.54	78.71
Latino	75.63	83.99	67.64	73.26
Asian	38.06	53.11	25.31	37.02
Pacific Islander	61.04	68.57	49.77	70.37
American Indian / Alaska Native	69.56	68.31	45.01	77.14
Two or More Races	46.56	56.37	34.42	54.34

DECOLONIZING REPRESENTATION

With this cross-categorical demographic data (for example, race, class, and geographic), it is therefore understandable that the focus of most urban education research, policies, and programs has been on Black and Latinx students, families, and communities. If we take a decolonizing approach to urban education — especially if we ask "who is represent-ed?" and "who is missing?" — largely missing in our analysis is a serious consideration of Indigenous students as well as Indigenous educators, families, and communities in urban ecologies.

There are a little over half a million American Indian and Alaska Native students in US public schools, constituting 1.04 percent of the total number of students in US public schools (see Table 1). Out of this total across the country, 21.2 percent (or about one out of five) American Indian and Alaska Native students are in urban public schools. According to the National Congress of American Indians (n.d.),

> American Indians and Alaska Natives may be described as the "Asterisk Nation" because an asterisk, instead of data point, is often used in data displays when reporting racial and ethnic data due to various data-collection and reporting issues, such as small sample size, large margins of errors, or other issues related to the validity and statistical significance of data on American Indians and Alaska Natives.

As a result, from a research, policy, funding, and programming view that is largely driven by demographic and statistical data, the number and percentage of Indigenous students — and their interests and concerns — in urban ecologies may be construed as relatively insignificant. In other words, our prevailing discourses in urban education may end up eclips-ing the unique and overlapping conditions and needs of Indigenous stu-dents in urban schools and communities (Brayboy 2005; Grande 2004; Smith, Tuck, and Yang 2019).

For those of us trained in Ethnic Studies and its linkages to multi-cultural education, critical race theory, and even postcolonial studies need to decolonize how we conceptualize urban education because our dominant frames can end up marginalizing significant insights and differences from Native American and Indigenous Studies (Byrd 2011; Dunbar-Ortiz 2015; Sleeper-Smith et al. 2015). Indigenous students and communities are not merely another racial, ethnic, or minority group within the US sociocultural and political fabric. Indigenous Peoples foreground self-determination, sovereignty, and treaty status in rela-tion to the US nation-state and government (Harjo 2014). According to Elizabeth Cook-Lynn and Craig Howe (2001, 151), "particularly rancorous and troublesome for many Ethnic Studies professionals is Native scholars' claim of First Nation status for Native enclaves within the United States." A central struggle for many racialized minorities is the recognition of their rights and belonging as legitimate citizens and members of the US nation-state, but the struggles for Indigenous Peoples are quite different. For Native American and Indigenous Studies scholars, "the nature of the study of ethnicity as social systems in the U.S. disputes, trivializes, denies, and co-opts citizenship claims and treaty rights within nation-to-nation relationships" (Cook-Lynn and Howe 2001, 151). More specifically, "Native populations in the United States do not consider themselves just social groups within a cultural system called America. Rather, they define themselves as holding specific tribal legal status within the nation of the United States." (Cook-Lynn and Howe 2001, 152)

Hence, it is deeply problematic when Indigenous bodies, experiences, and even concepts are erased or appropriated, even by critical scholars of urban education. For instance, in his book *For White Folks Who Teach in the Hood*, Chris Emdin (2016, 9) mobilizes "neoindigenous" to refer to marginalized urban youth because, for him, the term "moves beyond a literal biological or geographical connection and into more complex connections among the oppressed that call forth a particular way of looking at the world." Emdin admits that he does "not engage in the work of connecting indigenous and neoindigenous either to trivialize the indigenous experiences or exaggerate that of the nonindigenous" (14). He draws from "Indigenous and diasporic scholars" who contend that

> the ways we view those we consider "indigenous" must move beyond prescribed definitions issuing from colonial and imperial constructs and toward a more inclusive definition that considers how people categorize themselves based on their shared experiences with imperialism and colonialism in their varied forms.

Emdin (2016, 14) points to "the Aboriginal, the Maori, and the Indigenous American" [*sic*] and their experiences of colonialism and imperialism in "different ways across different contexts" in Australia, New Zealand, and the United States. He clusters Indigenous students as underperforming in comparison to white students, and links them in urban contexts: "These same achievement gaps exist between neoindigenous urban youth of color and their counterparts from majority-white schools with students of middle to high socioeconomic status" (14–15).

Emdin (2016, 26) is interested in ways to "provide teachers with a very different worldview" and "allow educators to go beyond what they physically see when working with urban youth." However, is it necessary for him to utilize the term "neoindigenous" as a "new lens and vocabulary" (Emdin 2016, 26) to accomplish this goal? What is gained intellectually, politically, and even pedagogically in such a move? And what is lost? Indeed, it is important to make connections across marginalized communities, especially Indigenous Peoples and racialized minorities for deeper understanding and even political solidarity within and across national lines. The intertwined historical and contemporary workings of imperialism, colonialism, white supremacy, capitalism, and militarism can serve as an important node for this crucial analytical connection. However, in Emdin's formulation, the term neoindigenous does not include the Indigenous. The new term draws from and connects to the old term, but does not include the people that it references. Since Emdin's focus is on the neoindigenous and more specifically Black youth in the inner-city, his work inadvertently erases Indigenous students in urban contexts.

Part of the move to decolonize urban education is to fight against the ongoing erasure of Indigenous Peoples in urban schools and communities, for instance, through our research data collection, analysis, and representation, and to resist the appropriation of Indigenous terms and concepts that excludes or distorts Indigenous Peoples, cultures, histories, and futurities. For ongoing research (McKinley and Smith 2019; Tomlins-Jahnke et al. 2019), how might the framing of urban education research, policy, curriculum, and teacher and administrator preparation shift if we centre learnings from Indigenous communities?

DECOLONIZING STRUCTURE

For historians of education in the United States, a starting point in our analysis of urban education is David Tyack's *The One Best System: A History of American Urban Education* (Tyack 1974). Other historians of urban education have since documented and analyzed case studies of urban school systems and contexts across the United States, such as Atlanta,

Baltimore, Boston, Chicago, Detroit, Houston, Los Angeles, Milwaukee, New York, Portland, and St. Louis, from the early 1800s to the recent past of the 1990s (Rury 2005). Yet, "little research has been done on the transition of American Indian children into urban schooling or the more general history of American Indians' experiences with public education" (Murphy 2010, 3). The scholarship on the history of Indigenous education in the United States is grounded in missionary schools, the Bureau of Indian Affairs' boarding schools, and other boarding and day schools. A small but growing body of academic and community-based scholarship has documented and analyzed the histories of Indigenous Peoples in urban schools and communities since the mid-1950s. The Indian Relocation Act of 1956 was pivotal in the "history of state-sponsored efforts at Americanization that for the first time sought the use of cities as a way of integrating American Indians into the mainstream of American life" (Rosenthal 2012, 51). To my knowledge, Stephen Kent Amerman's (2010) *Urban Indians in Phoenix Schools, 1940–2000* may be the only book-length historical study focused on American Indians in urban schools.

When critically examining the structural contexts of urban dynamics and politics, especially from a decolonizing perspective, one provocative and insightful frame that is gaining currency is the use of "plantation" as a technology linking the history and legacy of slavery to what has been taking place in urban schools and communities. In *Research in Urban Educational Settings,* editors Kimberly Scott and Wanda Blanchett (2011, xiii) shared a story about a prominent African American female scholar instructing them "to be mindful of how we conduct research in urban areas" because she has seen how "researchers treat urban sites as plantations." Unfortunately, some researchers come to urban sites to collect data and advance in their careers, without developing meaningful and reciprocal ties and relationships with communities and these communities often receive very little, if any, benefits from the researchers' work. It is not only in research where plantation dynamics take place. In his analysis of educational policy and decision making in St. Louis, Missouri in the early 2000s, Bruce Anthony Jones (2005, 9) forwards a "*plantation model* of policy design, development, and implementation [that] places high significance on understanding how history and issues of race affect the policy process" (original emphasis). His model consists of seven characteristics: the policy process is 1) driven by white men; 2) hierarchical and top-down; 3) characterized by arrogance, indifference, and paternalism; 4) unpredictable; 5) punitive; 6) inconsistent; and 7) driven by racial considerations (Jones 2005, 14). In the realm of urban educational policy, "the worldview through which policy manifests for the largely African American children and their families in the St. Louis community is a White male worldview" (Jones 2005, 19). In this case study, Jones lays bare the consequences of plantation politics in urban education: the beneficiaries are business and philanthropic organizations that hold mandate authority over decision making as well as the city government, the participating university, and consulting company. The victims of the plantation model of policy decision making are the students, parents, schoolteachers, and administrators.

In their article "Historically White Universities and Plantation Politics," T. Elon Dancy II, Kirsten Edwards, and James Earl Davis (2018, 177) argue that the "experiences of Black people on historically White campuses are best understood as 'continuities of colonial preoccupations.'" Connecting slavery and the plantation system as part of US settler colonialism, they trace Black subjugation through "the extraction of labor from the Black body without engaging the body as a laborer, but as property" and through the various ways "institutions use to police, control, imprison, and kill" Black people (180). They examine the positioning of "Africa as ontologically colonized" (180) and of Blacks as "(still) the slave and other than human" (185). Dancy, Edwards, and Davis (2018, 178) delineate three dimensions of anti-Blackness: "(a) interpretations of Black labor through colonial arrangements; (b) relationship between labor, ownership, and education; and (c) institutionalization of Black suffering." Reflecting colonial designs in contemporary contexts, they consider the "labor expectations placed on Black women in academia" as "reflective of domestic servitude" (183) and Black male bodies, especially in athletics, as "primarily generators of income and properties of entertainment" (184). Since settler colonialism ties together land and citizenship, the authors maintain that public education is "predicated on anti-Blackness" and is "a direct model of plantation politics" (187). Because the "maintenance of a public education system [is] dependent on property taxes," it functions as an institutionalized tool of dispossession, and limits access to higher education (Dancy, Edwards, and Davis 2018, 187). Lastly, if "White humanity is predicated on Black inhumanity," then Black experiences of "microaggressions, tokenism, impostorship, and racial battle fatigue attest to [their] psychological torment" (Dancy, Edwards, and Davis 2018, 188). When anti-Black violence takes place on campus, "the modus operandi prioritizes the public image of the White institution, not the assault on Black inhumanity" (Dancy, Edwards, and Davis 2018, 189).

This line of research that links racism, capitalism, and colonialism through the history and ongoing operations of plantation conditions remind me of the theory of internal colonialism embraced by Black and Chicano activists and intellectuals in the 1960s and 1970s and tied to the emergence of Ethnic Studies as an academic discipline. In his genealogy of the theory of internal colonialism, Ramón Gutiérrez (2004, 282) contends that "internal colonialism represented a radical break in thinking about race" because it posits racism as "deeply historical, rooted in the legacies of conquest and colonialism." Gutiérrez (2004, 284) adds that "Internal colonialism as theory grew out of the brutal urban conditions minorities faced," and was inspired by Third World revolutions and writings by Mao Tse Tung, Frantz Fanon, and Che Guevara. Moreover, it was "a modern capitalist practice of oppression and exploitation of racial and ethnic minorities ... characterized by relationships of domination, oppression, and exploitation" and underpinned by forced entry, cultural impact, and external administration (Gutiérrez 2004, 289–290). Within this framework, urban areas or "ghettos" largely populated by poor people of colour could be characterized as domestic colonies ridden by "hunger, illiteracy, disease, ... slums, cultural starvation, and the psychological reactions to being ruled over by others not of [their] kind" (Gutiérrez 2004, 286). While the hetero-patriarchal underpinning of the theory of internal colonialism has been heavily critiqued by feminists and queer people of colour, Gutiérrez (2004, 293) shows that the "utopian nationalist ideals" of resisting internal colonialism through "territorial autonomy, self-determination, community control, [and] an end to racism" remain crucial matters to fight for.

When I consider the historical and contemporary dynamics in Detroit, Michigan where I now live and work, how do I employ decolonizing approaches to the material structures that shape and impact urban lives and conditions? How might the analytical metaphor of plantation be generative (or not) in a city that is predominantly Black (that is, about 80 percent of the city population are African Americans), while the leadership of its city government, as well as that of the largest public-school district in the state, and the corporations, industries, and philanthropies shaping the economic livelihoods and social service systems of city residents is overwhelmingly white? With Detroit's history of white flight and governmental neglect and disinvestment (Mirel 1999; Sugrue 2014), how do we make sense of the relatively recent efforts by government, corporate, real estate, and philanthropic sectors to "revitalize" the city? How do these revitalization efforts entice white professionals and families to return to the city, while ignoring the ongoing demands for community development and sustainability of African Americans who have stayed in the city with very little support? How do these efforts address the ravages brought by school choice and voucher advocates such as Betsy DeVos who cut her political teeth in Michigan and now oversees the US Department of Education? How do we enact the difficult, yet necessary, simultaneous moves of radical critique and transformative possibility in urban education (DeNicolo et al. 2017; Gonzales and Shields 2015)?

DECOLONIZING AFFECT

When students and I read and discuss work on urban education, the students sometimes remark that they are feeling overwhelmed, angry, sad, frustrated, pessimistic, and defeated about the ongoing state of affairs. Consider the following features that characterize urban education as outlined by Kincheloe et al. (2006):

- Schools operate in areas with high population density.
- Schools are bigger and school districts serve more students.
- Schools function in areas marked by profound economic disparity.
- Urban school systems are undermined by ineffective business operations.
- Poor urban students are more likely to experience health problems.
- Urban schools experience higher student, teacher, and administrator mobility.
- Urban schools experience unique transportation problems.

- Teachers working in poor urban schools are less likely to live in the communities neighboring the schools than are teachers in suburban and rural systems. (xii)

Issues such as "underachievement, institutionalized white racism, segregation, poverty, teacher flight, poor teacher quality, inadequate material resources, failed reform efforts, preschool to prison pipeline, high student dropout rate" plague urban schools (Lomotey 2015, xiv).

For many researchers and advocates of urban education, documenting, contextualizing, examining, and addressing problems in schools and society has been our main intellectual, pedagogical, and political approach. We are deeply committed to addressing the historical and ongoing inequities that shape the educational and lived conditions of already marginalized groups. We take an anti-deficit view of urban students, families, and schools: "Rather than perceiving students and their families as inferior or deficient because they live in poverty, for instance, the point is to identify, study, and address structural forms of inequity that do not serve students well in education and beyond" (Milner and Lomotey 2014, xvi). We situate the problems and solutions in urban schools as intricately intertwined within the societies we are a part of. For many of us, this work is not only a scholarly and empirical project; it is inherently a moral, ethical, and activist commitment.

Hence, for those of us who work in urban education, point out the historical and ongoing inequities, and critique the language and structures that reinforce disparity and injustice, we might be perceived as what Sarah Ahmed (2010) calls being a "killjoy." According to Ahmed, a killjoy is seen as a "social threat:" "The killjoy is the one who comes between bodies that would be, or should be, in agreement. The killjoy is the one who gets in the way of an organic solidarity" (213). So, for instance, if there is a general agreement among policymakers, practitioners, and other advocates about resolving a problem in urban schools and communities, the person pointing out the agreement's limits, compromised position, and potential negative repercussions could be deemed as a killjoy. Ahmed (2010, 213) adds that "if ethics is to preserve the freedom to disagree, then ethics cannot simply be *about* affirmation, or *for* affirmation, understood as good encounters, as what increases the capacity for action" (original emphasis). In a democracy, how do we handle disagreements and the sometimes bad feelings that come with that? Individuals and collectives who "refuse the promise of happiness" through easy resolutions and skewed compromises end up becoming the killjoy or the "causes of bad feeling" (Ahmed 2010, 215). Ahmed (2010) is concerned about the act and impact of recovering in the pursuit of agreement: "to recover can be to re-cover, to cover over the causes of pain and suffering" (216). She is not interested in a perpetual state of melancholia that holds on to disagreement or bad feelings generated from disagreement. Rather she wants us to "attend to bad feelings not in order to overcome them but *to learn by how we are affected by what comes near ... as an ethical resource*" (216; original emphasis). She does not want these bad feelings as being "in the way"; instead, she wants us to "unlearn what we have learned not to notice" (215). She argues that this move is important "if we are to produce critical understandings of how violence, as a relation of force and harm, is directed toward some bodies and not others" (216).

Contrary to certain misinterpretations of Ahmed's critique of the promise of happiness, I do not think that the killjoy is fundamentally opposed to happiness, love, or even joy. I suggest that it is precisely due to their love for marginalized subjects that we "unlearn what we have learned not to notice" (Ahmed 2010, 215) even at the risk of generating bad feelings. In other words, it is from the place of love where the killjoy launches their critiques. I attend to emotions and feelings as part of decolonizing urban education in order to trouble the Cartesian split between mind and body — between the so-called logical mind and emotional heart — that underpins Western Enlightenment and rationality. This binary, if understood from Gloria Anzaldúa's (2015, 90) vantage point, limits the cultivation of "nuestras facultades that rely on inner knowledges" and the engagement with *el sitio y la lengua*. This decolonizing move — largely inspired by the praxis of feminists of colour — marshals affect, such as love and joy, as an embodied and epistemic resource to navigate urban terrains and dynamics and to serve disenfranchised students, families, and communities.

In their "Visions of Love in Urban Schooling, or A Love Letter from the Editors," Esther Ohito, Wanda Watson, Jamila Lyiscott, and Yolanda Sealey-Ruiz (2019, 147) write:

> rarely is it that the term urban is associated with the word "love."
> Even more pointedly, it is rare for the word love to connote

positive association with teaching, children, and urban schools, much less the teaching of children in urban schools. Those of us who use the term love in word and deed often have a deep understanding of society's disdain for those children — typically, Black, Brown, and/or poor children — who are restricted from an opportunity to experience the fullness of education.

Because love — alongside hope and care — is such a positive emotion, many of us gravitate to its affective power as a salve to the seemingly negative feelings generated by what is happening in urban schools and communities. It offers inspiration, nourishment, and sustenance to confront the ravages and persistence of epistemic, structural, and psychic violence against already marginalized folks. Love is revolutionary in the face of oppression. It functions as a shield to combat hate.

In addition to the word love, another word that is rarely associated with urban education is joy. Perhaps it is no coincidence that a woman of colour scholar, Sonia Nieto (2013), is one of the few who focuses on the joy of teaching and working with diverse students. In *Finding Joy in Teaching Students of Diverse Backgrounds*, she foregrounds "teachers who thrive" even when they "feel the relentless pressures associated with inequality, standardization, and constant references to the 'achievement gap.' In spite of the difficult school and societal contexts in which they may work, these teachers find joy in teaching" (xiii). In other words, finding joy in teaching, especially in urban schools and communities, is not about closing one's eyes and ears to structural disparity, epistemic violence, and relentless dehumanization that occur.

Finding joy is not the opposite of being a killjoy. Sarah Ahmed's (2010) concern is this: "The affective economy which associates joy with good things and pain with bad things might prematurely hold things in place. If we aim for joy, we aim to move beyond pain. Bad feelings are in the way of what gets beyond" (215). She is reticent about the urgent move toward agreement and resolution and the insistence to "get over" or "get beyond" what might cause discomfort, discord, or disagreement. Yet finding joy and being critical are not necessarily contradictory or opposites of each other. For Bettina Love (2019), "finding joy in the midst of pain and trauma is the fight to be fully human" (119), especially since "joy makes the quest for justice sustainable" (120). At the end of *Eloquent Rage*, Brittney Cooper (2018, 274) writes: "Joy ... is different from happiness, because happiness is predicated on 'happenings,' on what's occurring, on whether your life is going right, and whether all is well. Joy arises from an internal clarity about our purpose. My purpose is justice. And the fight for justice brings me joy."

CONCLUSION

I would like to end where I began in this essay: in student activism and the ongoing fight for Ethnic Studies, especially in light of the more recent attacks against critical race theory, as crucial and intertwined in our work to decolonize urban education. In the late 1960s, student activism across the country — such as the Third World Liberation Front protests in San Francisco and Berkeley, the walkout of Chicano high school students in East Los Angeles, and the Black student strike at the University of Wisconsin–Madison — demanded more relevant curriculum and more diverse faculty and students. Fifty years later, the institutional status of Ethnic Studies in PK–12 schools and higher education remains tenuous. In California, students staged a 10-day hunger strike at San Francisco State University in 2016, which resulted in the provision of additional funding close to half a million dollars in support of Ethnic Studies (Herrera 2016). In Arizona, students, educators, and community members protested the ban of Mexican American Studies in Tucson Unified School District, and filed a lawsuit, resulting in a federal judge ruling in 2017 that the state violated the students' First and Fourteenth Amendment rights (Strauss 2017). In Texas, students, educators, and community members also fought for the inclusion of Mexican American Studies in the official school curriculum, with the State Board of Education finally approving the course as a high school elective in 2018 (Swaby 2018). Students, educators, parents, and community supporters in other states, such as Colorado, Connecticut, Indiana, Kansas, Montana, New Mexico, Oregon, Rhode Island, Vermont, and Washington, are clamouring for Ethnic Studies as a necessary intervention for more diverse and inclusive curriculum. Fifty years later, Ethnic Studies and decolonizing urban education continue to be worth fighting for.

*A version of this text originally appeared in "Decolonizing urban education," Roland Sintos Coloma, *Educational Studies*, © 2020 Taylor &

Francis, reprinted by permission of the publisher (Taylor & Francis Ltd, http://www.tandfonline.com/journals/heds20).

References

Ahmed, Sara. 2010. *The Promise of Happiness*. Durham and London: Duke University Press.

Amerman, Stephen. 2010. *Urban Indians in Phoenix Schools, 1940–2000*. Lincoln: University of Nebraska Press.

Anzaldúa, Gloria. 1987. *Borderlands/la frontera: The New Mestiza*. San Francisco: Aunt Lute Books.

___. 2015. *Light in the Dark/luz en lo oscuro: Rewriting Identity, Spirituality, Reality*. Durham and London: Duke University Press.

Brayboy, Bryan. 2005. "Toward a Tribal Critical Race Theory in Education." *Urban Review* 37, 5.

Butler, Johnnella (ed.). 2001. *Color-Line to Borderlands: The Matrix of American Ethnic Studies*. Seattle: University of Washington Press.

Byrd, Jodi. 2011. *The Transit of Empire: Indigenous Critiques of Colonialism*. Minnesota: University of Minnesota Press.

Camarillo, Albert. 2007. "Cities of Color: The New Racial Frontier in California's Minority-Majority Cities." *Pacific Historical Review* 76, 1.

Carmona, Matthew, Steve Tiesdell, Tim Heath, and Tanner Oc. 2010. *Public Places — Urban Spaces: The Dimensions of Urban Design,* second edition. Oxford: Elsevier.

Collins, Patricia, and John Solomos (eds.). 2010. *The SAGE Handbook of Race and Ethnic Studies.* London and Thousand Oaks: SAGE.

Coloma, Roland Sintos. 2009. "'Destiny Has Thrown the Negro and the Filipino Under the Tutelage of America': Race and Curriculum in the Age of Empire." *Curriculum Inquiry* 39, 4.

___. 2012. "White Gazes, Brown Breasts: Imperial Feminism and Disciplining Desires and Bodies in Colonial Encounters." *Paedagogica Historica: International Journal of the History of Education* 48, 2.

___. 2013. "Empire: An Analytical Category for Educational Research." *Educational Theory* 63, 6.

___. 2017. "'We Are Here Because You Were There': On Curriculum, Empire, and Global Migration." *Curriculum Inquiry* 47, 1.

Cook-Lynn, Elizabeth, and Craig Howe. 2001. "The Dialectics of Ethnicity in America: A View from American Indian Studies." In *Color-Line to*

Borderlands: The Matrix of American Ethnic Studies, edited by Johnnella Butler. Seattle: University of Washington Press.

Cooper, Brittany. 2018. *Eloquent Rage: A Black Feminist Discovers Her Superpower*. New York: St. Martin's Press.

Curley, Stephen, Jeong-eun Rhee, Binaya Subedi, and Sharon Subreenduth. 2018. "Activism as/in/for Global Citizenship: Putting Un-Learning to Work Towards Educating the Future." In *Palgrave Handbook of Global Citizenship and Education*, edited by Ian Davies, Li-Ching Ho, Dina Kiwan, et al. London: Palgrave Macmillan.

Dancy II, T. Elon II, Kirsten Edwards, and James Davis. 2018. "Historically White Universities and Plantation Politics: Anti-Blackness and Higher Education in the Black Lives Matter Era." *Urban Education* 53, 2.

DeNicolo, Christina, Min Yu, Christopher Crowley, and Susan Gabel. 2017. "Reimagining Critical Care and Problematizing Sense of School Belonging as a Response to Inequality for Immigrants and Children of Immigrants." *Review of Research in Education* 41, 1.

Dunbar-Ortiz, Roxanne. 2015. *An Indigenous People's History of the United States*. Boston: Beacon.

Education and Urban Society. n.d. "Aims and Scope." journals.sagepub.com/aims-scope/EUS.

Elia, Nada, David Hernández, Jodi Kim, et al. (eds.). 2016. *Critical Ethnic Studies: A Reader*. Durham and London: Duke University Press.

Emdin, Christopher. 2016. *For White Folks Who Teach in the Hood...And the Rest of Y'all Too: Reality Pedagogy and Urban Education*. Boston: Beacon.

Gonzales, Sandra, and Carolyn Shields. 2015. "Education 'Reform' in Latino Detroit: Achievement Gap or Colonial Legacy?" *Race Ethnicity and Education* 18, 3.

Grande, Sandy. 2004. *Red Pedagogy: Native American Social and Political Thought*. Lanham: Rowman & Littlefield.

Gutiérrez, Ramón. 2004. "Internal Colonialism: An American Theory of Race." *Du Bois Review: Social Science Research on Race* 1, 2.

Harjo, Suzan (ed.). 2014. *Nation to Nation: Treaties Between the United States and American Indian Nations*. Washington: National Museum of the American Indian and Smithsonian Books.

Herrera, Jack. 2016. "10-day Hunger Strike = Victory for sfsu Students." *USA Today*, May 22, 2016. usatoday.com/story/college/2016/05/22/10-day-hunger-strike-victory-for-sfsu-students/37417869/.

Jones, Bruce. 2005. "Forces for Failure and Genocide: The Plantation Model of

Urban Educational Policy Making in St. Louis." *Educational Studies* 37, 1.

Journal of Urban Mathematics Education. n.d. "About the Journal." https://journals.tdl.org/jume/index.php/JUME/about.

Kincheloe, Joe, Kecia Hayes, Karel Rose, and Philip Anderson (eds.). 2006. *The Praeger Handbook of Urban Education*. Westport: Greenwood.

Lomotey, Kofi. 2015. "Foreword." In *Handbook of Urban Educational Leadership*, edited by Muhammad Khalifa, Noelle Arnold, Azadeh Osanloo, and Cosette Grant. Lanham: Rowman & Littlefield.

Love, Bettina. 2019. *We Want to Do More than Survive: Abolitionist Teaching and the Pursuit of Educational Freedom*. Boston: Beacon.

Maxwell, Lesli. 2014. "U.S. School Enrollment Hits Majority–Minority Milestone." *Education Week* 34, 1.

McKinley, Elizabeth, and Linda Tuhiwai Smith. 2019. *Handbook of Indigenous Education*. Singapore: Springer.

Milner, H. Ricard IV. 2012. "But What is Urban Education?" *Urban Education* 47, 3.

Milner, H. Richard IV, and Kofi Lomotey (eds.). 2014. *Handbook of Urban Education*. New York and London: Routledge.

Mirel, Jeffrey. 1999. *The Rise and Fall of an Urban School System: Detroit, 1907–81*, second edition. Ann Arbor: University of Michigan Press.

Murphy, Kimberly. 2010. *The Urban "Half": Resituating the History of Urban Relocation and Public Education*. UC Berkeley ISSI Fellows Working Papers. escholarship.org/uc/item/3vt690fq.

National Center for Education Statistics. 2013. "Table B.1.e.-1 Number and Percentage Distribution of Public Elementary and Secondary Enrollment by Percentage of Students in School Eligible for Free or Reduced-Price Lunch by School Urban-Centric 12-Category Locale and Race/Ethnicity: Fall 2013." nces.ed.gov/surveys/ruraled/tables/B.1.e.-1.asp.

National Congress of American Indian. n.d. "Data Disaggregation: The Asterisk Nation." ncai.org/policy-research-center/research-data/data.

National Journal of Urban Education & Practice. n.d. "Focus and Scope." tsu.edu/academics/colleges-and-schools/college-of-education/current-students/center-for-excellence-home/national-journal-of-urban-education--practice/overview.html.

Nieto, Sonia. 2013. *Finding Joy in Teaching Students of Diverse Backgrounds: Culturally Responsive and Socially Just Practices in U.S. Classrooms*. Portsmouth: Heinemann.

Ohito, Esther, Wanda Watson, Jamila Lyiscott, and Yolanda Sealey-Ruiz. 2019.

"Postscript: Visions of Love in Urban Schooling, or a Love Letter from the Editors." *Urban Review* 51.

Okihiro, Gary. 2016. *Third World Studies: Theorizing Liberation*. Durham and London: Duke University Press.

Organisation for Economic Co-operation and Development. 2013. "Definition of Functional Urban Areas (FUA) for the OECD Metropolitan Database." oecd.org/cfe/regional-policy/Definition-of-Functional-Urban-Areas-for-the-OECD-metropolitan-database.pdf.

Paddison, Ronan (ed.). 2001. *Handbook of Urban Studies*. London and Thousand Oaks: SAGE.

Pérez, Emma. 1991. "Sexuality and Discourse: Notes from a Chicana Survivor." In *Chicana Lesbians: The Girls Our Mothers Warned Us About*, edited by Carla Trujillo. Berkeley: Third Woman Press.

Powell, John. 2002. "A Minority-Majority Nation: Racing the Population in the Twenty-First Century." *Fordham Urban Law Journal* 29, 4.

Rosenthal, Nicholas. 2012. *Reimagining Indian Country: Native American Migration & Identity in Twentieth-Century Los Angeles*. Chapel Hill: University of North Carolina Press.

Rury, John. 2005. *Urban Education in the United States: A Historical Reader*. New York: Palgrave Macmillan.

Sayer, A. 1984. "Defining the Urban." *GeoJournal* 9.

Scott, Kimberley, and Wanda Blanchett (eds.). 2011. *Research in Urban Educational Settings: Lessons Learned and Implications for Future Practice*. Charlotte: Information Age Publishing.

Sleeper-Smith, Susan, Juliana Barr, Jean O'Brien, et al. (eds.). 2015. *Why You Can't Teach United States History Without American Indians*. Chapel Hill: University of North Carolina Press.

Smith, Linda Tuhiwai, Eve Tuck, and K. Wayne Yang (eds.). 2019. *Indigenous and Decolonizing Studies in Education*. New York: Routledge.

Strauss, Valerie. 2017. "Arizona's Ban on Mexican American Studies was Racist, U.S. Court Rules." *Washington Post*, August 23, 2017. washingtonpost.com/news/answer-sheet/wp/2017/08/23/arizonas-ban-on-mexican-american-studies-was-racist-u-s-court-rules/.

Sugrue, Thomas. 2014. *The Origins of the Urban Crisis: Race and Inequality in Postwar Detroit*. Princeton: Princeton University Press.

Swaby, Aliyya. 2018. "Texas Education Board Approves Course Formerly Known as Mexican-American Studies." *Texas Tribune*, April 11, 2018. texastribune.org/2018/04/11/texas-education-board-mexican-american-studies-course/.

Takaki, Ronald. 2008. *A Different Mirror: A History of Multicultural America*. New York: Bay Back Books.

Tomlins-Jahnke, Huia, Sandra Styres, Spencer Lilley, and Dawn Zinga (eds.). 2019. *Indigenous Education: New Directions in Theory and Practice*. Edmonton: University of Alberta Press.

Tyack, David. 1974. *The One Best System: A History of American Urban Education*. Cambridge: Harvard University Press.

UNICEF. 2012. "Chapter 1: Children in an Increasingly Urban World." In *The State of the World's Children 2012: Children in an Urban World*. unicef.org/media/84881/file/SOWC-2012-executive-summary.pdf.

Urban Area Criteria for the 2010 Census. 2011. 76 Fed. Reg. 53030-53043 (2011).

Urban Education. n.d. "Journal description." journals.sagepub.com/description/UEX.

Urban Review. n.d. About the Journal. springer.com/journal/11256.

Round 3

ON HEALING, WELL-BEING AND SUSTAINABILITY

Taking Care in the Work of Decolonizing Equity

In this final section, Ozioma Aloziem and Dr. V.C. Rhonda Hackett each explore the importance of and pathways for attending to our healing work while striving toward decolonial equity. Aloziem presents a framework for radical healing as a necessary means of both transforming educational institutions and healing from the impact of the racist, colonial harms that continue to happen in these settings. Drawing on critical race theory (CRT) and centring embodiment/embodied knowledge, Aloziem outlines four key components of Radical Healing as both a pedagogy and a practice: promoting collective healing, pedagogies of healing, teaching to transform, and radical self-care. This chapter underscores the importance of centring healing in higher learning as a means of realizing more equitable educational settings, particularly for racialized students. In the context of decolonial equity beyond the classroom, Aloziem's writing emphasizes that the work of redressing social injustice cannot be separated from our individual and collective healing as we are simultaneously experiencing and striving to transform the harms that social injustice creates.

Similarly, Dr. Hackett explores the importance of healing in decolonial equity work, focusing specifically on the experiences of peoples of African descent in the lands presently known as Canada. She reflects on the erasure, silence and colonial violence experienced by peoples of African descent in social work education and practice, and the impact of the perpetuation of anti-Black violence in media representations and everyday conversations that continue to shape how individuals, families, and communities of African descent are treated by social workers and social work educators and researchers. She presents witnessing and wellness as resistance — as pathways to healing in the face of colonial violence and refusing separation from self and each another. Providing examples of witnessing work done by and with women of African descent in so-called Canada, Dr. Hackett reflects on the importance of heart work in being able to engage with decolonial equity on one's own terms.

Together, these chapters emphasize the imperative of attending to our wholistic well-being in any effort to theorize, articulate, and contribute toward decolonial equity since the cost of experiencing, resisting, and transforming inequities is both embodied and collective.

7

A CALL FOR INTEGRATING RADICAL HEALING AND IMAGINATION INTO CRITICAL RACE EDUCATION

Ozioma Aloziem

In 2019 I found myself in Amsterdam with scholars from the United States, Jamaica, and the Netherlands. I had just finished my social work master's where I had been deeply immersed in critical race theory (CRT) and was excited to be using it to examine how race matters in a global context in order to imagine what a decolonial university could look like. I was imagining a new curriculum for social work education rooted in a decolonial approach to equity. On that trip, my mentor Dr. Frank Tuitt, a co-leader of the group, brought up Audre Lorde's (2007, 112) famous quote: "The master's tools will never dismantle the master's house. They may allow us temporarily to beat him at his own game, but they will never enable us to bring about genuine change." Is this true? Does this then require new frameworks and curricula to make systemic change? And are we not also tools? If so, what change must occur within us?

I'll be honest. Going into the trip I felt scared and unsure about the state of the world. This was 2019. Bolsonaro was elected president in Brazil, the Amazon was burning. A white supremacist live-streamed his attack on a mosque in New Zealand, Brexit was happening. We witnessed a surge in asylum-seekers at the US southern border, a surge in xenophobia, and a surge in ignorance and apathy. Everything felt so heavy, and I was starting to believe this was as bad as it could get. But just when I decided I'd feel this way forever, there was a switch.

Radical imagination is a tool to reimagine ourselves and our society time and time again. It's about having the audacity to live in the world as it is, while dreaming of something different, and believing that a dream is possible even when you cannot see it. It's being humble enough to ask questions of ourselves and of each other. It's being courageous enough to learn and unlearn. It's so different from what we learned in school, where we were taught how to analyze and analyze and analyze, which means taking things apart. But when are we taught how to put things back together? When do we learn how to construct something new that has never existed before, with no real roadmap or directions? Radical imagination is the instinct that was taught out of us but it is the skill we desperately need for a liberated future. It's a tool I've used to reimagine our current approach to education using a reimagined critical race theory.

Considering the ingrained and disembodying effects of oppressive systems on the mind, heart, body, and soul, we must deconstruct systems of oppression while simultaneously reconstructing systems of support that cultivate individual and community well-being. How can we respond to racism and oppression in restorative ways? I use critical race theory to offer a framework for radical healing and argue for the implementation of an emancipatory and embodied kind of education. Radical imagination invites us to consider a different approach to healing. Radical healing understands that complete change is necessary, that we don't accommodate to systemic oppression but resist and transform through growth and healing. We cannot have justice or a decolonized society if we don't reclaim and repair the human spirit. As a constructive criticism, and informed by my positionality and experience, I draw upon the work of queer BIPOC healers, teachers, cultural workers, grassroots activists, and leaders. I also use scholarship in the fields of higher education, Black feminist anthropology, psychology, and sociology. I offer an integrative, culturally responsive, critically conscious focus on healing as a decolonial, embodied approach to education. My intention is to highlight the limitations of our current education system and the current frameworks used to promote equity within them. Can we fill that void by decolonizing our educational spaces and by centring practices and ways of being that simultaneously promote critical consciousness, challenge oppression, and foster well-being? Is this not an act of racial and social equity? This chapter articulates what I have found to be healing throughout my educational journey and uses my experience as a theory for healing. Ultimately, I hope to use my reimagining of critical race theory to emphasize that promoting wellness is a crucial aspect of a decolonized and equitable educational environment. I encourage institutions and individuals to also imagine new ways of support to create inclusive environments where all participants can thrive.

Although this chapter primarily focuses on critical race theory and education, embodiment is at its core. Why is the body important? I'm constantly thinking about that conversation in Amsterdam: Are we not also tools? What change must occur within us? Bodies are centrally impacted by oppression; Morales (2013, 9) says, "No body stands outside the consequences of injustice. Our bodies are sites of struggle and transformation." Our bodies are tools and sites of resistance. When we do not own our bodies, when our bodies are intentionally made to be not ours, that is an act of colonization. So, a decolonial approach to equity, to me, would necessitate a return to body. I draw upon Prentis Hemphill's (2021) definition of embodiment as "what is currently practiced or habituated in us." It is also the process of becoming more aware of our practices and behaviours. A decolonial approach to equity recognizes that we are always embodying something. If we are not intentionally aware of what we are embodying, chances are we are embodying dominant and oppressive ways of being, thinking, feeling, and acting. I came to this realization after engagement with and around the work and teachings of Indigenous leaders, somatic practitioners, and healing centred social justice workers. These teachers and guides have helped me to understand that any justice movement must challenge traditional and oppressive ways of being while also returning us to more natural ways of being. A decolonial approach to equity is situated in and centred around connection.

When we fundamentally lack connection to ourselves and our emotions, to one another, to our work, to the food we consume and to the land we occupy, we can never be free and whole. No matter what we achieve, there will always be something missing. And if we don't feel connected, we don't feel accountable which leads to the destruction of ourselves and our world. Decolonial healing then becomes moving toward that state of connection. In all the anti-racist Black feminist liberation work I do, I think of emancipation as freeing our entire beings and getting to a place of connection, love, relationality, accountability, care, and tenderness. We do that by first loving ourselves and one another enough to know that we deserve better than the current state of things, and then by committing ourselves to the pursuit of justice, wholeness, radical love, and moral reimagination.

As a social worker, I am committed to struggling against oppression and the ways I internalize and embody myths and misinformation about my own identity and the identities of other people. I am committed to resisting the ways in which systems of oppression manifest in how I exist in my body and misinformation about my own identity and the identity of other people. I am committed to exercising as much agency as I can over my own body and experience. Our bodies are our containers and tell the story of who we are, who we've been, and what we have witnessed or been made witness to. So, when we work through our bodies, through somatics, affective engagement, and critical self-reflection, we are able to disrupt the embodied colonization, and do and feel new things.

A decolonial approach to equity has to recognize the places in ourselves where we have been taught or trained to divide and disconnect. I embrace a decolonial embodied approach to equity where liberation and healing are actually situated in ourselves. I am here because I am committed to the fight for racial equity and healing. But deeper than that, I am committed to restoring connection, to being fully in my body at all times, and to modelling what that means.

CRITICAL RACE THEORY AND EDUCATION

The United States' education system is rooted in a legacy of systematic subjugation and institutional oppression. Critical race theory (CRT) was created by racially and ethnically minoritized scholars to challenge and change systems of racial oppression (Delgado and Stefancic 2017; Ladson-Billings and Tate 1995; Solórzano 1997). Academics frame it as an emancipatory counterspace to engage in anti-racist forms of research to radically confront and transform systemic racism. Educators and researchers have used CRT to develop frameworks that examine and challenge racism in curricular structures, processes, and discourses

(Ladson-Billings and Tate 1995; Solórzano and Yosso 2002; Tuitt, Haynes, and Stewert 2018). However, these existing theoretical education frameworks have failed to fully consider the physical, mental, emotional, and psychological cost of this work and have ignored the role that healing can play in the fight for racial justice and decolonial equity in education. While CRT might attempt to be emancipatory, as bell hooks (1994, 61) shows: "theory is not inherently healing, liberatory, or revolutionary. It fulfills this function only when we ask that it do so and direct our theorizing towards this end." I was introduced to CRT as a tool for decolonizing institutions of higher education to promote more equitable learning spaces for students of colour. As such, I argue that CRT scholars must incorporate a praxis of healing to promote holistic wellness and well-being to make CRT truly liberating for racially and ethnically minoritized individuals and those committed to social justice work.

As a Black woman who has spent decades attending school in predominantly white spaces, I have experienced incredible harm throughout my educational career. I am intimately familiar with "weathering," a term coined by Arline Geronimus and colleagues to describe the long-term physical, emotional, mental, and psychological effects of racism and white supremacy (Geronimus et al. 2006). I've long suffered from "racial battle fatigue," the stress that comes with being a Black student in a white space (Smith 2014). It has been incredibly taxing, and I have not been offered very many ways to navigate this. Racially and ethnically minoritized students, Black students in particular, often work themselves to the point of severe illness in order to combat perceptions of intellectual inferiority (McGee and Stovall 2015). Jennifer Richardson (2018, 281) states that "marginalized students of color (particularly Black women) often feel (re)traumatized by academic spaces in which they may experience debates and/or critiques as uncomfortable, isolating and even violent." Weathering and racial battle fatigue can lead to damaging physiological and psychological strain (Smith, Yosso, and Solórzano 2011). As a social worker, I am also well aware of the high burnout rates of those within my profession. Shawn Ginwright (2015, 37) states that "one of the greatest challenges facing social justice work is the growing sense of spiritual emptiness and burnout." Pursuing higher education should not make students sick nor should pursuing a career committed to social justice.

THE RELEVANCE OF CRT AND
THE NEED FOR RADICAL HEALING

McGee and Stovall (2015) call on CRT to create a space that openly acknowledges the healing of those who have experienced racialized trauma. They call on CRT to develop a grounded theory of what this healing might look like. I have in part, attempted to do that here. I have also attempted to develop a framework that makes the application of CRT and the pursuit of social justice more sustainable. Radical healing is conceptualized here as a way to deconstruct systems of oppression while simultaneously reconstructing systems of support that cultivate individual and community well-being (Hicks Peterson 2018). Radical healing as both pedagogy and praxis allows both students and faculty alike to build our capacity for hope, critical consciousness, and social change in the midst of oppression (Hicks Peterson 2018).

Within this context, I construct radical healing in four parts (radical self-care, teaching to transform, pedagogies of healing, and collective healing) informed by existing research and centred around Yosso's (2002) six key tenets (discussed below) and several core questions: Considering the effects of oppressive systems on the mind, body, and soul, how do those hurt by oppression heal? How do individuals committed to social justice preserve their spirits when confronting systems of oppression? How can we respond to racism and oppression in ways that restore and retain hope and possibility? Radical healing can allow us to discover a radical notion of justice: wholeness.

Researchers like Daniel Solórzano (1997, 7) argue that CRT in education is "a pedagogy, curriculum, and research agenda that accounts for the role of racism in US education and works toward the elimination of racism as part of a larger goal of eliminating all forms of subordination in education." CRT applied to education has the ability to lessen educational inequity while exposing and challenging both micro and macro forms of racism disguised as traditional US schooling. According to Tara Yosso (2002), critical race theory in education should: 1) openly acknowledge the intercentricity of race and racism; 2) challenge dominant oppressive discourse; 3) promote social consciousness, social transformation, and social justice; 4) centre experiential knowledge; and 5) include interdisciplinary perspectives. The aim is to examine and challenge racism in curricular structures, processes, and discourses. As it stands historically, the implementation of courses and curriculum shifts like this have been met with resistance (Romero 2010; Watkins 2009).

While initial CRT curricular discourse may start with a very "radical" intent, when applied, it is often incredibly diluted before it reaches the people it is intended to benefit (Yosso 2002). Some approaches have only focused on curriculum as it pertains to materials taught in classes and have not given enough attention to structures and processes (Yosso 2002). Additionally, I argue that many approaches have not fully considered the ways in which racism impacts the spirit and what we embody. CRT in education should explicitly promote psychological well-being, collective action, and liberatory education (McGee and Stovall 2015). As such, I recommend that a CRT curriculum should also aim to engender hope and well-being by incorporating a radical healing framework (as illustrated in Image 1). This would decolonize traditional approaches to promoting equity within education by centring the promotion of critical consciousness *and* centring the body in order to promote individual and collective well-being.

Image 1: Radical Healing Tenets

Challenge dominant, oppressive discourse

Centre experiential knowledge

Engender hope and well-being

According to Yosso (2002), a CRT curriculum should...

Promote social consciousness, social transformaton and social justice

Include interdisciplinary perspectives

Openly acknowledge the intercentricity of race and racism

Image 2: Radical Healing Framework

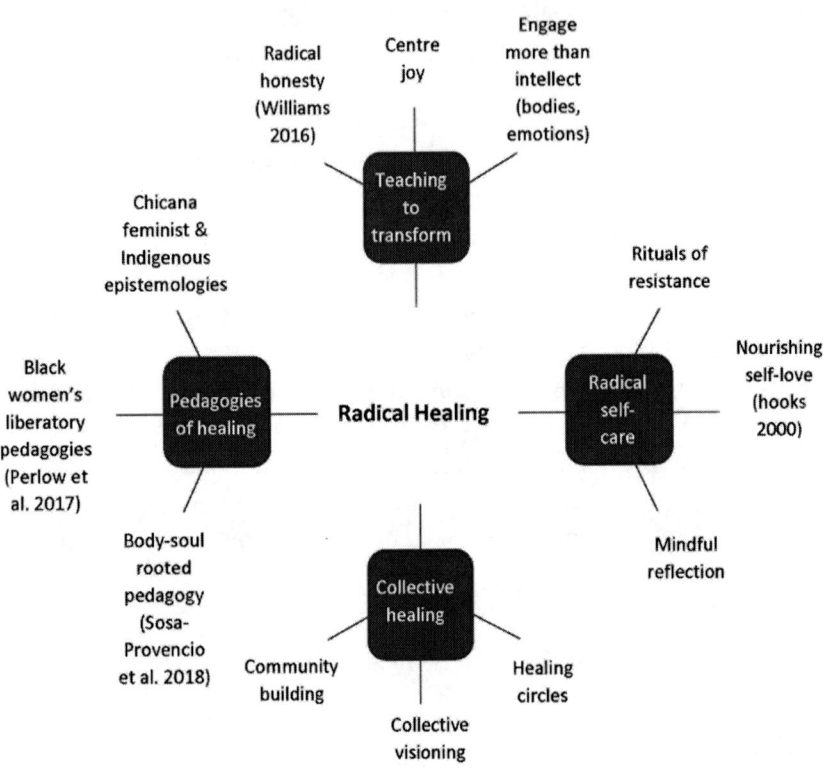

I propose the following as tenets of radical healing by applying Yosso's (2002) description of a Critical Race Curriculum and by synthesizing existing racial justice healing models. Radical healing should: 1) honour multiple epistemologies (ways of knowing) and ontologies (ways of being); 2) centre stories of individual and community resiliency in the face of systemic oppression; 3) identify and interrogate the ways in which racialized oppression undermines wellness and influences both individual and community healing; 4) utilize an interdisciplinary approach to capture the complexities of healing; 5) incorporate pedagogies for transformation; and 6) promote healing as an act of resistance. Radical healing is a nurturing framework that aims to promote and sustain individual and community well-being alongside social justice activism. Educators can apply this framework to decolonize classroom spaces and make them more equitable by using an iterative model centred around teaching to transform (hooks 1994), incorporating pedagogies of healing, encouraging radical self-care and promoting collective healing (as illustrated in Image 2). In the following sections, I present a visual framework for and further describe my model for radical healing in education.

TEACHING TO TRANSFORM

If educators are to teach about justice and freedom, they must also educate as a practice of freedom. bell hooks (1994, 13) states that to educate as a practice of freedom is to "teach in a manner that respects and cares for the souls of our students" and argues that this "is essential if we are to provide the necessary conditions where learning can most deeply and intimately begin." It is imperative that we return to the liberatory nature of learning (Chatmon and Watson 2018). We must recreate a model of education based on wholeness, belonging, social justice, and liberation. Teaching to transform means that educators strive to centre and explore healing as a path of resistance in order to challenge traditional academia which is rooted in white supremacy and the oppression of racially and ethnically minoritized peoples.

To transform classrooms, educators must remain committed to processes that promote holistic learning, growth, and well-being. To practice this commitment, I offer the following invitations: I invite educators to utilize a pedagogy of radical honesty — radical honesty is "a pedagogical practice of truth telling that seeks to challenge racist and patriarchal institutional cultures in the academy" (Williams 2016, 72). Classrooms can become transformational, regenerative, embodied spaces where education can be life giving, especially when they are places where the exchanging of truth is viewed as knowledge production and theory building. It is important to demonstrate the ways in which we are all consumers and producers of knowledge by promoting collective knowledge and experiences as learning resources and new visions of social change (Richardson 2018). This includes recognizing multiple ways of knowing. Educators can utilize a variety of resources that reflect the everyday lives of students including their languages, histories, and stories of resistance. These legacies of embodied resilience should specifically centre the ways in which oppressed groups have not only survived historical brutalities but thrived in spite of the harm they endured (Sosa-Provencio 2020). Embodied resilience is how we build the capacity within ourselves to look at our systems, organizations and communities, and are then able to start making changes in the material conditions of our lives (Shankar 2021).

I invite educators to attempt to reclaim and regenerate that which has been disrupted by colonization — love and joy. Joy allows this work to be pleasurable. According to Mari Matsuda (2017, 1126) "Attention to mental and physical health, care in how we resolve conflicts within our movements, incorporation of art, healing, music, dancing, and joy in all we do, allows us to remain strong as we struggle." Activist Valarie Kaur (2020) has created a framework for revolutionary love as a force for justice. Love and joy are both an affective and political tool (Hicks Peterson 2018). It's important for educators to teach in a way that acknowledges the harm that shifting paradigms can cause (hooks 1994). Beth Berila (2016, 122) states that "the dissonance that arises from learning about oppression is more than a cognitive one. It is an emotional and psychological one, because the ideas we are challenging are often embedded in the students' very sense of selves." Educators should encourage students to move beyond despair about oppression to radical imagination and hope.

I invite educators to move beyond merely engaging the intellect of their students and work to also engage their bodies and minds. We cannot separate political understanding and action from emotional, physical, and spiritual well-being (Williams, Owen and Syedullah 2016). This might look like incorporating consciousness-raising art, music, dance, or poetry. This could also look like integrating mindfulness or meditation. Breathing balances and centres the body. Meditation, critical self-reflection, and mindfulness are strategies for calling ourselves to the present in order to recognize how our emotional, physical, and spiritual bodies are showing up which allows us to develop ways of intentionally responding to stimuli without becoming reactive and also become more aware of what we are actively embodying. Trauma informed mindfulness exercises in classrooms, when integrated at the beginning (and when students can consent to it), allow students to self-regulate, become aware of their embodied experience, consider the ways in which they automatically react and practice concrete strategies for being present with discomfort which is crucial when participating in conversations about equity and justice (Hicks Peterson 2018). Classrooms should be egalitarian communal spaces of healing where assumptions are challenged, and accountability is upheld.

INCORPORATING PEDAGOGIES OF HEALING

Radical Healing requires transformative pedagogies that can nourish the body, mind, and spirit in the fight for liberation. I invite educators to incorporate pedagogies from racially and ethnically minoritized communities that challenge hegemonic knowledge production and validation. Educators should centre stories of individual and community resiliency in the face of systemic oppression. Strengths-based pedagogies, ancestral wisdom, connectedness, and critical consciousness have allowed critical education scholars and racially and ethnically minoritized communities to exist, resist, and persist (Sosa-Prevencio et al. 2018). Centring holistic pedagogies rooted in embodiment can disempower dominant ideologies and build the capacity to act toward social action (Sosa-Provencio et al. 2020).

For example, Sosa-Provencio et al. (2020) utilized spiritually embodied, land-based Chicana feminist and Indigenous epistemologies to develop body-soul rooted pedagogy, a transformative pedagogical framework for teacher education. This framework was created in response to the wounds that dominant schooling has inflicted upon the academic, psychological, emotional/spiritual well-being of marginalized communities. Body-soul rooted pedagogy positions educators as healers and encourages them to design curriculum to remedy the wounds caused by marginalization to promote wholeness of the mind, body, and spirit. It incorporates anti-colonial Indigenous and Chicana feminist frameworks that centre body and land as sites of knowing. They position the body as both birthplace of theory and anti-colonial text. They argue that for transformational education to occur, it must first contend with the body because of the disembodiment of racialized schooling (Arce 2016; Calderón et al. 2012; Elenes 2013; Elenes et al. 2001; Sosa-Provencio et al. 2020). Additionally, Black Women's Liberatory pedagogies are another example of embodied pedagogy. They explore the collective resilience and resistance that occurred as a result of slavery and the ways in which they can be used to promote wellness. Black feminist pedagogies centre the voices, stories, and experiences of Black women in order to challenge hegemonic knowledge production (Perlow et al. 2017). These pedagogies locate "healing at the center of our interactions not just with ourselves, but also with our students, coinvestigators/subjects, colleagues and others" (Richardson 2018, 283).

ENCOURAGING RADICAL SELF-CARE

Angela Davis reminds us that "self-care and healing and attention to the body and the spiritual dimension — all of this is now a part of radical social justice struggles" (as qtd. in van Gelder 2016, n.p.). She reminds us how transformative self-care can be in the radical healing process. Self-care and healing become radical when they are used as a form of resistance to hegemonic cultures and colonial structures; they allow us to consider how self-transformation can lead to lasting social change. These practices are also deeply political. As we work to decolonize our broader society, we must simultaneously work to decolonize our spirits. Radical self-care models social change from the inside out by decolonizing the spirit and working on self-transformation, healing, and hopefulness. Radical self-care allows one to refuel, become grounded, and find centre.

I invite educators to encourage students to commit to examining ways to strive as students and whole beings by promoting rituals of resistance, critical reflexive journaling and self-love to challenge practices of domination (hooks 1994). McGee and Stovall (2015) describe racial survival strategies as sophisticated sets of actions individuals develop to evade historical social problems. Racially and ethnically minoritized students often create these "toolkits" to protect themselves from the harms of weathering and racial battle fatigue. However, these toolkits and strategies are often created in response to harm that has been already caused. While these rituals of resistance can be imperative for survival; they can be transformational if viewed as scholarly strengths worth highlighting in the classroom. Rituals of resistance don't necessarily have to be responses to attacks. They can be self-nourishing habits. This might look like leisure pursuits such as running, yoga, dance, or hiking, or creating things like music, graffiti, spoken word poetry, or activist art. These nurturing habits, when practised consistently and holistically over time, can create shifts in the psyche.

I invite educators to both participate in and create space for critical self-reflection. To effectively participate in social change, we must consider who we are and the ways in which we come to see the world. It's important to be able to understand who and how we are, and how that impacts our worldviews, relationships, behaviours, and perspectives (Goodman 2020). We must consistently reflect on our values, beliefs, desires, and goals in order to develop effective critically conscious approaches to social justice work. Self-reflection also allows us to check in with ourselves to determine the things needed to sustain us in the long run. To ignore our pain is to remain disconnected and disembodied, which causes great violence to ourselves. Deeply knowing ourselves has the power to bring down systems of oppression that depend on us remaining strangers to ourselves and one another. However, we must move beyond naming our pain and be willing to engage in the appropriate forms of self-care that are needed in response.

I invite educators to promote self-love. The reason self-care is radical is because it puts the power of "re-establishing wellbeing into the hands of the people whose wellbeing is being threatened" (Hicks Peterson 2018, 98). Radical healing provides nourishing self-love which is profoundly important especially for those subjugated to structural violence. As I said earlier in this chapter, we must love ourselves and one another enough to know that we deserve better than the current state of things, that we deserve lives that are more than just in the quest for societal transformation; we must all view ourselves as instruments of love and transformation (Neville 2018).

PROMOTING COLLECTIVE HEALING

If educators are to provide spaces for students to unpack and deconstruct their experiences in the world, they should also be committed to providing spaces where students can engage in both individual and collective healing. Collective and individual self-care practices are necessary to counteract the ways in which well-being suffers when confronted with the realities of oppression. They become necessary forms of "resistance, resilience and rebuttal" (Hicks Peterson 2018, 98). We must explore the entanglements of individual well-being with community well-being and how they connect to racism and oppression. I invite educators to attempt to foster collective healing through healing circles, appreciative inquiry, and collective visioning. Students should be allowed to engage in activities that restore collective well-being, meaning, and purpose which can build agency, voice, and action (Ginwright 2010). When educators promote community building and collaboration, this fosters collective self-care which creates room to exchange stories, find shared beliefs and ways in which we embody resistance and love as radical acts of social justice. This creates space for healing and love which can be profoundly powerful in social justice spaces or learning environments (Pour-Khorshid 2016).

Research shows that having space to exchange experiences with same-race peers or friends reduces the stress of racialized experiences (McGee and Stovall 2015). This might include utilizing healing circles or places for individuals to gather to tell their stories, offer testimony and imagine more justice-oriented futures. Healing circles are places to share in pain and resistance, in experience and mutual understanding. These are spaces where same-raced individuals can share concerns, beliefs and solutions for healing and for resisting oppression (Richardson 2018). When racially and ethnically minoritized students are able to exchange stories in these spaces, they are provided a certain sense of relief (Hill 2009). Appreciative inquiry seeks to locate and highlight the life giving forces of the individual, group, or society's existence at its most positive source (Cooperrider and Whitney 2011). As people become actively aware of their strengths, talents, and passions they are then able to act more effectively and deliberately toward desired objectives or realities.

Collective visioning relies on utilizing the wisdom and resilience of the collective to imagine a better society and promote community accountability (Neville 2018). Mari Matsuda (2017, 1214) underscores the importance of what she calls utopian visioning: "envisioning a world so much more humane and delightful than the one we currently inhabit is theory, is criticism, is politics. It is strategic." We can't let go of the idea that good things are possible. Hope takes courage to claim. It's a radical and political decision but is actually an act of defiance against a state that would rather we not dream or imagine or feel; as such, doing so is an important act. We're afraid to have hope but we have to step out of just protecting ourselves because this vision is collective.

For students and folks committed to social justice to create a better society, they must first be able to imagine it for themselves and one another. It takes a lot of creativity and strength to imagine a world that does not exist. It's even harder when you're living in a world filled with so much suffering and oppression. And yet, there are a multitude of innovative solutions for the many issues we face. No one of us will have all the answers nor should we expect ourselves to. Instead, it's important to be as creative as we can be, together. It's important to activate radical imagination again and again. Engaging in collective visioning allows us to truly reimagine education and determine goals and strategies for achieving that vision. If we can't articulate a vision, we have no idea what direction we're headed in, and no way to evaluate whether our current tactics will help us get there. So, we dream because we deserve it, because we can't afford not to. We have to show up for the vision. Williams, Owens and Syedullah (2016, 198) proclaim: "If we can't dream greater, we are only demanding lives that are just outside of intolerable."

IMPLICATIONS

Researchers have noted the ways in which racism and intersecting forms of oppression impact our education system and materialize in health disparities and life opportunities for racially and ethnically minoritized individuals (Hardy 2013; McGee and Stovall 2015). Racially and ethnically minoritized individuals are collectively hurt by oppression but are not defined by it. Additionally, the pain caused by racism isn't exclusive to racially and ethnically marginalized peoples. White people also experience a certain kind of racial tax. Frantz Fanon (2008) wrote about the psyche of colonized people and argued that people in positions of power suffer from an illness of moral consciousness. Racism emits a toxicity that causes harm that everyone must constantly work to heal from. And, as bell hooks (1994, 43) states, "there can be, and usually is, some degree of pain involved in giving up old ways of thinking and knowing and learning new approaches." Centring healing benefits all; however, it especially benefits racially and ethnically minoritized students. This makes their educational experience more bearable which makes higher education that much more equitable considering the emotional labour these students are often tasked with in addition to their scholarly efforts (McGee and Stovall 2015).

CRT provides an excellent framework for naming and combatting oppression. While this can be incredibly emancipatory, this in and of itself isn't liberation. I believe what is missing is a focus on preserving our spirits. We must be sure to centre healing as we do the work. Healing is an act of resistance. It is political action (Lorde 1988). It is what must occur alongside all the dismantling. We must create a praxis of healing to build as we break down; otherwise, I worry about what will remain in the wake. As members of academia, we must find ways to thrive not just academically as scholars, but as whole beings. Decolonizing educational spaces promotes more equitable and transformational learning environments for all.

CONCLUSION

During the last quarter of my social work program, I tried to describe my racialized academic experience. I thought that naming my pain might lead to some sort of redemption. The more I tried to give voice to these truths, the more I struggled. I attempted to synthesize these accounts into a fluid narrative for a class assignment and fell to pieces. I wondered: how do I make language accountable for the truths of my racialized experience? Then I considered what lay underneath that desire for accountability — a longing for healing. I wondered if healing is something that can be granted or if it is something that is sought, that is continuously created in the pursuit of a fully realized self. In the same way that bell hooks (1994) came to theory for healing, I too turn to theory for healing. We need a pedagogy that gives voice to pain and prevents one from being paralyzed by it. I desire a praxis that keeps me (and everyone committed to social justice work) moving forward through despair and doubt, past anger, and disappointment. Pour-Khorshid (2016, 30) proclaims: "we must create the spaces we need to empower ourselves, to sustain ourselves, to heal ourselves in solidarity with others through the reflexive praxis necessary to build collectively in love." Radical healing promotes wellness and creates this space in a way that challenges white supremacy and contends with historical, psychological, emotional, mental, and physical trauma.

Healing is too often left out of "proper" academic pedagogy and methodology (Richardson 2018). To work toward creating social justice, we must commit to the ongoing work of liberating ourselves. We must value our well-being as much as we value social justice. Research must consider investigating the empirical dimensions of healing in social justice settings as well as the harm caused to racially or ethnically minoritized students engaged in activist or social justice efforts. Radical healing should be considered a legitimate goal of critical race theory and a Critical Race Education, not simply a way to assist with anti-oppression efforts. The academy must consider work that incorporates healing as not only valuable but necessary. We must all value healing as a political path to freedom. We must activate our radical imagination to develop new theories and ways of being that are anchored by our attempts at naming systemic oppression and practices by which we might collectively engage in healing resistance that transforms the world as we currently know it (Haga 2020). Critical race theory has given us the language to ask: "what's wrong?" We must now have the courage to ask: "what if?" and "why not?" and "with who?" We must merge new ways of knowing with new ways of being with one another and ourselves, as bell hooks (2005, 174) urges: "when we choose to heal, when we choose to love, we are choosing liberation. This is where all authentic activism begins."

References

Arce, Martin. 2016. "Xicano/Indigenous Epistemologies: Toward a Decolonizing and Liberatory Education for Xicana/o Youth." In *"White" Washing American Education: The New Culture Wars in Ethnic Studies*, edited by Denise Sandoval, Anthony Ratcliff, Tracey Buenavista and James Marin. Santa Barbara: Praeger.

Berila, Beth. 2016. *Integrating Mindfulness into Anti-Oppression Pedagogy*. New York: Routledge.

Calderón, Dolores, Dolores Bernal, Lindsay Huber, et al. 2012. "A Chicana Feminist Epistemology Revisited: Cultivating Ideas a Generation Later." *Harvard Educational Review* 82, 4.

Chatmon, Christopher, and Vajra Watson. 2018. "Decolonizing School Systems: Racial Justice, Radical Healing, and Educational Equity inside Oakland Unified School District." *Voices in Urban Education* 48.

Cooperrider, David, and Diane Whitney. 2011. *Appreciative Inquiry: A Positive Revolution in Change*. San Francisco: Berrett-Koehler.

Delgado, Richard, and Jean Stefancic. 2017. *Critical Race Theory: An Introduction*, third edition. New York: NYU Press.

Elenes, C. Alejandra. 2013. "Nepantla, Spiritual Activism, New Tribalism: Chicana Feminist Transformative Pedagogies and Social Justice Education." *Journal of Latino/Latin American Studies* 5, 3.

Elenes, C. Alejandra, Francisca Gonzalez, Dolores Bernal, and Sofia Villenas. 2001. "Introduction: Chicana/Mexicana Feminist Pedagogies: Consejos, Respeto, y Educación in Everyday Life." *International Journal of Qualitative Studies in Education* 14, 5.

Fanon, F. 2008. *Black Skin, White Masks.* New York: Grove Press.

Geronimus, Arlene T., Margaret Hicken, Danya Keene, and John Bound. 2006. "'Weathering' and Age Patterns of Allostatic Load Scores among Blacks and Whites in the United States." *American Journal of Public Health* 96, 5.

Ginwright, Shawn A. 2010. *Black Youth Rising: Activism and Radical Healing in Urban America.* New York: Teachers College Press.

___. 2015. "Radically Healing Black Lives: A Love Note to Justice." *New Directions for Student Leadership* 148.

Goodman, Diane. 2020. "Cultural Competence for Equity and Inclusion." *Understanding and Dismantling Privilege* 10, 1.

Haga, Kazu. 2020. *Healing Resistance.* Berkeley: Parallax Press.

Hardy, Kenneth. 2013. "Healing the Hidden Wounds of Racial Trauma." *Reclaiming Children and Youth* 22, 1.

Hemphill, Prentis. 2021. *The Embodiment Institute.* instagram.com/p/CJJM2kVAvdh/.

Hicks Peterson, Tessa. 2018. "Self-Awareness and Radical Healing." In *Student Development and Social Justice.* London: Palgrave Macmillan.

Hill, Marc. 2009. "Wounded Healing: Forming a Storytelling Community in Hip-Hop Lit." *Teachers College Record* 111, 1.

hooks, bell. 1994. *Teaching to Transgress: Education as the Practice of Freedom.* New York: Routledge.

___. 2005. *Sisters of the Yam: Black Women and Self-Recovery.* Boston: South End Press.

Kaur, Valarie. 2020. *See No Stranger: A Memoir and Manifesto of Revolutionary Love.* London: One World.

Ladson-Billings, Gloria and William F. 1995. "Toward a Critical Race Theory of Education." *Teachers College Record* 97, 1.

Lorde, Audre. 1988. *Burst of Light: Essays by Audre Lorde.* Ithaca, NY: Firebrand Books.

___. 2007. "The Master's Tools Will Never Dismantle the Master's House." In *Sister Outsider: Essays and Speeches.* Berkeley: Crossing Press.

Matsuda, Mari. 2017. "The Next Dada Utopian Visioning Peace Orchestra: Constitutional Theory and the Aspirational." *McGill Law Journal/Revue de droit de McGill* 62, 4.

McGee, Ebony O., and David Stovall. 2015. "Reimagining Critical Race Theory in Education: Mental Health, Healing, and the Pathway to Liberatory Praxis." *Educational Theory* 65, 5.

Morales, Aurora. 2013. *Kindling: Writings on the Body.* Palabrera Press.

Neville, Helen. 2018. "Afterword: Giving Life—Black Women's Liberatory Praxis." In *Black Women's Liberatory Pedagogies*, edited by Olivia Perlow, Durene Wheeler, Sharon Bethea, and BarBara Scott. London: Palgrave Macmillan.

Perlow, Olivia, Durene Wheeler, Sharon Bethea, and BarBara Scott (eds.). 2017. *Black Women's Liberatory Pedagogies: Resistance, Transformation, and Healing Within and Beyond the Academy*. London: Palgrave Macmillan.

Pour-Khorshid, Farima. 2016. "HELLA: Collective Testimonio that Speak to the Healing, Empowerment, Love, Liberation, and Action Embodied by Social Justice Educators of Color." *Association of Mexican American Educators Journal* 10, 2.

Richardson, Jennifer L. 2018. "Healing Circles as Black Feminist Pedagogical Interventions." In *Black Women's Liberatory Pedagogies*, edited by Olivia Perlow, Durene Wheeler, Sharon Bethea, and BarBara Scott. London: Palgrave Macmillan.

Romero, Augustine F. 2010. "At War with the State in Order to Save the Lives of Our Children: The Battle to Save Ethnic Studies in Arizona." *The Black Scholar* 40, 4.

Shankar, D. 2021. *Embodied Resilience.* Embodied Social Justice Certificate Program.

Smith, William A. 2014. *Racial Battle Fatigue in Higher Education: Exposing the Myth of Post-Racial America.* Washington: Rowman & Littlefield.

Smith, William A., Tara J. Yosso, and Daniel G. Solórzano. 2011. "Challenging Racial Battle Fatigue on Historically White Campuses: A Critical Race Examination of Race-Related Stress." In *Covert Racism*, edited by Rodney D. Coates. London: Brill.

Solórzano, Daniel G. 1997. "Images and Words that Wound: Critical Race Theory, Racial Stereotyping, and Teacher Education." *Teacher Education Quarterly* 24, 3.

Solórzano, Daniel G., and Tara J. Yosso. 2002. "Critical Race Methodology: Counter-Storytelling as an Analytical Framework for Education Research." *Qualitative Inquiry* 8, 1.

Sosa-Provencio, Mia A., Annemarie Sheahan, Shiv Desai, and Shawn Secatero. 2020. "Tenets of Body-Soul Rooted Pedagogy: Teaching for Critical Consciousness, Nourished Resistance, and Healing." *Critical Studies in Education* 61, 3. DOI: 10.1080/17508487.2018.1445653.

Tuitt, Frank, Chayla Haynes, and Saran Stewart. 2018. "Transforming the Classroom at Traditionally White Institutions to Make Black Lives Matter." *To Improve the Academy* 37, 1.

van Gelder, S. 2016. "The Radical Work of Healing: Fania and Angela Davis on a New Kind of Civil Rights Activism." *Yes Magazine*, February 19, 2016. yesmagazine.org/issue/life-after-oil/2016/02/19/the-radical-work-of-healing-fania-and-angela-davis-on-a-new-kind-of-civil-rights-activism.

Watkins, William. 2009. "Black Curriculum Orientations: A Preliminary Inquiry." In *New Curriculum History*, edited by Bernadette Baker. Rotterdam: Brill Sense.

Williams, Angel Kyodo, Lama R. Owens, and Jasmine Syedullah. 2016. *Radical Dharma: Talking Race, Love, and Liberation*. Berkeley: North Atlantic Books.

Williams, Bianca. 2016. "Radical Honesty: Truth Telling as Pedagogy for Working Through Shame in Academic Spaces." In *Race, Equity, and the Learning Environment: The Global Relevance of Critical and Inclusive Pedagogies in Higher Education*, edited by Frank Tuitt, Chayla Haynes, and Saran Stewart. Sterling: Stylus Publishing.

Yosso, Tara. 2002. "Toward a Critical Race Curriculum." *Equity and Excellence* 35, 2.

8

CENTRING SUBJECTIVITY

Witnessing and Wellness

V.C. Rhonda Hackett

SELF-LOCATION

I am an arrivant (Hackett 2019; Petillo 2020) of African Caribbean descent to this nation now called Canada. I arrived on the lands called Tkaronto as a child migrant with my older siblings to reunite with my mother. I have continued my learning about the many Nations who have cared for those lands including the Mississaugas of the Credit, the Haudenosaunee, the Huron-Wendat, the Chippewas, and the Anishnaabeg. I am the first Black Assistant Professor in the School of Social Work at the University of Victoria, located on the traditional territories of the ləkʷəŋən peoples, the Songhees and Esquimalt Nations and W̱SÁNEĆ Nations.

Indigenous Peoples have been on Turtle Island since time immemorial. This truth is foundational to the exploration of the histories and experiences of people of African descent in what is now called Canada. The historical and ongoing presence of Indigenous Peoples on Turtle Island informs my arrival to these lands. The specificity of the violence enacted against Indigenous Peoples on Turtle Island and against people of African descent on these lands reflects the brutality of enslavement and ongoing colonialism. I will anchor my discussion of resistance of anti-Black violence, insistence on healing for peoples of African descent, and the possibilities of decolonial equity within this context of historical enslavement and ongoing colonial violence.

The Equity Myth (Henry et al. 2017) clearly articulated the problem of inequity experienced by Indigenous and racialized people at universities within the Canadian context. Specifically, Ramos and Li (2017, 56) found that among the professoriate, racialized and Indigenous faculty are underrepresented and have lower earnings over time, with Black women professors earning the least. Their research also notes that these indicators of inequity have increased over time even though Canadian universities claim to support equity and diversity. These indicators of inequity also serve to highlight the rareness of Black women professors at Canadian universities. White supremacy declaws and renders inconsequential Offices of Equity, Diversity, and Inclusion (EDI) usually set up in higher education to respond to individual incidents of racism as well as the issue of racism on campus. The problem is that EDI can deflect from the institutional racism supporting inequitable access to university employment and education.

We are more than halfway through the United Nations proclamation of the International Decade of People of African descent (2015–2024; UNESCO 2014), and it is important to reflect on the issues of inequity facing people of African descent. Importantly, the UNESCO (2014) declaration highlights experiences of inequity, disadvantage, and inhumanity as anchored in the legacy of enslavement and colonialism. I focus my reflections particularly in the discipline of social work and offer my proposal of what can be enacted for more liberating approaches that support people of African descent within social work. More specifically, in response to inequity in social work, I explore anti-Black violence experienced by people of African descent in higher education through Black feminist thought (BFT) and critical race theory (CRT). I am interested in examining the sustainability of the well-being of people of African descent through practices that place our stories at the centre of our struggles for liberation.

SITUATING SOCIAL WORK

Social work has only recently begun to account for the ways in which its ideas about welfare for oppressed peoples masked its complicity of enacting dominant ideologies of colonialism. The Canadian Association of Social Workers (CASW; 2019) has acknowledged its role in supporting and enacting harmful assimilationist practices against Indigenous

Peoples in its apology for, and complicity in, anti-Indigenous violence. These histories of social work's violence toward vulnerable communities are surfacing, along with histories of Black people enacting social welfare within Black communities while navigating the legacies of enslavement and colonialism (Chapman and Withers 2019). Furthermore, social work has failed to recognize the social welfare practices of communities of African descent and actively excluded peoples of African descent from gaining access to services and to social work education. This kind of inequitable omission of Black people works to erase our presence from social work history(ies) (Hackett 2019) and simultaneously views our pain and suffering as a spectacle to be viewed without care.

Beyond spectatorship or the literal sense of looking or seeing, there is witnessing, a practice that helps to (re)construct narratives from experience that counter misrepresentations of the oppressed. Specifically, telling our stories and centring our knowledges provides important counternarratives to the dehumanizing stereotypes and identities projected unto people of African descent that are naturalized by white supremacy. Therefore, within our storytelling is the refusal to be separated from our selves. Storytelling is an important component of CRT that centres the experiences of the oppressed to speak their truth and confront silence and erasure (Delgado et al. 2017).

STORYING OUT

The institutionalization of violence and brutality against Black peoples, now more widely available on various media platforms, has spotlighted the naturalizing of the simultaneous reliance on and entrenchment of anti-Black violence. Included in this anti-Black violence is the state violence perpetrated through the overrepresentation of Black children and families in the care of child welfare (Phillips and Pon 2018), incarceration, and educational pushout. Maynard (2017) presents an intersectional analysis of the overrepresentation of Black people in carceral spaces, including the pushout of Black students from educational spaces, and demonstrates how these examples of carceral state violence and dehumanizing treatment of Black people exemplified in these institutions exists in concert with the legacy of enslavement and colonialism. Under these conditions our stories often get erased, minimized, or overlooked.

There is a current frenzied state of many people who are not of African descent, who have suddenly become aware of anti-Black violence and have the desire to reckon with the deadly enactments of directed white supremacy, but who instead display and enact a spectatorship for Black pain. I have witnessed, in social work, the moments when people of African descent are being "talked about" by others who are not of African descent and who do not acknowledge our presence in shared spaces, those who consciously erase our presence by writing us out of the story, and those who minimize our contributions. Being talked about is a painful experience to deal with individually or collectively, and also to witness in the media or in person.

People of African descent don't often get to tell our own lived stories, underscoring the importance and influence of representations of Blackness that are constituted within and from institutions of child welfare, education, policing, and mainstream media. However, these institutions often lack the contextualization of Black life and the inequitable social, political, and economic circumstances that shape Black life. For example, child welfare's overrepresentation of children and families of African descent normalizes its overseeing and surveillance approach that focuses on individual responsibility instead of relational accountability. Moreover, in social work, there is a way in which those who are not descendants of African people consume these representations of Blackness (hooks 2015a), which are treated as extracted commodities to be discarded or exchanged as expertise about people of African descent.

I further contend that "talking about" influences representations of people of African descent in social work education, research, and practice that are often constructed through a colonial lens employing an individual deficit orientation rather than a strengths-based perspective. This colonial deficit orientation presents anti-Black state violence of systemic inequity and disadvantage as depoliticized, de-historized, and decontextualized individual problems and failures (Hackett 2019) that rationalize interventions based on the deployment of fix, save, and rescue discourses. Thus, social work's support for the use of these colonial interventions upon, and representations of, people of African descent contributes to the spectatorship of our lives.

To attend to the injury involved in talking about another is to attend to who is rendered vulnerable in those situations. For example, the act of "talking about" usually omits the voices of those being discussed and prevents those voices from being heard, as they cannot immediately or directly speak back to what is being said about them when they are excluded from the discussion(s). Additionally, when the content of the discussion is violent but viewed as neutral, then the risk to, and impact on, the listener who is from or most like the group being "talked about" must be taken into account. In other words, there is a subject who experiences both the violence of the content being discussed as well as the violence of being "talked about," who must be ethically engaged.

People of African descent are also faced with being treated as invisible and discounted in social work when we speak up or resist going along with dominance. The response from people of non-African descent is often silence, unresponsiveness to the resistance, and pretending as though nothing was said. These types of responses ride alongside dehumanizing representations of people of African descent; they are used to eliminate and silence resistance to domination. It is a move that erases people of African descent from the present moment when ignored, from the past when there is silence about what was said, and from the future with the ongoing treatment of unbelonging. The absence of people of African descent from the history of social work, the inequitable access to social work education in predominantly white universities, the underrepresentation of Black faculty (Henry et al. 2017), and the expert stance of researchers who talk about people of African descent who are not from the community, all contribute to erasing people of African descent from social work. I propose interrupting this anti-Black violence by taking up the experiences of people of African descent through the practice of witnessing. I explore recentring the subjectivity of people of African descent by employing witnessing and wellness as resistance.

WITNESSING

Witnessing is being seen in the fullness of our humanity and refusing to be viewed as separate from each other. Erasure and a stance of expertise in talking about people of African descent amount to spectatorship reliant on colonial representations of Black people. However, when social work makes subjectivity and ethical relations critical to its work, it can hold space for the practice of witnessing. A move toward witnessing is one that necessarily returns subjectivity to people of African descent. Witnessing involves the centrality of subjectivity and ethics (Hartman

1997), which differentiates it from spectacle. This focus on subjectivity demands being in ethical relation, which challenges the expert stance and the consumption of the spectacular in colonial social work's fix, save, and rescue risk assessments, interventions, and research. The witnessing of the subjectivity of people of African descent can unsettle social work's colonial gaze. For example, Hartman's (1997) refusal to repeat violent scenes in her writing about slavery and terror that decentralize subjectivity demonstrates an ethical path of witnessing that could be utilized in decolonial social work, especially in relation to the lives of women of African descent in the lands now called Canada.

The legacy of "care" without subjectivity in power over relations was exemplified in the Domestic Scheme that targeted and managed the migration of young Black women without children from the Caribbean to take care of middle-class families in Canada (Calliste 1994; Lawson 2013). In the construction of the Domestic Scheme, Black women were employed with an expectation of providing care despite receiving little to no care from the state or its agents, reflecting state-sanctioned neglect, erasure, and dehumanization. As an agent of the state, social work continues to demonstrate a lack of care toward Black women and their families and communities. In colonial social work, care in relationships is enacted through power when social workers take up an expert stance as the knower inattentive to difference and specificity. Encounters in care are influenced by race, class, ability, sexuality, and gender in relation to who provides and receives care (Raghuram 2019). Importantly, denaturalizing the essentializing of care in social work can help to unhinge it from the legacy of undervalued servitude assigned to people of African descent. Relationships of care are possible when we challenge the comfort of treating people of African descent like objects — seen but overlooked — even when anti-Black violence is the topic of discussion. Hill Collins (2009) centres the subjectivity and political actions of Black women when she highlights the everyday resistance to white supremacy and dominance of a domestic worker surviving and taking care of themselves and their family.

The positionality of the witness or the spectator can highlight the possible distance from the risk of experiencing anti-Black violence and can mask the complexity of the power involved in the relationship. Therefore, witnessing in social work must be relational, meaning that social workers ought to be connected to or part of the communities that they work within. Attending to how we are in relation to each other is never neutral and is always a reflection of the intersectionality of our positionalities. I propose that witnessing can help social work to account for our ethical enactment of power with, and the centralizing of, subjectivity.

My positionality as an arrivant here on Turtle Island, and specifically on the traditional territories of the ləkʷəŋən peoples, is not neutral. I am literally and figuratively standing upon lands that have practices of witnessing already employed in ceremonial activities. One of the most significant sets of witnessing events that have taken place in this country now known as Canada is the Truth and Reconciliation Commission. The witnessing of the stories of survivors of residential schools by the Truth and Reconciliation Commission of Canada (TRC; 2015) stands as a powerful example of centralizing the humanity of Indigenous people impacted by Canada's ongoing colonialism. The TRC (2015) noted that the principle of witnessing is shared by various Indigenous Peoples across Turtle Island and described witnessing as being able to accurately recall and share the event and its importance with others. In social work, the exploration of witnessing has primarily been utilized by Indigenous scholars articulating decolonizing approaches to knowledge production (see, for example: Richardson 2012; Thomas 2015).

I want to also acknowledge that my exploration of witnessing in relation to people of African descent is happening in the context of local scholarship focused on witnessing within Indigenous cultures. For example, Kwagu'ł scholar Sarah Hunt provides an exploration of witnessing as methodology. Alongside addressing issues of power and positionality, Hunt (2018, 283) offers the following knowledge about witnessing from her traditional practice: "witnessing is a part of a larger system of maintaining an oral culture, and just as the role of a dancer or singer is embodied, so too is the role of the witness." Furthermore, they provide a complex understanding of the role and responsibilities of witnessing specifically as a duty in relation to stories of violence, highlighting the importance of addressing relational power hierarchies. Hunt (2018) centres not only the voices of the people experiencing violence, but also addresses issues of power differences in relation to the ways in which knowledge is constructed and by whom. Importantly, for Hunt, witnessing is not about speaking for another but rather working to emphasize and augment the silenced voices. I embrace embodied witnessing in the following discussion of witnessing by people of African descent as it supports an intersectional understanding of witnessing.

WITNESSING OURSELVES

As described earlier, witnessing is a complex practice that engages an intersectional lens, and attends to issues of power and positionality as well as the role of the witness. In addition to these elements, witnessing for communities of African descent in what is known as Canada has also included documenting the silenced voices of arrivants of African descent. In the next section, I present examples of the ways in which people of African descent, especially women, have undertaken this work of witnessing/visibilizing as an act of resistance, refusal, and reclamation.

Silvera (1989) utilized an oral history methodology in witnessing the lives of working-class African Caribbean women in Toronto. She made more visible the voices of domestic workers from the Caribbean, along with the violence in their lives, helping to augment their words, presence, and lived experiences. Gooden (2008) documented the organizing activities in communities of African Caribbeans in Toronto, as they confronted the often-denied reality of anti-Black violence. She bore witness to the history of English-speaking African Caribbeans organizing over the span of eighty years, whose life experiences were otherwise unattended to in the history of what is now known as Canada. In addition to amplifying the silenced voices, witnessing has supported the documentation of previously untold and neglected stories of the presence of people of African descent arriving in what is now known as Canada.

These examples of bearing witness in Black communities directly oppose the historical erasure of people of African descent. Additional examples of witnessing of and by Black women include the work of Bristow (1994) which visibilized the presence of women of African descent as they recounted more than three hundred years of Black arrivants across Canada, while Cooper (2006) reignited the life and slave narrative of Marie Joseph Angelique testifying to the reality of slavery in Canada. More recently, Nelson's (2020) witnessing revives the agency of the enslaved to flee enslavement but also the heterogeneity of ethnicities among people of African descent through the exploration of runaway slave advertisements in Québec.

In addition to text, the audiovisual medium is yet another potent method used to bear witness to the erasure of the experiences and silencing of narratives of people of African descent navigating anti-Black violence. For example, the widespread use of cellphone cameras has transformed the possibilities of witnessing, helping to make resistance more visible. This technology also helps community members to define the narrative of people of African descent and increases access to the content for a wider audience. A difficult question, then, is how do we witness the horror enacted without dehumanizing and terrorizing each other as the viewers? The issues of representation and spectacle continues to haunt visual witnessing (Nelson 2010). However, according to Richardson (2020, 5) "black witnessing is reflexive, yet reflective. It despairs, but it is enraged too." The importance of maintaining the humanity of the subject in Black witnessing remains paramount when what is being witnessed is the horror of brutality and death. Richardson (2020) imbues Black witnessing within advocacy for rights and connects the numerous terrorizing events of anti-Black racism across time in a manner that illustrates the specificity and importance of this practice.

This long history of witnessing has been employed to maintain the subjectivity of people of African descent on Turtle Island against the ongoing anti-Black violence of erasure and silencing. Maintaining our subjectivity through witnessing one another is an important approach in the fight against persistent inequalities and the terrors of white supremacy. However, there is an accompanying toll of exhaustion and heartbreak that also needs to be counteracted. What does staying in the fight and nurturing well-being look like under these dehumanizing conditions? I turn now to the exploration of wellness and the care for self and community as resistance to highlight what is already being practised by people of African descent in the fight against anti-Black violence and the inequities it perpetuates.

WELLNESS AS RESISTANCE

There is no place free from white supremacy and anti-Black violence, which means that it is important to create spaces for staying well and healing in the fight for equity, justice, and liberation. Domination that is systemic and intricately woven together (Hill Collins 2009) continues to be directed at people of African descent with horrific outcomes. As increased attention to anti-Black racism across Turtle Island and around the world has demonstrated, racism is not only bad for our health, it is deadly (Etowa and McGibbon 2012; Williams 2012). Not surprisingly, the well-being of Black people is also not taken seriously within an untrustworthy healthcare system as noted in Washington's (2007) examination of the history of enslavement, non-consensual experimentation, and ongoing mistreatment of Black people in health care. Additionally, environmental racism meted out to Black and Indigenous Peoples (Waldron 2020) identifies the normalization of targeted systemic racism. Unfortunately, Black women are also dealing with the "weathering" effects of racism (Williams 2012) which reflects early breakdown of the body. It is a decidedly political act to care for ourselves (Lorde 1984) not from individualism but from wholeness, and as part of being in community.

There is nothing consensual about living and dying in the face of hate and dehumanization for generations and having to fight against institutionalized anti-Black violence every step of the way. As people of African descent continue to be forced to live and die under these conditions, strategies for survival become necessary. Some of these strategies are not sustainable or good for us, while other strategies support our wellness. Given that knowledge about wellness is connected to and derived from the lived experiences of Black people in the community, wellness as resistance is not abstract and instead reflects healing of the self in relation to community.

Since we are affected by systems of domination, we can also be complicit in replicating them with each other. This kind of lateral violence in communities can inhibit us from working together in community and can impede our individual and collective healing. However, there is no need to postpone attending to healing as it is necessarily interconnected to being well. hooks (2015b, 7) states it clearly: "living as we do in a white-supremacist capitalist patriarchal context that can best exploit us when we lack a firm grounding in self and identity (knowledge of who we are and where we have come from), choosing 'wellness' is an act of political resistance." She holds that involvement in Black liberation struggles necessarily includes taking up the process of self-discovery to heal our wounds. The following are examples of Black women attending to wellness as resistance in which their subjectivity is central to their approaches to healing.

Richardson (2017) discusses radical self-care inside and outside of the classroom using healing circles. A significant intention of the healing circle is to talk back to the dehumanizing representations of Black women and reconstruct counternarratives of self-identity that help to decolonize the mind. Another component of well-being as resistance is reflected in the exploration of love and joy in the lives of participants of the healing circle. In centring well-being, she argues that the political is personal, such that challenging dominant representations simultaneously reclaims individual self-identity and enacts collective resistance.

Another example of centring well-being can be found in Caldera's (2020) exploration of work and self-care. She explains that theory helped her to find healing as she explored the ways in which her health was being affected by white supremacy and patriarchy. During the pandemic caused by the COVID-19 virus, she began the challenge of resting and attending to self-love. Black Feminist Thought (BFT) helped her to understand that the stereotype of working hard was an individually outlined route to financial autonomy that did not address systemic inequities for people of African descent. She reflected on capitalism, in that "it forces us to neglect our personal and communal well-being for the sake of thriving industries and robust economies" (711–712). She asserts that her self-care helped her to fight capitalist exploitation and to turn toward heart work instead of hard work.

Expressing what is in our heart is political and, for Melonas (2021), letter writing is an activity of heart work. According to Melonas (2021) letter writing is an activity of radical self-care, as it creates space to build community, to bear witness, and to slow down. She provides an affirming discussion of letter writing among Black women and explores it as resistance. She also affirms that letter writing challenges neoliberalism's expectations of increasing speed that ride on harmful stereotypes of Black women tirelessly working. Letter writing, she contends, invites self-care, taking time and slowing down; additionally, she argues that it is collective. She points out that the choice to participate in exchanging words of care through letter writing and receiving constitutes an act of collective care rather than an exercise in neoliberal informed individual care for self. Melonas (2021) exploration of letter writing between Audre Lorde and Pat Parker provides an example of how engagement in letter writing creates space to share strategies of wellness as resistance, like slowing down, and making time to be vulnerable and still, and to practice self-care, all of which directly challenge the stereotypes about and disposability of people of African descent, particularly Black women.

These responsive practices are some examples of creative ways in which marginalized peoples, particularly women of African descent, resist anti-Black violence. Such approaches demonstrate commitment to sustainable care for ourselves and each other, and support participation in community. Joining together as a community to resist dominance is an important but partial outcome. Working toward consciously stopping the violence we enact through our ways of being, knowing, and doing with ourselves and one another is challenging, yet offers opportunities for sustainable wellness.

A signature practice in social work is critical reflection for transformative change of the self and the collective in the fight for more equitable life chances and choices now and in the future. Years ago, I co-facilitated a support group for Black women during a conflict about which population of women a health centre was developed to support. The employees wanted to specifically create a space for Black women's health and wellness that would address the health inequities that Black women experienced. The Board of Directors, on the other hand, had other ideas. At the time, the small staff were threatened with being permanently locked out of the centre and responded by occupying the offices with support from community members. As co-facilitators, we decided not to make a choice between protesting and healing. We saw the well-being and healing of Black women as resistance, so we continued to offer the support group inside and alongside the protest and occupation of the health centre. The protest and occupation were also a demonstration of community standing together across differences to create transformative change.

The development of collective responses to the exclusion of people of African descent from equitable participation in society has a long history of collective mutual aid at the community level. Another example of wellness on a community scale, albeit economic wellness, is made visible in Gordon Nembhard's (2014) examination of the history of African American cooperative movements. Smaller scale versions of economic mutual aid include the Susu, a form of banking that can be found in communities of African descent throughout the diaspora, focused on rotating loans of saved money among community members based on trusted relationships, until everyone has had a turn. These practices of well-being at the community level demonstrate that wellness as resistance is also visible in community responses to inequity.

IMPLICATIONS FOR DECOLONIAL EQUITY

Decolonial equity means addressing anti-racism and decolonization. Universities and social workers need to account for the specificity of different historical contexts and experiences of colonialism and racialization. Their wilful ignoring of racism and colonialism highlights the problems of the EDI industry and how it continues to support the status quo.

While this chapter has focused on the experiences of communities of African descent broadly and women of African descent specifically, I remain mindful of what the knowledge presented here means in relation to walking alongside Indigenous Peoples in the work of decolonizing equity. The history of enslavement and colonialism has affected how we come together in community as Black and Indigenous Peoples (Smallwood 1999) and working well together is not a given. In the context of specific histories of enslavement and colonialism, trust and relational engagement that centre subjectivity and accountability urge us to witness each other with care. One of the pathways we must travel to this work is to confront the ways that we have internalized the violence of enslavement and colonialism that tries to separate us from ourselves and each other. Acknowledging the ways in which colonialism has attempted to falsely separate us as mutually exclusive groups and ignored our intertwined histories on and beyond Turtle Island can aid us in the process of what Audre Lorde (1984) refers to as recognizing ourselves in each other.

The simultaneous centring of Blackness and Indigeneity understands our lives and life chances and choices as being in ethical relation, rather than in competition. Likewise, centring anti-Indigenous and anti-Black racism together allows us to train our collective attention and action on the violence of racism and colonialism that informs our shared and unique experiences of inequity, and also to share our strategies for resistance, witnessing, and wellness. I would clarify that to recognize the impact of racism and colonialism is not to centralize them, but to isolate them as the sources of the structural inequities we face.

Strategies of decolonial solidarity and decolonial equity (strategies of resisting, witnessing, and wellness) help to counter the impact of ongoing colonialism and legacies of enslavement, including forced separations from each other and ourselves, by overriding the normalization of disconnected individualized responses to intersectional systemic anti-Black racism. Additionally, acknowledging the sources of these lived structural inequalities also means attending to caring for our whole being, including our bodies, since experiences of anti-Black racism and resistance to colonialism are embodied experiences. I think that the integration of our subjectivity and wellness as people of African descent is inseparable from our engagement in the struggle for decolonial equity and against systemic inequities. Centring Indigeneity and Blackness (as interconnected rather than equivocated) highlights the inequities of colonialism and racism and offers us a path together anchored in decolonial solidarity, land back, and futurities informed by decolonial equity.

CONCLUSION

Since equity work, like Blackness, is externally imposed, I come to it on my own terms. Creating spaces where we can be our whole selves and where we do not have to let go of our humanity is a critical act of both resistance and wellness. As I close this chapter, I sit with the offerings of Caldera (2020) about heart work and the ways that it both invokes and celebrates a reclamation of who we are by slowing down and moving toward our wholeness in relation to one another. Attending to heart work offers us the opportunity to build congruent relationality both within and among our communities and ourselves. Heart work reminds us that our wholeness and healing are vital to sustainable responses to ongoing colonization and racism.

References

Bristow, Peggy. 1994. *We're Rooted Here and They Can't Pull Us Up: Essays in African Canadian Women's History.* Toronto: University of Toronto Press.

Caldera, Altheria. 2020. "Challenging Capitalistic Exploitation: A Black Feminist/Womanist Commentary on Work and Self-Care." *Feminist Studies* 46, 3.

Calliste, Agnes. 1994. "Race, Gender and Canadian Immigration Policy: Blacks from the Caribbean, 1900–1932." *Journal of Canadian Studies* 28, 4.

Canadian Association of Social Workers. 2019. *Statement of Apology and*

Commitment to Reconciliation. casw-acts.ca/files/Statement_of_Apology_
and_Reconciliation.pdf.

Chapman, Chris, and A. J. Withers. 2019. *A Violent History of Benevolence:
Interlocking Oppression in the Moral Economies of Social Working.* Toronto:
University of Toronto Press.

Cooper, Afua. 2006. *The Hanging of Angélique: The Untold Story of Canadian
Slavery and the Burning of Old Montréal.* New York: Harper Perennial.

Delgado, Richard, Jean Stefancic, and Angela Harris. 2017. *Critical Race
Theory: An Introduction,* third edition. New York: NYU Press.

Etowa, Josephine, and Elizabeth McGibbon. 2012. "Race and Racism as
Determinants of Health." In *Oppression: A Social Determinant of Health,* edited by Elizabeth McGibbon. Black Point/Winnipeg: Fernwood Publishing.

Gooden, Amoaba. 2008. "Community Organizing by African Caribbean
People in Toronto, Ontario." *Journal of Black Studies* 38, 3.

Gordon Nembhard, Jessica. 2014. *Collective Courage: A History of African
American Cooperative Economic Thought and Practice.* University Park:
Pennsylvania State University Press.

Hackett, V. C. R. 2019. "African Caribbean Presence: Decolonizing Social
Work Education." *Intersectionalities: A Global Journal of Social Work
Analysis, Research, Polity, and Practice* 7, 1.

Hartman, Saidiya V. 1997. *Scenes of Subjection: Terror, Slavery, and Self-Making
in Nineteenth-Century America.* New York: Oxford University Press.

Henry, Frances, Enakshi Dua, Carl James, et al. 2017. *The Equity Myth:
Racialization and Indigeneity at Canadian Universities. Vancouver:* UBC
Press.

Hill Collins, Patricia. 2009. *Black Feminist Thought: Knowledge, Consciousness,
and the Politics of Empowerment,* second edition. Abingdon: Routledge.

hooks, bell. 2015a. *Black Looks: Race and Representation.* Abingdon:
Routledge.

____. *2015b. Sisters of the Yam: Black Women and Self-Recovery.* Boston: South
End Press.

Hunt, Sarah. 2018. "Researching within Relations of Violence: Witnessing as
Methodology." In *Indigenous Research: Theories, Practices and Relationships,*
edited by Deborah McGregor, Jean-Paul Restoule, and Rochelle Johnston.
Toronto: Canadian Scholars' Press.

Lawson, Erica. 2013. "The Gendered Working Lives of Seven Jamaican
Women in Canada: A Story about 'Here' and 'There' in a Transnational
Economy." *Feminist Formations* 25, 1.

Lorde, Audre. 1984. *Sister Outsider*. Freedom: Crossing Press.

Maynard, Robyn. 2017. *Policing Black Lives: State Violence in Canada from Slavery to the Present*. Black Point/Winnipeg: Fernwood Publishing.

Melonas, Desireé. 2021. "'Hey Mama,' 'Dear Sister,' 'Sister Love': Black Women's Healing and Radical Self-Care Through Epistolary Work." *Journal of Women, Politics & Policy* 42, 1.

Nelson, Charmaine. 2010. *Representing the Black Female Subject in Western Art*. New York: Routledge.

___. 2020. "A 'Tone of Voice Peculiar to New-England.'" *Current Anthropology* 61, S22.

Petillo, April. 2020. "Sketching Arrivantcy: Self-Naming Toward Decolonized Solidarity Across Indigenous and Black Divides." *Frontiers: A Journal of Women Studies* 41, 2.

Phillips, Doret, and Gordon Pon. 2018. "Anti-Black Racism, Bio-Power, and Governmentality: Deconstructing the Suffering of Black Families Involved with Child Welfare." *Journal of Law and Social Policy* 28, 1.

Qwul'sih'yah'maht (Robina Thomas). 2015. "Honouring the Oral Traditions of the Ta't Mustimuxw (Ancestors) through Storytelling." In *Research as Resistance: Revisiting Critical, Indigenous, and Anti-Oppressive Approaches*, second edition, edited by Lesley Brown, and Susan Strega. Toronto: Canadian Scholars' Press.

Raghuram, Parvati. 2019. "Race and Feminist Care Ethics: Intersectionality as Method." *Gender, Place & Culture* 26, 5.

Ramos, Howard, and Peter S. Li. 2017. "Differences in Representation and Employment Income of Racialized University Professors in Canada." In *The Equity Myth: Racialization and Indigeneity at Canadian Universities*, edited by Frances Henry, Carl James, Peter Li, et al. Vancouver: UBC Press.

Richardson, Allissa. 2020. "Bearing Witness While Black: African Americans, Smartphones, and the New Protest #journalism." London: Oxford University Press.

Richardson, Cathy. 2012. "Witnessing Life Transitions with Ritual and Ceremony in Family Therapy: Three Examples from a Métis Therapist." *Journal of Systemic Therapies* 31, 3.

Richardson, Jennifer. 2017. "Healing Circles as Black Feminist Pedagogical Interventions." In *Black Women's Liberatory Pedagogies: Resistance, Transformation, and Healing Within and Beyond the Academy*, edited by Olivia Perlow, Durene Wheeler, Sharon Bethea, and BarBara Scott. London: Palgrave Macmillan.

Silvera, M. 1989. *Silenced: Talks with Working Class Caribbean Women about Their Lives and Struggles as Domestic Workers in Canada*, revised edition. Toronto: Sister Vision Press.

Smallwood, Arwin. 1999. "A History of Native American and African Relations from 1502 to 1900." *Negro History Bulletin* 62, 2/3.

TRC (Truth and Reconciliation Commission of Canada). 2015. *The Final Report of the Truth and Reconciliation Commission of Canada*. Winnipeg.

UNESCO. 2014. "International Decade of People of African descent (2015–2024)." en.unesco.org/decade-people-african-descent/why

Waldron, Ingrid. 2020. *Environmental Racism in Canada*. Canadian Commission for UNESCO's IdeaLab. Ottawa.

Washington, Harriet. 2007. *Medical Apartheid: The Dark History of Medical Experimentation on Black Americans from Colonial Times to the Present*. New York: Anchor Books.

Williams, David R. 2012. "Miles to Go Before We Sleep: Racial Inequities in Health." *Journal of Health and Social Behavior* 53, 3.

CLOSING THE CIRCLE

Billie Allan and V.C. Rhonda Hackett

Through this edited collection, we have sought to gather up a knowledge bundle to help support and nourish the work of those engaged in equity work, particularly those relatives who are living the inequities they seek to transform. We aimed to centre BIPOC voices, recognizing the ways in which equity work and the construction of in/equity in settler colonial states is deeply racialized. As the presence of EDI offices and personnel rapidly expand in institutions across Turtle Island, we sought to challenge conceptualizations of equity and equity work in ways that recognized the colonial machinery that has, and continues to, set the terms of whose voices, knowledges, and presence are valued, suppressed, or ignored. We longed for a gathering of voices that could reconceptualize equity through a decolonial lens that could position our needs as in relation rather than in competition, while also trying to guard against an equivocation of all oppressions (Tuck and Yang 2012).

As wise scholars like Dr. Cindy Blackstock (2019, 856) note, decolonial theoretical approaches are inherently limited since "by definition these approaches still put the coloniser at the centre of the enterprise." We recognize the challenges of decolonial approaches, including the potential entrapment in Eurocentric frameworks, the focus on colonial institutions, policies and practices that can leech away the energy also needed to turn to ourselves (and as BIPOC relatives, to each other), and the ever-present risk of forwarding notions of decolonizing that ignore Indigenous Peoples (Smith et al. 2021), undermine Indigenous sovereignty (Tuck and Yang 2012) or further anti-Black racism (Garba and Sorentino 2020). However, we argue that working to foster transformation within colonial institutions necessitates a decolonial analysis that makes visible the policies, practices, and organizational cultures that explicitly or implicitly further colonial relations of power, privilege, violence, silence, and harm. Likewise, it means visibilizing policies, practices, and organizational cultures that are antidotal and seek to not only neutralize the root system of colonialism but to enrich the soils in which we can sow and nourish the carefully protected knowledge of our Ancestors, both past and future.

The authors who have generously lent their gifts to this collection have emphasized the importance of relationship, relationality, and relational accountability, as well as the necessity of a decolonial analysis that can contextualize, historicize, politicize, and collectivize our equity efforts to avoid recycling colonial constructs (Hackett 2016). They have also underscored the necessity of attending to affect or heart-based knowing, and to the healing work involved in managing the impact of equity work on our spirits, hearts, minds, and bodies.

The chapters presented here emphasize the importance of centring Indigenous sovereignty and redressing anti-Black racism in decolonial approaches to equity, while also highlighting the tensions between these aims, particularly in relation to land. For example, the arguments presented by Dr. Shauneen Pete and Dr. Kathy Hogarth invoke the debates illustrated in the writings of scholars like Tuck and Yang (2012) and Garba and Sorentino (2020), and those of Lawrence and Dua (2005) and Sharma and Wright (2008-09); the writings of Drs. Pete and Hogarth simultaneously deepen dialogue about what decolonizing equity and equitable decolonizing means and what this work demands, of everyone.

DECOLONIZING EQUITY MATTERS RIGHT NOW

There is a powerful reckoning unfolding in higher education in the lands presently known as Canada, visible in the newly released *Igniting Change* report (Smith et al. 2021) commissioned by the Federation of Social Sciences and Humanities. This report and the consultations that informed it were led by an esteemed group of scholars tasked with developing recommendations to help forward Equity, Diversity, Inclusion and Decolonization (EDID) within the Federation, its annual Congress, and its member Associations and affiliates. The authors describe their recommendations as "a recognition of the harm caused by, and the need to move away from, the injurious performativity of conventional EDI committees and technocratic checklists that result in superficial change" (Smith et al. 2021, 18). In the spirit of nurturing deep and lasting change, many of their recommendations emphasize capacity and relationship building through (un)learning about equity through a decolonial lens, centring anti-racism and anti-colonialism in all its efforts, undertaking relational accountability, centring subjugated knowledges, and attending to responsibility to local Indigenous Peoples, languages, and territories (Smith et al. 2021, 62).

A 2019 national survey by Universities Canada assessing the state of EDI efforts and action found near parity in senior university leadership positions among women and men (49 percent and 51 percent, respectively), suggesting some positive movement in gender equity. However, this same study found that racialized and Indigenous Peoples account for only 8 percent and 3 percent of senior leaders, illustrating how white women continue to be the primary beneficiaries of EDI efforts (Academic Women's Association 2019; Chenier 2020). Research by esteemed scholar, Dr. Malinda Smith, illustrates even deeper disparities in leadership roles among Canada's "elite" research universities (known as the U15), in which visible minority men and visible minority women accounted for 8.7 percent and 0.9 percent of the executive leadership teams of U15 presidents respectively, with the remaining positions occupied by white men and white women (Academic Women's Association 2019). The Universities Canada study found that these inequities were consistent along the pathways that lead to senior leadership roles; among full-time faculty of which Black and Indigenous faculty members accounted for 1.9 percent and 1.3 percent of all full-time faculty, and worse, only 3.0 percent and 0.9 percent of doctorate holders respectively.

Despite the seeming proliferation of EDI offices and personnel in postsecondary education, the Universities Canada (2019) survey also found that 71.7 percent of institutions surveyed indicated that they had no EDI action plan or strategy (26.9 percent) or that their EDI action plan or strategy was in development (44.8 percent). We argue that the relatively recent emergence of EDI work in these institutions provides an important opportunity to disrupt the re-inscription of colonial conceptualizations of equity that favour institutional risk management and limited liability over relationality, masquerade multiculturalism as anti-racism, and ignore the glaring matter of Indigenous sovereignty, Indigenous lands, and the responsibilities of reconciliation.

Beyond issues of equitable access and representation, decolonizing equity also aims to redress the cultural tax (Padilla 1994) and the physical, emotional, and spiritual exhaustion and injuries faced not only by BIPOC faculty, but by BIPOC students and staff as well. Canton (2013, 2) states that "'cultural taxation' is a stealth workload escalator for faculty of color. And like stress, it can be a silent killer of professional careers and aspirations." Cultural taxation, the racism and colonialism imbued within it, and the inequities it creates, can be fatal for more than our careers. The implications of decolonizing equity for our health, well-being, and sustainability are reflected in the voices of multiple contributors in this text in their calls for, and focus on, healing. Within and beyond the context of postsecondary education, decolonizing equity could be understood as an act of harm reduction, health promotion, and reconciliation for and with Indigenous Peoples, Black peoples, and racialized peoples. As several chapters within this text illustrate, equity as diversity and inclusion manifested through ravenous efforts to recruit BIPOC faculty, staff, and students will fail if the institutions themselves do not address the injurious practice of continuing to "welcome" Black, Indigenous, and racialized peoples into deeply unwelcoming spaces.

As Terry Gardiner's chapter illustrates, the act of creating environments of welcome requires an understanding of what we are standing on and in relation to. It also requires careful attention to representation, not as tokenizing inclusion, but as a necessary means of ensuring a meaningful indication of invitation and reflection of self for those who have faced the invisible "keep out" and "no trespassing" signs of mainstream institutions, organizations, and broader society for generations. At a fundamental level, representation as reflection helps to make visible and anchor our intergenerational presence in places that would suggest we never before existed; it is an expression of our resistance, beauty, and power.

The writing of Pike, alongside contributors Bourgeois and Booth demonstrates the work that is *already* happening in community and the importance of integrating decolonial equity in governance to support and ensure its presence in practice. As they describe the visioning for and creation of the Toronto Birth Centre (TBC), the authors illustrate the importance of equity work that is driven by, and accountable to, community as well as the transformative power and beauty of centring Indigenous knowledge systems in organizations that serve not only

Indigenous Peoples, but all peoples. Their approach to decolonial equity directly challenges the epistemic racism embedded in settler colonialism to not only assert, but demonstrate, how much Indigenous ways of knowing, being, and doing have to offer to everyone in dreaming of and striving toward equity beyond colonialism. Learning *from* and not just about Indigenous ways of knowing, being, and doing reflects a decolonial ethic and relational accountability to the places and spaces we reside, love, learn, and labour in — it also demonstrates a deep respect for the incredible nuance, maturity, and beauty of Indigenous knowledge systems.

DECOLONIAL EQUITY REQUIRES DECOLONIAL SOLIDARITY

Decolonial solidarity and decolonial equity invite us to see ourselves as in relation rather than in competition; but to do so, we must "see" (bear witness to) ourselves. We must turn inward to be in that conversation. In other words, we need to account for our ways of knowing, being, and doing in relation. Decolonial solidarity offers more than resisting inequitable life chances and choices; it can disrupt and problematize the settler/Indigenous binary that fails to account for the specificity of the presence, knowledge, and lived realities of African descendants (Dei 2017; 2018). When the settler in this context is everyone who is not Indigenous to Turtle Island, what does accountability look like from the unaccounted in consensual decolonial solidarity? The settler/Indigenous binary constructs Black life and death as equivalent to whiteness and complicity in settler colonization (Dei 2017). The complicated history and legacy of the African diaspora as stolen people on stolen land is dehistoricized, depoliticized, and decontextualized in this tightly knotted binary. This settler/Indigenous binary at a minimum does not generally address racism and specifically does not address anti-Black racism (Dei 2017). Secondly, it erases the experiences and realities of people who identify as both Black and Indigenous. Additionally, this binary removes Indigeneity from the reality of people of African descent, who were historically forcibly separated from homelands by the centuries of enslavement and currently by the realities of neoliberalism. Finally, the binary forecloses on knowledge and experiences of colonialism as empire building across many lands.

Decolonizing equity work is not easy; in fact, it can be quite painful as we confront what Grandmother Madeline Dion Stout (2018, 67) describes through the Nehiyaw word *kitimakisona* — a poverty of unmet needs. These unmet needs are rooted in colonization (Dion Stout 2018) and might be understood and recognized in many ways, including unmet needs in terms of having our humanity, dignity, voices, choices, histories, and knowledges not only acknowledged, but upheld, and unmet needs in terms of life choices and chances. As we often note in our own work and in our own relationship of decolonial solidarity, it can be challenging to bear witness to the unmet needs or suffering of another when your own unmet needs and suffering feels unacknowledged. These challenges are distinctly rooted in a perceived economy of scarcity — a dynamic that readily plays into "pie politics" of equity and a sense that there is only so much (change, opportunity, acknowledgement, care) to go around; this can result in a sense that if one person or group's concerns are centred, it somehow displaces, erases, or minimizes the concerns of another. These dynamics can be particularly painful when experienced between or among Black, Indigenous, and racialized communities where lateral violence can spread like fire, effectively draining us of the energy needed for collective and collectivizing change and relieves those who benefit from colonial inequities from doing any of the work.

What does decolonial solidarity look like, feel like, and demand of us in a shared effort toward decolonizing equity? In addition to, or perhaps as a kind of, *kitimakisona* [poverty of unmet needs] (Dion Stout 2018), the desire for decolonial solidarity can reveal a poverty of stories that we have about one another within and between BIPOC communities. This draws back to Dr. M. Jacqui Alexander's (2005, 269) insistence that we must:

> become fluent in each others' histories, to resist and unlearn an impulse to claim first oppression, most-devastating oppression, one-of-a-kind oppression, defying-comparison oppression. We would have to unlearn an impulse that allows mythologies about each other to replace *knowing* about one another. We would need to cultivate a way of knowing in which we direct our social, cultural, psychic, and spiritually marked attention on each other. We cannot afford to cease yearning for each others' company. (original emphasis)

Yet yearning for one another's company will not prevent the injuries that we can experience or cause in our efforts to seed, nurture, and sustain our relations. Instead, we must also develop practices of repair for when we cause harm, or the painful moments in which, as Dr. Janet Smylie (personal communication, 2013) says, our traumas bump into each other. Practices of repair reflect a desire for non-disposability which does not mean tolerating violence or abuse. As we have suggested elsewhere (Hackett et al. 2020) in drawing on the work of Nehiyaw scholar, Dr. Michael Hart, decolonial solidarity and the desire for non-disposability require us to recognize one another as both *being* and *becoming* — holding each other in the light of who and how we are, and recognizing that we are always in the process of becoming who and how we are going to be.

It is important to distinguish practices of repair with those of reconciliation that, according to Moyo (2021, 268)

> requires constant compromise on the part of the aggrieved, who are supposed to forgive and forget, to "move on," as the saying goes, even as the past remains entrenched in the present. In these arrangements, the aggrieved are pressured to heal, to become friendly, to make the perpetrators comfortable and assimilate to master narratives, and to continue living in the same environments under the same systems that have harmed them instead of completely unlearning the ways that brought on these problems in the first place.

Practices of repair reflect a desire and commitment to remain in community with one another and a recognition that we are all interconnected (Minogiizhigokwe 2010; Moyo 2021), whether we choose intentionally and carefully (meaning in a manner full of care) to be in community or not. Dr. Alexander (2005, 283) states: "the fact of the matter is that there is no other work but the work of creating and re-creating ourselves within the context of community." Practices of repair require attention to values and teachings of relationality, relational accountability, self-in-relation, and a fundamental refusal to participate in the dehumanization of one another or the sacrifice of our own or each other's dignity. Practices of repair necessarily centre the heart and spirit, while recognizing the impact of harm or violence on the body and mind; they invite ceremonies of acknowledgement and what might be described as clearing away or cleaning off the psychospiritual impacts of the injury experienced. This may include ceremonial practices such as cedar brushing, smudging, or sweats, and reconnecting with All Our Relations by visiting with the lands and waters around us.

As noted in Dr. Hackett's chapter, practices of witnessing are critical to the work of healing and undoing harm, not only because they invoke the collective, but because they enact a recognition of one's humanity, dignity, and spirit. Critical reflexivity is a fundamental component of practices of repair, requiring a turn inward to reflect on and account for our own thoughts, words, and actions, and to account for where we are in our own healing journey.

HOW WILL WE KNOW?

Decolonizing equity also raises the issue of metrics in terms of how institutions, communities, or organizations will evaluate their actions toward advancing or fostering equity. For example, equity measures such as recruitment, retention, outreach, education, and conflict resolution might be assessed by the extent to which they deepen, resist, or transform colonial power relations and the inequities that they fertilize. Like cultural safety paradigms (and unlike efforts to identify Canada's top diversity employers), decolonial equity efforts ought to be assessed by those who are the target of and subject to colonial inequities.

The progress toward or practice of decolonial equity must be *felt* — it demands attention, as Ozioma Aloziem asserts, to the heart and spirit; it must include, as Dr. Roland Coloma describes, an ethic of love and joy. It is also important to remember that decolonial equity work will be felt by everyone, including those who have been the beneficiaries of colonial inequities. There is a need for active anti-racism, critical reflexivity, relational accountability, and practices of repair to help attend to the affective or heart-based realities of decolonial equity work.

Dr. Shauneen Pete describes the work of the decolonizing as unfolding on Indigenous territories and therefore accountable to Indigenous Peoples. As such, in evaluating or assessing our decolonial equity efforts, we must ask: how do equity efforts engage and square with local Indigenous Nations and communities on whose territories institutions and organizations are built? How do they respect and reflect the teachings of these local Nations and communities related to practising and living equity? How do equity efforts honour the sovereignty, well-being, and sustainability of the Indigenous Peoples on whose territories we are undertaking our work? What lies ahead? Such measures also require consideration of how to centre accountability to Indigenous Peoples and territories, and directly address the colonial violence of anti-Black racism.

The chapters in this book demonstrate a multitude of entry points into imagining and enacting decolonial equity and decolonial solidarity, while holding space for the complexity and complications of the realities that shape our relationships with one another. Seeding and nurturing relations of decolonial solidarity in the pursuit of decolonial equity requires nuance in navigating issues of mutual desire and consent. Do we desire to walk together? Are our relations deeply rooted in reciprocity, balance, and consent (not to a standard of perfection, but in a practice of respect and relationality)? How do our intentions and motivations account for our respective and collective healing? Since the idea of this book was first birthed, our shared world has witnessed a revolution of refusal — refusal of anti-Black racism that has for centuries amounted to a steady, state-driven genocide not only in the nation-states we call Canada and the United States, but around the world. We have witnessed the refusal enacted by Indigenous youth and communities who stood strong in the beauty of their gifts to turn up the volume on centuries-old fights to protect traditional territories and to uphold original instructions as caretakers and relatives of the Earth and all of her inhabitants. We have also witnessed incredible pain, loss, and grief through the theft and murder of beloved relatives through state-sanctioned police brutality and gross acts of murder and violence unabashedly rooted in anti-Black, anti-Indigenous, and anti-Asian racism. We have witnessed an unfathomable loss of life to the COVID-19 pandemic that has reflected, manifested, and deepened health, social, economic, and political inequities. As our shared world struggles through the pandemic and state-based responses, the severity of the inequities it has created or exacerbated seem incomprehensible. Where do we go from here?

Building on the efforts of generations of resistance by peoples of African descent, the Black Lives Matter movement has galvanized a global understanding of colonial violence and the ways that it manifests in anti-Black racism. After centuries of resistance and decades of inquiries, reports, and protest (NIMMIWG 2019; RCAP 1996; TRC 2015), the efforts of generations of Indigenous Peoples have worked to create a growing anti-colonial consciousness across so-called Canada. In the face of an abhorrent surge in anti-Asian racism during the pandemic, Asian activists and community members have laboured hard to keep each other safe, resist anti-Asian violence driven by the hateful political rhetoric of so-called global leaders, and to uplift their histories and make clear the colonial roots of anti-Asian racism across Turtle Island. In the context of our shared histories of resistance to colonial violence, we have a considerable amount to offer to one another in visioning for and moving toward decolonial equity through decolonial solidarity.

In our shared experience within our school and in the professional and community spaces we occupy, decolonial equity can be painfully slow work because it follows an Indigenous ethic of focusing on the *how,* or the process involved in doing the work as a necessary way of ensuring that the *what* or outcome of the work is meaningful, usable, and accountable. We believe that it requires what Dr. Alexander (2005, 283) refers to as "revolutionary patience" and a decolonized sense of time. We are surrounded with knowledge that can aid us in this journey; it lies in the blades of grass, the lapping waves of the ocean, and among the *ahnungoog* or star relations visible in the night sky; it rests in our blood, our bones, our songs, our dreams, our memories, and in our relations with one another. As noted within this text, our pathways forward to decolonial equity are accountable to All Our Relations, including our more-than-human relations. Through this lens, perhaps decolonizing equity is nothing new at all, but rather something very old; something that already lives in the knowledge systems of these lands. Nuu-chah-nulth scholar, Chaw-win-is (in Riecken and Edmunds 2018, n.p.), states: "we've lived in a particular way for thousands and thousands and thousands of years that didn't deplete our resources, that didn't deplete our salmon, we lived in a way that ensured our survival. [...] We didn't have a five-year plan, we had a fifty to a hundred year plan." This sentiment is echoed in the words of Inuk scholar, Aviaq Johnston (in Carreon-Alarcon et al. 2018, 375):

> You know, if you look back at those black-and-white photos of Inuit, their whole lives depended on the environment around them. No one was wealthy nor impoverished. If one person had more than they needed, they shared with those who were strug-

gling. If one person was impoverished, it was likely that the whole village was impoverished. Life was hard, but people were happy, at peace with the world. When non-Inuit came to our homeland, they saw Inuit as a rare species, barbaric and ancient. [...] And suddenly, people who survived and thrived in one of the harshest environments in the world for thousands of years were deemed to be stupid because papers and pens somehow meant intelligence.

There is no doubt that collectively and systematically rooting out and breaking down the epistemic racism that underpins our social institutions and broader society is a critical component of decolonial equity work.

Decolonial Equity emerged as a means to articulate our longing for and efforts to create workplaces and community spaces that we can bring ourselves into without feeling like we are complicit in injuring our own spirits, betraying the dreams of, and our responsibilities to, our Ancestors (past and future), or supporting environments that naturalize colonial harms, including the active erasure of our presence. As Black and Indigenous scholars, decolonial equity is neither conceptual nor optional; it is an act of resistance, survival, and well-being. It aims to refuse colonial tactics of divide and rule, the false face of multiculturalism, and disingenuous efforts toward reconciliation and reparation; it instead seeks to articulate the ways in which our histories, futurities, well-being, and efforts to reimagine and nurture equity are woven together. As we close the circle, we return to where we began with a vision of centring BIPOC voices in authoring visions of decolonial equity. With an intention that our desire and labours be rooted in our responsibilities to and love for our Ancestors (past and future) and All Our Relations, we have sought to lift up our words and those of the contributors to this text from a space of critical hope and desire for something more than concepts of equity borne of colonialism could ever offer us: a reflection of ourselves. *Chi miigwetch.*

References

Academic Women's Association. 2019. "The Diversity Gap in 2019." University of Alberta. uofaawa.files.wordpress.com/2019/06/u15-senior-leadership-awa-diversity-gap-2019.pdf.

Alexander, M. Jacqui. 2005. *Pedagogies of Crossing: Meditations on Feminism, Sexual Politics, Memory and the Sacred.* Durham: Duke University Press.

Blackstock, Cindy. 2019. "Revisiting the Breath of Life Theory." *British Journal of Social Work* 49, 4.

Canton, C. 2013. "The 'Cultural Taxation' of Faculty of Color in the Academy." *California Faculty Magazine.* https://www.calfac.org/wp-content/uploads/2021/07/The-Cultural-Taxation-of-Faculty-of-Color-in-the-Academy.pdf.

Carreon-Alarcon, Clark, Aviaq Johnston, Bryan, Brittany Walker, and Emma Bronson. 2018. "Racialized and Indigenous Youth: A Call for Change." In *Racism and Anti-Racism in Canada*, edited by David Este, Liza Lorenzetti, and Christa Sato. Black Point/Winnipeg: Fernwood Publishing.

Chenier, Ele. 2020. *Radical Inclusion: Equity and Diversity Among Female Faculty at Simon Fraser University. Academic Women of SFU.* www2.unbc.ca/sites/default/files/sections/equity-diversity-inclusion/radicalinclusion-aug312020.pdf.

Dei, George J. S. 2017. "Blackness and Colonial Settlerhood: A Purposeful Provocation." In *Reframing Blackness and Black Solidarities Through Anti-Colonial and Decolonial Prisms.* Cham: Springer.

Dion Stout, Madeleine. 2018. "Atikowisi miýw-āyāwin, Ascribed Health and Wellness, to Kaskitamasowin miýw-āyāwin, Achieved Health and Wellness: Shifting the Paradigm." In *Determinants of Indigenous Peoples' Health: Beyond the Social*, edited by Margo Greenwood, Sarah de Leeuw and Nicole Lindsay. Toronto: Canadian Scholars.

Garba, Tapji, and Sara-Maria Sorentino. 2020. "Slavery is a Metaphor: A Critical Commentary on Eve Tuck and K. Wayne Yang's 'Decolonization is Not a Metaphor.'" *Antipode: A Radical Journal of Geography* 52, 3.

Hackett, V.C. Rhonda. 2016. "Families Building Nations, or Nations Building on Families? An Exploration of How African Caribbean Immigrants (Re) Construct Family in the Context of Immigration and Oppression in Canada." Doctoral dissertation, University of Toronto.

Hackett, V.C. Rhonda, Amoaba Gooden, Billie Allan, and Devi Mucina. 2020. "Walking Together: Indigenous and Black Perspectives on Decolonizing Education." In *S'Tenistolw: Moving Indigenous Education Forward*, edited by Todd Ormiston, Jacquie Green, and Kelly Aguirre. Nanaimo: JCharlton Publishing.

Lawrence, Bonita, and Enakshi Dua. 2005. "Decolonizing Antiracism." *Social Justice* 32, 4.

Minogiizhigokwe (Kathleen Absolon). 2010. "Indigenous Wholistic Theory: A Knowledge Set for Practice." *First Peoples Child & Family Review* 14, 1.

Moyo, Otrude. 2021. *Africanity and Decolonizing Discourses: Ubuntu Emerging Perspectives*. Cham: Palgrave Macmillan.

NIMMIWG (National Inquiry into Missing and Murdered Indigenous Women and Girls). 2019. *Calls for Justice*. Ottawa, ON. mmiwg-ffada.ca/wp-content/uploads/2019/06/Calls_for_Justice.pdf.

Padilla, Amado. 1994. "Ethnic Minority Scholars, Research, and Mentoring: Current and Future Issues." *Educational Researcher* 23, 4.

RCAP (Royal Commission on Aboriginal Peoples). 1996. *Volume 1: Looking Forward, Looking Back*. Ottawa: Canada Communication Group.

Riecken, Ted, and Emma Edmunds (co-hosts). 2018. "Indigenous Resurgence in Education with Chaw-win-is." *Learning Transforms Podcast*, March 3, 2018.

Sharma, Nandita, and Cynthia Wright. 2008–09. "Decolonizing Resistance, Challenging Colonial States." *War, Crisis & Transition* 35, 3.

Smith, Melinda, Irene Golfman, Marie Battiste, et al. 2021. *Igniting Change: Final Report and Recommendations*. Ottawa: Federation of the Social Sciences and Humanities.

TRC (Truth and Reconciliation Commission of Canada). 2015. *Truth and Reconciliation of Canada: Calls to Action*. Winnipeg. gov.bc.ca/assets/gov/british-columbians-our-governments/indigenous-people/aboriginal-peoples-documents/calls_to_action_english2.pdf.

Tuck, Eve, and K. Wayne Yang. 2012. "Decolonization is Not a Metaphor." *Decolonization: Indigeneity, Education and Society* 1, 1.

Universities Canada. 2019. *Equity, Diversity and Inclusion at Canadian Universities: Report on the 2019 Study*. <]univcan.ca/wp-content/uploads/2019/11/Equity-diversity-and-inclusion-at-Canadian-universities-report-on-the-2019-national-survey-Nov-2019-1.pdf.

CONTRIBUTORS

Billie Allan, MSW, PhD is an Assistant Professor in the School of Social Work at the University of Victoria. Billie is a Two Spirit Anishinaabe scholar from Sharbot Lake, Ontario, whose research work is focused on Indigenous health and well-being, including the impact of racism and child welfare on the health and well-being of Indigenous Peoples. She is the co-author, along with Dr. Janet Smylie, of *First Peoples, Second class Treatment: The Role of Racism in the Health and Well-Being of Indigenous Peoples in Canada.*

V.C. Rhonda Hackett, MSW, RSW, PhD is an Assistant Professor in the School of Social Work at the University of Victoria. Rhonda is an African Caribbean social work scholar whose work is informed by extensive social work practice experience and a decolonizing theoretical lens woven from the offerings of critical race theory, Black Feminist Thought, and Indigenous thought. Her scholarship is focused on advancing understanding of the lived experiences and knowledge of African Caribbean peoples living in the lands currently known as Canada, including matters of family and community well-being.

Kathy Hogarth, PhD is a Professor and Dean of the Lyle S. Hallman Faculty of Social Work at Wilfrid Laurier University. Dr. Hogarth previously served as an Associate Professor in the School of Social Work at Renison University College and Special Advisor, Anti-Racism and Inclusion, Office of the Vice-President, Research and International at the University of Waterloo. Much of her work in academia over the past two decades has been focused on building community and institutional capacity related to equity for and with historically marginalized populations. She is co-author of the recently released *A Space for Race: Decoding Racism, Multiculturalism, and Post-Colonialism in the Quest for Belonging in Canada and Beyond.*

Ozioma (Ozy) Aloziem, MSW is an Igbo scholar situated at the intersection of multiple ways of knowing. Originally raised on Omaha land, she has been a visitor on Arapaho and Cheyenne territories since 2015. As a critical Black Feminist, Ozy prioritizes racial and gender equity in her scholarship and activism. She uses this focus to amplify voices of marginalized communities that are left on the fringes of both academic research and global conversation. Ozy believes in engaging in critical research as a radical act of freedom. Presently, her research is centred around radical healing, liberatory pedagogy, and Black women's well-being.

Roberta Pike, MSW, is Anishinaabekwe from Henvey Inlet First Nation and the Executive Director of the Toronto Birth Centre.

Cheryllee Bourgeois, AM, is a Cree-Métis Aboriginal Midwife working under the exception of the Ontario Midwifery Act. She is one of the original co-lead creators of the Toronto Birth Centre and Past President of its Board of Directors. She is also an Assistant Professor in the School of Midwifery at Ryerson University.

Sara Booth, RM, is a Registered Midwife and settler, former Board Member, and current Clinical Director of the Toronto Birth Centre.

Terry Gardiner, MSW was born in Montréal, grew up in the Caribbean, studied in the United States and Canada, and is a dancer, early childhood educator, and social worker. He engages with many knowledges in building bridges of communication and relationship in and across communities. Terry is currently the Director of Student Programs at the University of Toronto Faculty of Law.

Shauneen Pete, MEd, PhD is nehiyawin from Little Pine First Nation in Treaty 6 territory (Saskatchewan, Canada). She is currently Professor in Leadership Studies at the University of Victoria and previously served as both the Vice-President (Academic) and Interim President at First Nations University of Canada as well as the Executive Lead: Indigenization at the University of Regina.

Roland Sintos Coloma, MA (Educational Administration), MA (Cultural Studies in Education), PhD is Assistant Dean and Professor of the Division of Teacher Education and co-director of the Kaplan Center for Research on Urban Education in the College of Education at Wayne State University in Detroit, Michigan, USA. His research and teaching focus on urban and global education; history, cultural studies, and education; race, sexuality, and diaspora. He is currently working on two book projects: a manuscript on history, empire, and education; and an encyclopedia volume on diversity, democracy, and social justice in education.

OmiSoore Dryden, PhD, a Black queer femme, is the James R Johnston Chair in Black Canadian Studies, Faculty of Medicine, and the co-lead of the new national organization — The Black Health Education Collaborative. Dr. Dryden engages in interdisciplinary scholarship and research that focuses on Black LGBTQI communities, blood donation systems in Canada, anti-Black racism in health care, medical education, and Black health curricular content development. OmiSoore has published in peer-reviewed journals and book collections and has an edited collection (with Dr. Suzanne Lenon): *Disrupting Queer Inclusion: Canadian Homonationalisms and the Politics of Belonging* and the co-authored commentary (with Dr. Onye Nnorom): *Time to Dismantle Systemic anti-Black Racism in Medicine in Canada* in the *Canadian Medical Association Journal.*

INDEX

Ahmed, Sara, 4-5, 24, 27-29, 30-31, 34,
    112, 118-119, 147-149
Alexander, M. Jacqui, 34, 36, 201-202, 205
Anzaldúa, Gloria, 132, 148
anti-Black
    anti-Blackness, 3, 144
    racism, 2, 5, 6, 187-188, 191, 196, 197,
        200, 204
    violence, 145, 158, 179, 180-184, 186-
        188, 190
anti-colonial, 3, 6, 12, 105, 169, 205
anti-Indigenous, 6, 29, 110, 181, 192
assimilation, 41, 48, 53-54, 57

Black Panther Party, 5
Blackstock, Cindy, 26-27, 120-121, 196

Canada
    "from Sea to Sea", 64
    history of racism, 68-70
    two solitudes, 65
circle, 102, 124
    as a practice of equity, 14
    healing, 99, 172, 188-189
collective visioning, 171-173
colonial-decolonial matrix, 65
contractual benevolence, 48-50, 54
critical race theory, 140, 150, 159-162,
    164, 174-175, 180-181
    See also CRT

critical reflection, 73, 190
    critical reflexivity, 203
    critical self-reflection, 162, 168, 170,
    self-reflection, 171
CRT, 162- 165, 173, 180-181
    See also critical race theory
cultural safety, 92-93, 95, 203
cultural tax, 13, 51-52, 54, 199
cultural taxation, 48, 51, 199

decolonial equity, 86, 95, 96, 103-106,
    118-119, 123, 191
    allies in, 104-105
    allyship in, 105
    approaches, 111, 161-162
    implications, 191
    in practice, 103, 123
    Indigenous knowledge, 95, 106
    Indigenous perspective, 86
    leadership, 103
    meeting local, Indigenous and cultur-
        al needs, 96
    mutual aid as a cornerstone, 6
    perspective, 118
    work, 118-119, 123
    See also decolonizing equity; equity
decolonial leadership, 103
decolonial solidarity, 36, 191-192, 200,
    201, 204-205
decolonizing affect, 146-148

decolonizing equity, 6, 8, 10, 12, 22-23, 31, 33-34, 35, 42, 61-62, 65, 67, 76, 199-201, 206
    challenges to, 67
    metrics, 203-204
    praxis, 54, 56-57
    See also decolonial equity; equity
diversity, 1, 3, 4, 11, 13, 23-24, 34, 37, 51, 57, 65, 89, 133, 199
    as "image management", 24
    "diversity workers", 29, 31, 32
    and the status quo, 1, 4
Domestic Scheme, 184

EDI, 12, 35, 37, 180, 191, 196, 198
el sitio y la lengua, 132, 134, 148
embodied resilience, 166-167
embodiment, 161-162, 169
enslavement, 63, 66, 68-69, 179, 180, 181, 186, 188, 191, 200
    See also slavery
epistemic ignorance, 48
epistemic racism, 11, 31, 200, 206
equity,
    as balance, 26-31
    as diversity and inclusion, 199
    as fair treatment, 62
    as *nibi*, 33
    as water, 26, 28, 30
    control mechanisms, 54
    decolonial approach to, 161-162
    "equity/diversity regime", 11
    "equity myth", 12
    for Indigenous People, 95
    in Indigenous communities, 87-88
    in workplaces and public discourse, 23
    Indigenous approach, 26

    local, 33
    practitioners, 118
    principles of, 121
    work, 105-106, 116, 126, 199
    See also equity, diversity, and inclusion; decolonial equity; decolonizing equity, EDI
equity, diversity, and inclusion, 1, 3, 12, 17, 20, 40-41, 43, 62, 180, 197
    See also EDI; equity

Gause, C.P., 48, 50-51

healing, 126-127, 162, 173, 175, 188, 190, 203
    centring, 172
    circles, 99, 172, 188-189
    collective, 171-172
    decolonial, 162
    epistemological, 11
    praxis of, 173
    radical, 160, 164-167, 169, 171, 174
heart work, 189, 192
Hunt, Sarah, 185-186

inclusion, 4, 11, 14, 23-25, 44, 46, 73, 121, 134, 199
Indigenization, 49, 60, 62-63, 70-71, 73, 76
Indigenous midwifery, 92, 94, 97
Indigenous sovereignty, 4, 10, 17, 51, 53, 55, 56, 73, 140, 196, 197, 198, 204
Itapisinowin, 83, 89

joy, 149-150
    love and, 148, 168, 189, 203

"killjoy", 147-148, 149

kitimaskisona [poverty of unmet needs], 201

Kuokkanen, Rauna, 48, 50-51, 55

land, 2, 10-11, 54-55, 64, 69, 70-71, 86, 92, 144, 161, 169, 192, 200
    acknowledgments, 52, 55-56, 104
    and colonization, 66, 111
    and decolonization, 47, 54, 71
    See also territories
Laenui, Poka, 54-55
love, 148-149, 162, 168, 171-172, 174, 175
    and joy, 148, 168, 189, 203
    self-love, 170, 171, 189

Minogiizhigokwe, 11, 14, 20, 22, 26-27, 29
multiculturalism, 3, 23, 37, 46, 65, 198, 206
mutual aid, 5, 190

nation-state, 4, 31, 35, 60-61, 63-66, 69, 75, 140-141, 204
necropolitics, 63, 72
"neoindigenous", 140-141
nuestras facultades, 132, 148

overrepresentation, 34, 110, 119, 181, 182

pie politics, 26, 31, 34, 200
plantation, 143-145
politics of distraction, 28, 35
practices of repair, 202-203

racial battle fatigue, 145, 163, 170
radical healing, 160, 164-167, 169, 171, 174
    radical healing tenets (image), 165

radical healing framework (image), 166
radical imagination, 160, 168, 172, 175
recruitment, 11, 23-24, 40-41, 43, 48-49, 54, 57, 114, 203
resistance, 74-75, 96, 116, 166-167, 170-173, 175, 179, 183-184, 186-192, 199, 204-206
    collective, 189
    rituals of, 170
    wellness as, 6, 188-190
resurgence, 53, 55-56, 83, 89, 91, 97

self-care
    radical, 170-171, 188, 189
    collective, 171
self-determination, 55, 91-93, 103, 105, 129, 133, 140, 145
settler, 200
    colonial, 76
    colonialism, 41, 47, 57, 144
    decolonization, 41, 56-57
    deconstructing, 70-71
    identity, 72
    logics, 42-43, 45, 48
seventh-generation principle, 100
slavery, 1-2, 63, 68-69, 71, 143-144, 169, 184, 186
    See also enslavement
social work
    Black and Indigenous social workers, 114-115, 127
    Black and Indigenous social work students, 115, 119
    Black and Indigenous social work students, practitioners and staff, 115
    Canadian Association of Social

Workers, 180-181
  colonial, 181
  decolonial, 184
  history, 119-121, 181, 183
  peoples of African descent in social
    work education, 157, 181-182
  profession, 108, 113
  visionaries, 120-121
  witnessing in, 184
spectatorship, 181-182, 183
storytelling, 42, 124, 181

territories, 21, 27, 31, 33, 47, 56, 198,
    203-204
  See also land
The Equity Myth, 180
Thobani, Sunera, 11-12, 23, 64
Thomas Bernard, Senator Dr. Wanda,
    120-121
Truth and Reconciliation Commission of
    Canada, 12, 43, 49, 61, 73, 104, 185
Tuck, Eve and Yang, K. Wayne, 54-55, 71,
    86, 196-197

Ubuntu, 76
underrepresentation
  Black and Indigenous students in
    postsecondary, 109-110, 112
  Black faculty, 183
  in helping professions, 110, 113
  in social work, 34
United Nations Declaration on the Rights
    of Indigenous Peoples, 43, 56, 91
urban
  defining "urban", 134-136, 139
  education, 132, 134-139, 146-147
  schooling, 148-149

"weathering", 163, 170, 188
wellness as resistance, 6, 188-190
whiteness, 65-68, 72, 75, 113, 200
witnessing, 181, 183-187, 191, 203

Zapatista, 74